Institutions and Innovation

Interests, Identities, and Institutions in Comparative Politics

———

The post–Cold War world faces a series of defining global challenges: virulent forms of conflict, the resurgence of the market as the basis for economic organization, and the construction of democratic institutions.

The books in this series take advantage of the rich development of different approaches to comparative politics in order to offer new perspectives on these problems. The books explore the emerging theoretical and methodological synergisms and controversies about social conflict, political economy, and institutional development.

———

Institutions and Innovation

Voters, Parties, and Interest Groups in the Consolidation of Democracy—France and Germany, 1870–1939

MARCUS KREUZER

Ann Arbor

THE UNIVERSITY OF MICHIGAN PRESS

2004   2003   2002   2001   4   3   2   1

A CIP catalog record for this book is available from the British Library.

Library of Congress Cataloging-in-Publication Data

Kreuzer, Marcus, 1964–
        Institutions and innovation : voters, parties, and interest groups
    in the consolidation of democracy—France and Germany, 1870–1939 /
    Marcus Kreuzer.
            p.   cm.
        Includes bibliographical references and index.
        ISBN 0-472-11186-8 (cloth : alk. paper)
        1. Political parties—France—History.   2. Pressure
    groups—France—History.   3. France—Politics and
    government—1870–1940.   4. Political parties—Germany—History.
    5. Pressure groups—Germany—History.   6. Germany—Politics and
    government—1871–1933.   7. Germany—Politics and
    government—1933–1945.   I. Title.
    JN2997 .K74   2001
    320.943'09'034—dc21   00-011812

Contents

Preface

In writing this book, I became deeply indebted to history. History came to my rescue for the first time in early 1989. During that winter and spring, glasnost and perestroika toppled not just communist regimes but also most proposals that had been carefully drafted for the dissertation-writing seminar in which I participated at Columbia. Witnessing the emergence of brand-new liberal democracies and free markets quickly jaded my enthusiasm to contribute yet another study on how the Greens were going to solve the solid-waste crisis and reform bureaucratic parties. Yet this new-found excitement quickly yielded to the sobering realization that CNN-style headline history lacks the data sets, the secondary sources, and the distinct outcomes required for the effective deployment of the methodological apparatus that modern social science demands. Faced with the predicament of joining the ranks of transitologists, I was rescued by history a second time when somebody pointed out that the very same issues that kept us rushing for the newspaper each morning had made their historical debut in interwar Europe. The possibility of studying democratization through historical examples offered a tempting solution to the methodological problems posed by analyzing the present day transitions to liberal democracy. The passage of 70 to 80 years provided distinct outcomes and voluminous political histories that together enabled the formulation of a theoretically informed, methodologically self-conscious comparative study.

The political histories of interwar Europe offered more than just redress to methodological problems. They also suggested two key factors affecting the fate of interwar democracies. First, they placed an inordinate amount of attention on political parties. This emphasis might be explicable by the fact that interwar democracies lacked corporatist arrangements, constitutional courts, or supranational organizations, which nowadays act as rival channels to parties for the representation of societal interests. Much more than nowadays, interwar parties were the principal game in town for assisting citizens, voluntary associations, and economic interest groups to voice their interests and for keeping politicians, bureaucrats, and generals accountable. In short, interwar parties constituted the principal democratic fulcrum on which societal actors could leverage their political influence. Second, the general importance of parties stands in striking contrast to the actual leverage they offered citizens in different countries. In some countries, parties acted like voter-oriented, innovative entrepreneurs, while in others they behaved like inert, inward-looking bureaucratic behemoths. This difference in the willingness to innovate and take risks was particularly pronounced across French and German parties, which is one reason (further reasons are listed in the introduction) that I concentrate my analysis on these two countries. Interestingly enough, the centrality of parties and their entrepreneurialism increasingly emerge as themes in the analysis of postcommunist societies; thus, we might indeed learn a few lessons from history.

While history inspired this book, it did not readily divulge compelling explanations. Many strictly historical explanations were either unnecessarily exceptionalist or complex in accounting for the differing innovativeness of parties and the varying leverage they offered societal groups. On this front, the vast American literature on Congress and its rapidly growing comparative offspring provided invaluable insights. It gratifyingly integrates formal institutional analysis with rational choice models and provides extremely compelling and empirically thoroughly tested accounts of how formal representative institutions structure the choices of political actors. This literature provided the indispensable theoretical road map for piecing together the innumerable but highly scattered references about political institutions made by historical monographs. Once these institutional fragments were linked together, it became apparent that institutional incentives were key for explaining the varying innovativeness of parties.

These efforts to trespass back and forth between history and political science would not have been possible were it not for the support that I received from many different sources. I obtained generous financial support from the Canadian Social Science Council, Canadian Institute for Peace and Security Studies, Columbia University, DAAD (German Academic Exchange), Council for European Studies, Mellon Foundation, and Institute for Human Sciences (Vienna, and Villanova University). The MTA's Capital Improvement Funds are to be thanked for restoring the tracks and rolling stock of New York subways to the point where I could actually get some work done on my daily rides to and from Brooklyn.

I received intellectual advice and much-needed moral support from Mark Kesselman, Lisa Anderson, Jeffrey Olick, and Robert Paxton, who also generously served on my dissertation committee. I would like to thank Chuck Myers, Kevin Rennells, and Eric Dahl for their help in preparing the final manuscript. Mark Lichbach, in turn, used all his intellectual breadth to situate the argument more comfortably in the different theoretical literatures from which it draws. Mark Zacher kindly and persistently nudged me to get done and reminded me that scholarship is equal parts perspiration and inspiration. I counted 20 singled-spaced pages of comments I received over the years from anonymous referees. The best way I can thank them is to point out that their comments delayed the manuscript's completion by over two years. Were it not for their many small and large criticisms, this would have been a different book. Thanks also to *Comparative Politics* for permission to reprint parts of "Electoral Institutions, Political Organization, and Party Development: French and German Socialists and Mass Politics," vol. 30, no. 3 (April 1998): 273–92, and *Social Science History* for permission to reprint "Money, Votes, and Political Leverage: Explaining Electoral Performance of Liberals in Interwar France and Germany," vol. 23, no. 2 (summer 1999): 211–40.

In navigating the perilous waters of interdisciplinary scholarship, support was at first difficult to find but ultimately all the more generous and rewarding. Stathis Kalyvas had just traveled these difficult waters and shared his lessons as well as recommendations of first-rate Mediterranean restaurants. As a long-standing and accomplished practitioner of historically grounded social science, Ira Katznelson reassured me that doing history is not only okay but also of profound intellectual significance. Finally, the comments of Peggy Anderson were unrivaled in their insightfulness, subtlety, and above all thoroughness. They helped retrieve insights from muddled passages that even I could no longer retrace; they added invaluable historical nuances; and their wit and kindness always served as a welcome morale booster. Maybe her generous style of commenting explains why it has been such a pleasure to read the works of her fellow historians.

Books rest on more than just financial patrons and intellectual mentors. The interest and perseverance propelling this endeavor would have been unthinkable without my parents, Harald and Edda Kreuzer. I owe them deeply for their constant encouragement, persistent support, and early reminder that intellectual curiosity has payoffs far more rewarding and lasting than even the most lavish Wall Street salary. My wife, Pam Loughman, on the other hand, deserves credit for her gentle insistence that I periodically ignore my work and appreciate the other joys of life—a task recently made easier by the arrival of Lucas and Julia. As my editor in chief, Pam helped guide me through more than just the stylistic complexities of the English language.

Abbreviations

ADGB	Allgemeiner Deutscher Gewerkschaftsbund
	General Federation of German Trade Unions
ALP	Action libérale populaire
	Liberal Popular Action
ANR	Association nationale républicaine
	National Republican Association
BdL	Bund der Landwirte
	Agrarian League
BVP	Bayerische Volkspartei
	Bavarian People's Party
CGT	Confédération générale du travail
	General Confederation of Labor
CNBLP	Christlich-Nationale Bauern- und Landvolkpartei
	Christian-National Peasants' and Farmers' Party
DDP	Deutsche Demokratische Partei
	German Democratic Party
DNVP	Deutschnationale Volkspartei
	German National People's Party
DVP	Deutsche Volkspartei
	German People's Party
KPD	Kommunistische Partei Deutschlands
	German Communist Party
KVP	Konservative Volkspartei
	Conservative People's Party
NSDAP	Nationalsozialistische Deutsche Arbeiterpartei
	National Socialist German Workers' Party
PCF	Parti communiste français
	French Communist Party
PDP	Parti démocrate populaire
	Democratic Popular Party

PPF	Parti populaire français
	French Popular Party
PR	Proportional representation
PSF	Parti social français
	French Social Party
Radicals	Parti radical
	Radical Party
SFIO	Section française de l'internationale ouvrière
	French Socialist Party
SPD	Sozialdemokratische Partei Deutschlands
	German Social Democratic Party
UIE	Union des intérêts économiques
	Association of Economic Interests
URD	Union républicaine démocratique
	Republican Democratic Union
USPD	Unabhängige Sozialdemokratische Partei Deutschlands
	Independent Social Democratic Party of Germany

Introduction: History, Politics, and Institutions

At the turn of the century Max Weber, Moisei Ostrogorski, and Robert Michels observed the rapid growth of parties and prophesied that their inertia would obstruct democratization. Half a century later, E. E. Schattschneider, Joseph Schumpeter, Maurice Duverger, and Giovanni Sartori argued that modern democracy had indeed become party democracy but that it owed its democratic qualities to the innovativeness and entrepreneurialism of parties. This reversal, from viewing parties as bureaucratic behemoths that endanger democracy to regarding them as responsive entrepreneurs advancing democracy, underscores the close but little-studied relationship between political innovation, party development, and democratic performance. The question of how parties became risk-taking entrepreneurs contributing to the development of democracy is an eminently historical one, which explains why it has received little attention from political scientists. Political scientists primarily study parties in established, Western democracies, where they already behave like innovative, voter-oriented entrepreneurs. This ahistorical perspective means that insufficient attention is paid to factors facilitating and impeding the erstwhile advent of entrepreneurial parties so central for the proper functioning of democracy.

France and Germany provide two special opportunities for studying the development of competitive parties. Since the late nineteenth century, their political histories have been significantly shaped by political parties and their deficiencies. French and German parties are accused of having impeded democratization by having been undisciplined, doctrinaire, controlled by economic interest groups, autocratic, and unable to govern. These indictments add up to a more general failure of parties to innovate and properly translate voter preferences into policy outcomes. Furthermore, France and Germany provide a central clue for what shapes the development of entrepreneurial parties. In rebuilding their democracies after 1945, German and French politicians agreed that the ineffectiveness of parties had undermined their interwar democracies and that their ineffectiveness could be traced to poorly designed electoral and parliamentary procedures. They recognized that it was not just parties that affected democracy but that the particular constitutional configuration of democracy also influenced the proper functioning of parties. They consequently set out to re-engineer parties by changing the constitutional environment under which they operate (Williams 1958; Fromme 1960; Oberreuter 1990). The insight that politicians gained after 1945 from the malfunctioning of interwar parties was not available to politicians in 1870–71 when France and Germany introduced universal male suffrage and when parties in the modern sense did not yet exist. The absence of any ex ante knowledge about the effects of institutions on parties only made these effects more open-ended and hence significant (Schanbacher 1982; Albertini 1961; Duverger and Seurin 1955).

Unlike political scientists, historians have analyzed the link between institutional design, the innovative capacity of parties, and democratic performance. They are attentive to these three elements and weave them into their larger historical narratives. Despite this attention, the causal interconnections between these three elements are insufficiently explained. Existing historiography is characterized by a peculiar disjuncture. On the one hand, innumerable party monographs and electoral histories provide highly particularistic accounts of how institutional and noninstitutional factors affect the internal politics and development of parties.[1] Unfortunately, these studies do not systematically analyze the effects of institutions, nor do they pay specific attention to the role parties play, in the two countries' democratic performance. On the other hand, macrohistorical accounts in the form of either national histories or cross-national comparisons engage the issue of democratization but often view parties as epiphenomenological proxies of large-scale, sociohistorical forces. They treat parties as organizationally undifferentiated, single unitary actors that are unaffected by institutions.[2] Neither historical perspective explicitly studies how institutions structure the internal decision making of parties and thereby affect their capacity to innovate and respond to changes in their political environments.

The notable exception is the work undertaken by Ferdinand Hermens in the 1940s and 1950s. Yet he attributed Weimar's collapse so single-mindedly to its electoral system that subsequent scholars found it difficult to look beyond his institutional reductionism and give due consideration to his more valuable insights (Hermens 1941). This state of affairs is regrettable for three reasons. First, advances in the study of electoral systems allow us to place Hermens's argument on a much firmer and more differentiated theoretical basis, while 50 years of extensive historical research now permits a methodologically self-conscious comparative analysis. Second, democratic transitions in Eastern Europe and Latin America have put the role of parties during democratic consolidation back on the scholarly agenda (Mainwaring and Scully 1995). Third, recent debates in French and German historiography have questioned previous exceptionalist accounts (Blackbourn and Eley 1984; Passmore 1993; Russo 1991). The explicit comparison of parties and electoral politics in both countries will help to differentiate similar and dissimilar elements within this subplot of French and German history.[3]

The Puzzle: Similar Historical Contexts,
Different Political Consequences

Conceptually, this study hinges on a comparison of how French and German parties responded to changing historical circumstances. And innovation will be evaluated in terms of how readily parties adapted themselves to four sets of historical circumstances: mass politics, interwar economic crisis, electoral volatility, and fragmentation. A quick review of these four circumstances underscores the rationale for comparing French and German parties. It also demonstrates that despite their similar deficiencies, German parties proved even less entrepreneurial than their French counterparts.

Mass politics constituted the most significant and enduring factor challenging French and German parties. It was set in motion by universal male suffrage and the industrialization that transformed the social and organizational basis of electoral politics. Mass politics confronted French and German parties with similar exigencies for modernizing their organizations, political platforms, and campaigning styles. Before 1914, French and German parties responded to these exigencies in similar ways by establishing effective national organizations, articulating distinct ideological profiles, and becoming increasingly entrepreneurial in their electioneering strategies. After 1918, however, French and German parties responded in a strikingly different manner to the continued challenges of mass politics. Germany's established parties—the Sozialdemokratische Partei Deutschlands (German Social Democratic Party, SPD), Deutsche Demokratische

Partei (German Democratic Party, DDP), Deutsche Volkspartei (German People's Party, DVP) and Deutschnationale Volkspartei (German National People's Party, DNVP)—became far more inert than before 1914. Their programs became more dogmatic, their organizations increasingly bureaucratized and less participatory, and their campaigning style less innovative and entrepreneurial. Conversely, France's established parties— Section française de l'internationale ouvrière (French Socialist Party, SFIO), Parti radical (Radical Party), and Union républicaine démocratique (Republican Democratic Union, URD)—continued along their pre-1914 trajectory. They debated and periodically reformed their electoral platforms, expanded their organizations without lessening grassroots involvement, and modernized their electioneering strategies.[4]

Economic turmoil in the interwar years constituted a second challenge confronting parties. The French and German interwar economies were highly volatile and rocked by a series of economic crises. These crises politicized economic issues on an unprecedented scale, posing a short-term programmatic challenge for parties that interacted with the long-term effects of mass politics on their ideological development. The postwar inflation raised troubling questions for liberals of how to reconcile their deflationary orthodoxy with the need to minimize its unequal distributional consequences. The Great Depression confronted socialists with the challenge of rethinking their Marxist orthodoxies and adopting new Keynesian policies that promised to alleviate unemployment. And the agricultural crisis compelled conservatives to reconsider their objections to rural relief programs. I do not deny that the problems in the economy, in foreign policy, and in legitimacy were much greater for a defeated Germany with a changed regime than for a victorious France with an unchanged constitution. Nevertheless, these well-known differences should not obscure others that are often missed: French parties readily modified their agendas, organizations, and electioneering practices while German parties failed to adapt theirs.

Throughout the book, the innovative capacity of parties is assessed primarily in terms of their responses to mass politics and to the interwar economic crisis. I would like to supplement this historical benchmark with a few aggregate, quantitative measures, presented in table 1. Volatility and fragmentation are used as proxy indicators for the constraints interwar historical contingencies imposed on parties. Electoral continuity, polarization, breakaway parties, and start-up parties, in turn, are meant to express how innovatively parties responded to these constraints.

Electoral volatility measures the vote shifting between parties. It can be viewed as a proxy measure for various short-term historical circumstances destabilizing voter allegiances. Table 1 shows that France's interwar volatility of 13.7 percent and Germany's of 17.8 percent were both considerably higher than the European average of 9.9 percent for the same period. Yet while French and German voters both frequently shifted their allegiances, they realigned themselves in very different ways. These different realignment patterns manifest themselves in the electoral continuity of established parties and the vote share of extremist parties (i.e., polarization). These patterns can serve as a measure for the adaptiveness of parties. French voters switched between established parties. In the last interwar election, in 1936, France's established parties managed to maintain 88.2 percent of the seats they had won in the first interwar election. They also lost only a modest amount of their parliamentary strength to extremist parties, which won on average only 5.1 percent of the seats. The ability of France's established parties to woo each other's voters assured the electoral continuity and limited polarization and ultimately can be taken as an indicator of their innovativeness. Germany's unsettled voters, on the other hand, defected at ever increasing rates from established parties beginning already in 1924 (Jones 1988). By 1932, Weimar's older, established parties,

TABLE 1. Realignment and Fragmentation Patterns, 1919–39

	Third Republic	Weimar Republic
Realignment patterns		
Volatility	13.7	17.8
Continuity of established parties[a]	88.2%	44.3%
Seat share of extremist parties[b]	5.1%	32.2%
Fragmentation patterns		
Effective number of parliamentary parties	7.2	6.0
Breakaway parties[c]	14	8
Start-up parties[c]	5	8

Source: Falter, Lindenberger, and Schuman (1986); M. Schlesinger (1989, 45, appendix); Bartolini and Mair (1990, appendix).

[a]Calculated as seats won in the last election as percentage of seats won in the first election. In Weimar, 1919 results were used for first election and 1932 results for last election. The average given is based on DDP, DVP, SPD, and DNVP. The average increases to 49.6% if the Zentrum and BVP are included.

[b]Classified as extremists; in Germany, KPD, USPD, NSDAP, DVFP, and DNVP (after 1930); in France, PCF, Parti d'unité prolétarienne, Parti social français (PSF) (after 1936), Parti agraire.

[c]Only counting parties winning at least one seat. Breakaways are formed through defections from existing parties, whereas start-up parties are formed de novo.

which had founded the Republic, retained only 44.3 percent of their original parliamentary strength in 1919. They also lost a disproportionate
amount of their support to extremist parties like the Kommunistische
Partei Deutschlands (German Communist Party, KPD) and the Nationalsozialistische Deutsche Arbeiterpartei (National Socialist German Workers' Party, NSDAP). The polarization became particularly striking after
1930, when extremist parties won on average 54.4 percent of the votes,
compared to only 14 percent before 1929. The dramatic electoral loss of
Weimar's established parties provides a measure for their ossification and
inability to compete with new start-up parties.

Fragmentation provides another measure of historical contingencies
capturing especially societal cleavages. It is a somewhat imperfect measure
of historical circumstances because the number of parties also is determined by institutional constraints. Yet fragmentation still is worth a brief
consideration, because the type of fragmentation we can observe—factionalism or segmentation—provides insights into how intransigent and risk-
averse actors are in dealing with each other. According to Laakso and
Taagepera's measure of effective number of parties (N_s), both party systems displayed extremely high levels of fragmentation.[5] The magnitude of
France's 7.2 parties and Weimar's 6.0 parties becomes apparent when compared to the N_s 2.4 that Taagepera and Shugart report for 44 democracies
in the early 1980s (1989, 83–84). France's and Germany's high levels of
fragmentation, however, mask two very different types of fragmentation.

The French fragmentation can be described as fluid factionalism. It
was characterized by weakly cohesive parties that permitted ambitious
politicians to advance their political careers by setting up their own parties. Of France's 19 new interwar parties, 14 formed as breakaways from
existing parties. The other five parties, in turn, were start-ups formed
entirely de novo.[6] These start-up parties were even more insignificant and
ephemeral than many breakaway parties. What offset the brittle quality of
the French party system, however, were the frequently changing electoral
alliances like the Bloc national, Union nationale, Cartel des gauches, or
Front populaire, through which parties cooperated. In this context, factionalism thus attests to the entrepreneurialism of French politicians.

German fragmentation, on the other hand, resembled rigid segmentation. The eight breakaway parties were far less numerous than in France
and were mostly the result of expulsions (four out of eight) rather than
politically ambitious faction leaders. Weimar also had a slightly higher
number of start-up parties (eight) than France, which, moreover, won a
far greater share of the votes. Parties like the Wirtschaftspartei, the Land-

bund, the Volksrechtspartei, and above all the NSDAP were significantly larger than any of their French counterparts.[7] Weimar parties also engaged in little electoral cooperation, since it was not necessary under proportional representation (PR). Michaela Richter nicely captures this segmentation when characterizing Weimar parties as pursuing "mobilization strategies which aimed both to create strong 'boundaries' around their constituencies and to develop a 'siege mentality' among their supporters. . . . The point . . . was less to mobilize hitherto untapped sources of support than to ensure the absolute loyalty and solidity of a party's traditional electoral base" (1986, 120). Segmentation underscores the intransigence and ideological rigidity of German politicians, especially for incumbent politicians. This inflexibility reflected timidness, risk aversion, and lack of imagination much more than it did deeply held political passions and principles.

French and German parties thus differed fundamentally in their innovative capacity, especially after 1918. This difference played a crucial role for the distinct ways in which the two countries responded to mass politics, interwar economic turmoil, volatility, and fragmentation. We thus face the *puzzling disjuncture between the fairly similar historical conditions shaping development of parties and the very different political consequences resulting from the parties' response to these conditions.* Historical differences like Germany's lost war, regime change, or severe economic depression account for some variance in the two countries' political performance, but, as subsequent chapters show, they cannot account for all or even most of it. If anything, with Germany's final democratization in 1918, the two countries became even more alike at the same time as the innovative capacity of their parties diverged more than ever.

The principal explanation can be found in how electoral mechanisms structure a politician's three principal activities: securing a candidacy, mobilizing resources, and winning votes. Elections are among the most highly regulated of political activities, so we should expect the specific nature of these regulations to affect the collective actions of politicians inside parties, their relationships with economic interest groups, and their interaction with voters. In other words, electoral mechanisms affect the conduct of politicians at the pre-electoral stage, when they fight over nominations and court economic interest groups, as well as in the electoral marketplace, when they finally woo voters.

Moreover, electoral mechanisms provide a compelling starting point for explaining French and German party development. Both countries used the same double ballot system until 1918. Under this system, election

on the first ballot was possible for the candidate winning an absolute
majority (greater than 50 percent). If no candidate obtained such a majority, elections were decided by a runoff ballot and plurality. After 1918, the
Third Republic kept the double ballot system, whereas Weimar introduced one of the purest forms of PR ever designed. The empirical chapters
(chapters 3 to 6) explain cross-national differences in the electoral fortunes
of four sets of ideologically paired parties: socialists, liberals, conservatives, and fascists.

Legal provisions other than those found in the electoral law also affect
how entrepreneurial a politician will be in carrying out his representative
tasks. Executive-legislative relations, parliamentary committee structures,
geographic divisions of power, constitutional review, and referenda are
additional institutions that have to be analyzed to fully explain what historians call the national histories of interwar France and Germany or what
political scientists label political systems or democratic performance. This
book does not study such extra-electoral institutions and instead limits its
analysis to the performance of individual parties within the electoral arena.

The electoral performance of individual parties arguably played a key
role for the overall political stability of France and Germany, but the two
should not automatically be equated. Explaining actions of individual parties tells us little about the legislative process, the role of bureaucrats and
judges, or the hidden powers of the military and captains of industry. We
therefore have to be careful before relating the effects of electoral institutions to the performance of entire political regimes. But their centrality has
been widely recognized. The French prime minister Aristide Briand
declared that the double ballot system had "rendered his country and its
republic one of the largest services. It installed the regime and consolidated
it" (cited in Cotteret 1960, 11). In Germany, in turn, the list of scholars and
public commentators attributing Weimar's woes to PR was long indeed. It
even included Oswald Spengler, who added PR to his otherwise mostly
metaphysical reasons for the decline of the Occident (Pollock 1932, 250).
In a decidedly less anecdotal fashion, the conclusion addresses how the
focus on electoral politics affects our ability to draw more general insights
for the performance of democracy in interwar France and Germany.

Combining Historical Narrative with
Theoretical Generalizing

Social scientists generally see little virtue in adding historical context, per-
ceiving it as pesky background noise standing in the way of edifying theo-

retical parsimony. The previous section, however, identified French and German party development as a historical phenomenon, without being too historical to preclude generalizations. It showed that we need an explanatory framework that incorporates the highly contingent forces pushing the development of parties forward while simultaneously providing a systematic account of how mechanical, transhistorical electoral procedures translated these historical forces into such different political outcomes. I will first elaborate the obstacles to such an interdisciplinary framework before specifying its particular variables.

The central obstacle to combining historical and social science research comes, I would suggest, from an overly strict observance of disciplinary boundaries. This intellectual segregation contributes to the respective disciplinary orthodoxies that an explanation has to conform *in its entirety* to either an idiomatic, interpretive logic or a generalizing, axiomatic one. Of course, many scholars do not subscribe to this disciplinary segregation and refuse to make uniform, undifferentiated theoretical claims for all the variables they employ. Nevertheless, the disciplinary divide is deep enough and common enough to require closer attention before a more ecumenical alternative is proposed.

Most political scientists have difficulties treating historical phenomena because they see themselves as primarily concerned with discerning the systematic from the random. As Sewell (1996, 258–59) points out, the commitment to generalize requires finding units of analysis, not unlike in the physical world, that are qualitatively equivalent and independent of chronologically prior events. These requirements make it difficult for political scientists to analyze phenomena that change through time or interact with sequentially prior events. Criticizing King, Keohane, and Verba for subscribing to such assumptions, Sidney Tarrow observes that "the function of qualitative [historical] research is not to peel away layers of non-systematic fluff from the hard core of systematic variables, but also to assist researchers to understand shifts in the value of systematic variables" (1995, 472). Tarrow makes an important point. King, Keohane, and Verba (1994, 101) come close to conceding Tarrow's point in quoting O'Hear: "There may be no true universal theories, owing to conditions differing markedly through time and space; this is a possibility we cannot overlook. But even if this were so, science could still fulfill many of its aims in giving us knowledge and true predictions about conditions in and around our spatio-temporal niche."[8]

The assumption of operating within a temporal niche is perfectly suitable for analyzing many political phenomena, but it becomes problematic when studying historical processes that extend across historical niches and whose chronological sequencing affects outcomes (Collier and Collier 1991, 27–39; Kiser 1996, 254). The assumption of time as a constant even permeates the work of historically minded social scientists. Skocpol (1979), North (1990), and Levi (1981), for example, consider something as historical because it occurred in the past and not because it extends through time (Sewell 1996). This neglect of time makes it difficult to differentiate between meaningful sounds in the historical background, which matter, and ahistorical background noise, which is genuinely irrelevant. Mass politics, for example, indisputably influenced party development, yet political scientists would treat it as a historical, nonsystematic factor, something as random as the eye color of voters. This disregard for time may be attributable to an overextended analogy between the physical world (where the theoretical models originate) and the social world (where they are applied). Morris Cohen captured this point when observing that "if we have the mechanical or physical coordinates of a body or physical system, we do not need to inquire into its past history to determine its future course. . . . Organic [i.e., societal] phenomena are not so independent of time. A tree bears the evidence of an injury to it a century ago when it was a young shoot" (Cohen 1947, 118). Cohen's point that the past has an even more persistent and unchangeable influence on society than on inanimate nature is pertinent for articulating a theoretical framework suitable for explaining party development.

Historians, on the other hand, are interested in explaining historical persons, events, and changes within structures, rather than identifying general phenomena, which precludes them from observing systematic regularities. The historian's subject matter thus has the exact opposite properties of cases: they are unique (hence lacking any possible equivalence) and are linked to chronologically prior events (thus incapable of ever being independent). Historians' interest in the historically embedded prevents them from observing possible regularities across space. The neglect of such a possibility frequently produces exceptionalist explanations that risk overestimating historical particularities and neglecting the systematic, cross-national factors.[9] King, Keohane, and Verba (1994) are correct in pointing out that such historical and qualitative research frequently lacks the methodological self-consciousness necessary to increase confidence in exceptionalist claims.

Having indicated the limitations of historical analysis, however, it is important to resist the all-too-common and highly unfortunate canard that historians, by virtue of not pursuing lawlike generalizations, engage in mere storytelling. This haughty caricature overlooks the fact that historians pursue distinct explanatory objectives that go well beyond recounting just "one damn thing after another" (H. A. L. Fisher, cited in Burnham 1994, 59). Historiographical debates, for example, about the origins of fascism concern themselves with generalizing about chronological proximity and sequencing of historical events to a particular outcome. To what degree was Nazism the product of the Protestant Church's subordination to the state in the sixteenth and seventeenth centuries, the failed "bourgeois revolution" in the nineteenth century, the Great Depression in the twentieth century, or the particular sequencing of these and other events? *Historians focus on the chronological rather than spatial regularities.* They generalize along the durable-transient continuum rather than the systematic-random. They are concerned with historical continuities and discontinuities, periodization, or what we social scientists call path dependence. Historical research takes place at the edges of temporal niches to see when qualitative changes over time amount to a change in kind (i.e., mark a genuine disjuncture or period). Or it takes place across temporal niches to investigate whether or how long the causal impact of specific events extends through time. In either case, historians display a concern for the very temporal regularities and irregularities that social scientists ignore. If historians can be said to own a variable, it would be time.

Historical and social scientific research thus clearly conform to distinct explanatory logics whose respective strengths nicely complement each other. I therefore pursue a more ecumenical course that involves two steps. First, I relax the assumption that an explanation has to conform in its entirety to a single explanatory logic. Rather than tarring all variables with the same broad epistemological brush, I ascribe distinct explanatory specifications to individual variables. I assign an axiomatic, generalizing logic to institutions and agency (e.g., actors defined as rational utility maximizers) and attribute a narrative logic to socioeconomic developments and political events. As the next section demonstrates, this strategy rests on the assumption that agency and institutions are less time-sensitive and more static variables than socioeconomic/political events and consequently more amenable to generalizations.

Second, I configure the individual variables into a joint explanatory framework. The goal of this framework is not to produce lawlike, predictive generalizations that would themselves be sufficient for explaining party development (Katznelson 1997; Lichbach 1997).[10] The impact of historical factors on party development makes such an objective impossible. Instead, these generalizations most closely correspond to what economic sociologists and cognitive psychologists term analysis of causal mechanisms (Elster 1989; Hedström and Swedberg 1998a, 1998b). "To explain an event . . . takes the form of citing an earlier event as the cause of the event we want to explain together with some account of the causal mechanism connecting the two events" (Elster 1989, 3). In this case, the psychological properties of agents making decisions and the mechanical incentives of electoral mechanisms will provide the causal mechanisms for explaining why French and German politicians responded differently to socioeconomic changes and political events whose similarity has been underestimated. In other words, they will provide a systematic account for how mass politics, electoral volatility, and levels of fragmentation were translated into such different organizational trajectories, polarization and realignment patterns, and types of fragmentation.

Theoretical Potential of Different Variables

Specifying different explanatory logics for individual variables rests on the assumption that variables have distinct properties and that these properties affect their potential to either generalize across space or account for change across time. It therefore is necessary to elaborate on the static, "transhistorical" and hence generalizable qualities of agency and institutions and the dynamic, historical and mutable characteristics of socioeconomic factors.

Rational choice theorists have demonstrated the enormous theoretical potential of agency. In focusing on utility maximization, they have identified a psychological constant with recurring and hence generalizable properties. Rational choice theorists focusing on electoral politics have identified the benefits of office holding (i.e., prestige, income, policy influence, career advancement) as discrete, readily identifiable, and largely unchanging goals that politicians seek to maximize (Downs 1957; Mayhew 1974; J. Schlesinger 1975). Utility maximization and office seeking are theoretical constructs that are, of course, not immutable constants and are not entirely autonomous from historical circumstances (Monroe 1991; Tsebelis 1990, 31–36; Simon 1985). They constitute, however, a realistic empirical approximation of electoral politics from the late nineteenth century onward. Historians, following contemporaries like Michels, Weber, and Ostrogorski, discuss the advent of political careerism and professionalism during this period. As the first chapter will show, office-seeking politicians did not emerge instantaneously and uniformly across the political spectrum. Nevertheless, from the 1890s onward, there was a significant behavioral convergence of politicians around the self-interested, office-seeking model discussed by rational choice theorists.

Agency alone, however, is insufficient for explaining French and German party development. *While politicians might all be utility maximizers and office seekers, they still differ with regard to various nonpsychological factors.* They differ in their resources, levels of information, and organizational cohesion. Variance across such nonpsychological endowments underscores that politicians act in highly contingent economic, technological, and organizational contexts. Overlooking an actor's context inevitably yields "undersocialized," "underinstitutionalized," and purely static explanations (Granovetter 1985; Taylor 1993). Put differently, without configuring agency with institutional and socioeconomic variables, it would be impossible to assign probabilities to the payoffs politicians seek to realize.

As a variable, political institutions closely resemble agency. Their mechanical properties create consistent and recurring incentives and constraints that are constant even across "temporal niches." Their constitutional status assures institutions' considerable durability and provides them with a degree of formalism that makes them analytically discrete and readily identifiable. There are few reasons to assume that the incentives and constraints of electoral mechanisms have changed since the turn of the century. Historical monographs from the interwar period, for example, report numerous complaints by politicians about the constraints that electoral procedures imposed on them. This anecdotal evidence is very consistent with the institutional effects that the literature on electoral systems has demonstrated across countries (Rae 1967; Taagepera and Shugart 1989; Lijphart 1994; Cox 1997).

Yet, just like agency, institutions alone are insufficient for explaining party development. The ultimate, political consequences of institutional constraints depend on their interaction with noninstitutional factors. A candidate's resources, for example, influence the degree to which logistical requirements created by electoral mechanisms will constrain his actions. Institutions interact with purposive actors *and* historically contingent factors. Overlooking the interaction between institutions and agents yields overinstitutionalized explanations, while neglecting the interaction between institutions and historical factors leads to static explanations.

This dual reductionism is particularly pronounced in the literature on electoral systems, which correlates the number of parties, their parliamentary size, or any other quantifiable outcome with various electoral mechanisms.[11]

Socioeconomic and political factors lack the durable and recurring properties that would make them amenable to the kind of theorizing undertaken by rational choice and institutional theorists. Class structures, economic conditions, wars, or political crises are dynamic and historical variables that either do not repeat themselves or change over time. These factors differ markedly today from the turn of the century and even changed during the period of our analysis. They lack anything equivalent to the mechanical properties or psychological constants of the other two variables. Furthermore, socioeconomic and political factors are analytically less discrete and identifiable than institutions. Institutional taxonomies, for example, are far less controversial than occupational categorizations.

Yet, for all their theoretical limitations, socioeconomic and political factors are enormously important in explaining French and German party development. Historians and political observers around the turn of the century widely agreed that socioeconomic changes as well as political events like the First World War transformed notable politics into mass politics and constituted a profound structural and qualitative transformation of electoral politics. Such changes made voters less deferential, shifted the relative distribution of resources, and transformed voter preferences. They are crucial for understanding the different historical opportunities to which politicians responded.

While socioeconomic and political factors provide the crucial dynamic that is missing in rational choice models or institutional explanations, they too are insufficient for explaining party development (Sartori 1969). They played a crucial role in inducing, without causing, the organizational trajectories and realignment patterns of French and German parties. They do not provide a "rock bottom" or "ultimate explanation" of party development but only account for the possibility of its occurrence (Taylor 1993, 91–92). Socioeconomic factors cannot explain outcomes but help to "cut down the feasible set of abstractly possible courses of action and reduce it to a vastly smaller subset of feasible actions" (Elster, cited in Cohen 1994, 9). Furthermore, a purely socioeconomic explanation runs the risk of stressing historical contingencies to the point of producing exceptionalist explanations. It therefore is important to check for possible regularities across time and space to avoid the geographic and temporal reductionism that characterizes exceptionalist explanations.

Research Design and Different Case Configurations

To explore fully the theoretical potential of agency and institutions requires close attention to methodological considerations. The central goal of every research design is to maximize the confidence that the explanatory variables actually cause the outcomes observed on the dependent variable. This general goal raises specific methodological issues when applied to qualitative research based on few cases ("small N"), such as is undertaken in this book. King, Keohane, and Verba (1994) identify three possible sources of biased inferences: selection of cases, endogeneity, and omitted variables. I briefly discuss how these three problems are addressed.

Selection Bias.   The selection of cases on the dependent variable is a common source of bias in qualitative research. The small number of cases prevents random or large N sampling. Qualitative research also is often problem-driven, leading investigators to select cases that have a particular outcome in common. Such case selection creates a bias by eliminating variance on the dependent variable, which is necessary to actually observe the causal effects of the independent variable (King, Keohane, and Verba 1994, 128–48). I seek to avoid such selection bias by choosing my cases on the independent variable and truncating French and German party development into two historical periods (1870–1914 and 1918–1933/39). This strategy assures variance on the independent variable (i.e., PR versus double ballot) and on the dependent variable (i.e., different historical contexts, organizational trajectories, fragmentation, and realignment patterns).

Endogeneity Bias.   Endogeneity, in turn, refers to inferences that are biased by wrongly estimating the causal direction. Endogeneity bias occurs when the dependent variable has a feedback effect on the independent variable or when the independent variable subsumes factors that are causally prior (King, Keohane, and Verba 1994, 187–205). Fortunately, King, Keohane, and Verba illustrate this problem with Weimar's fragmented party system. They point out that the common attribution of this fragmentation to the permissive effects of its PR system overlooks that Germany's fragmented society led to the adoption of PR in the first place (1994, 189–90). Thus, it was societal cleavages that caused party fragmentation because they chronologically precede the choice of PR. This charge has to be taken seriously because it echoes the wider criticism that institutional theories ignore the origins of institutions.

I control for such endogeneity bias by analyzing the actual decision-making process leading to the adoption of PR. In other words, I submit King, Keohane, and Verba's implicit premise that institutional preferences are sociologically determined to historical scrutiny. Such scrutiny points to three problems with King, Keohane, and Verba's argument.

First, Imperial Germany's old double ballot system was even more permissive ($N_s = 8.01$ for 1903–14) than the PR system ($N_s = 5.7$). Consequently, there would have been little need to change the old electoral system if a more accurate representation of Germany's fragmented society had been the central concern. Second, Weimar's 1919 constitutional assembly, which selected the electoral system, was less fragmented ($N_s = 3.97$) than the party system produced in 1920 by its choice of electoral system ($N_s = 5.7$). It seems implausible to assume that the constitutional assembly would draft electoral procedures more permissive than required for assuring the representation of its members. Third, there is little evidence to be found for political pressures exerted on the constitutional assembly that could directly be tied to concerns for political inclusion and exclusion. The clearest evidence for the absence of such political pressure was the decision to delegate districting and choice of allocation formula to a nonpartisan, civil service agency. Since these features had a potentially significant effect on the representativeness of the electoral system, it is unlikely that politicians would have delegated their design if they were primarily concerned with the accurate representation of societal cleavages (Schanbacher 1982, 50–52).

In this context, it also important to remember that in 1918 Europe had virtually no prior experience with PR. Its precise political consequences were not well understood, making it difficult to attribute its choice to pre-existing societally induced preferences. If anything, preferences for PR were shaped simply because it was not the old double ballot. The old double ballot system had become discredited at the national level because the districting (unchanged since 1870) vastly overrepresented rural areas and because of the regime censitaire still used in some Länder elections. By 1914, politicians had come to conflate these two electoral procedures—districting and voting qualifications—with the entire electoral system and thus ended up changing it rather than reform its malfunctioning components (Schanbacher 1982, 130).

This example illustrates the larger point that the choice of institutions is first of all a political process in which the multiplicity of institutional effects, goals other than vote maximizing, and insufficient information shape the institutional choices far more than societal cleavages (Shvetsova 1998). The choice of institutions therefore is sufficiently indeterminate to establish that their causal effects are independent of causally prior factors. In a similar vein, Ellen Immergut observed that the "origins of institutions are chronologically independent from the actors and their strategies. That is, institutions are constraints created by political actors engaged in a struggle for power. However, the actors that participate in the battles over institutional design are only rarely identical to those that participate in later policy conflicts. Thus the view that institutions are somehow congealed societal structures is not especially helpful" (1992, 85).

Omitted Variable Bias.   The most serious source of biased inferences is the omission of variables that are causally significant. This omitted variable bias also is referred to as the issue of controlling for alternative variables (King, Keohane, and Verba 1994, 168–84). Failure to address it leaves a high degree of uncertainty over whether connections "between dependent and independent variables . . . suggest only association but not cause" (Laitin, cited in Kalyvas 1996, 15). The omitted variable bias also creates a particularly thorny problem for explanations incorporating temporal variables. I address this source of bias by multiplying the number of cases and configuring them into sets of comparisons that try to reduce bias resulting from omitted systematic variables as well as historical events.

For simplicity's sake, I so far have equated case with country. This is common practice even though there are many other ways to specify a case. Ragin rightly argues that "the term case and the various terms linked to the idea of case analysis are not well defined in social science" (1992, 1). The subsequent analysis disaggregates each country into four actors— socialists, liberals, conservatives, and fascists—and two time periods, 1870–1914 and 1918–1933/39. One case therefore becomes one party during a time period. This case specification makes sense since I am interested in the development of individual parties over time. It also increases the number of cases and permits three different sets of comparisons.

Before continuing with my different case configurations, I need to briefly digress and explain why the Catholic Zentrum (Center party) is not included in this study. Its omission could be considered by many as biasing inferences, especially since it was the largest party in the German Empire and remained one of the three largest in the Weimar Republic.[12] It principally has been excluded because there is no comparable party in France. On two occasions, French Catholics formed a clerical party. In 1902, Jacques Piou founded the Action libérale populaire (Liberal Popular Action, ALP), and conservative deputies created in 1928 the Parti démocrate populaire (Democratic Popular Party, PDP) (Delbreil 1990; Le Béguec 1992, 43–45). These parties are not comparable with the Zentrum since the ALP quickly floundered and the PDP never won more than a handful of seats. Kalyvas (1996) provides an interesting explanation for the failure of clerical parties in France. The Zentrum also cannot be reclassified as a conservative or liberal party, given its confessional nature and cross-class support. In short, the Zentrum was a distinct feature of the German party landscape, and this raises the question of how its omission skews the analysis of other German parties.

The exclusion of the Zentrum creates two potential problems for my argument. First, many traditional explanations contend that the prominence of Germany's confessional divide significantly contributed to the rigid segmentation of parties and their lack of entrepreneurialism (Lepsius 1973). They consequently would fault mine for spuriously attributing the risk taking of parties to institutional incentives rather than the constraints imposed by Germany's religious cleavage. I would contend that the confessional divide made the German political landscape more fluid by introducing a cultural dimension that cut across the constitutional, regional, and economic divides. In the early 1870s, for example, anticlericalism formed the basis for cooperation between liberals and Protestant conservatives. This cooperation softened the economic and constitutional issues that otherwise divided these two groups. From the late 1870s onward, the Center party emerged from its isolation during the Kulturkampf and became the quintessential swing party. Generally, it aligned itself with conservatives on economic and social policy issues and with Progressives and even Socialists on civil rights and military matters (Craig 1978, 57, 97, 279). The Zentrum widened the alliance possibilities and required German politicians to engage in intricate strategic maneuvering. It thereby added to the entrepreneurialism of German politicians rather than subtracted from it.

Second, various historians argue that the Zentrum's very size and role as a swing party make it a key element for understanding the performance of the Weimar Republic. Jürgen Falter (1991) and others have shown that religion was the strongest predictor of the Nazi vote, with Protestants far more likely than Catholics to support Hitler. John Zeender (1963) demonstrated that the refusal of Bavarian Catholics, who broke away in 1919–20 to form the Bayerische Volkspartei (Bavarian People's Party, BVP)—a Bavarian Zentrum—to vote for the Zentrum's candidate, Wilhelm Marx, prevented his defeat of Hindenburg. Such explanations implicitly fault mine for overlooking how the Zentrum affected the strategic interdependence of parties and thereby shaped the dynamic of the German party system. This criticism overlooks that my analysis focuses on electoral and pre-electoral activities of individual parties, where the strategic interdependence of parties is far smaller than in post-electoral activities like coalition formation, legislative bargaining, and cooperation among different branches of government. The Zentrum, for example, had no discernible impact on how other parties recruited candidates and mobilized resources. And its influence on other parties' vote getting was arguably limited. In the Weimar Republic, the Catholic vote was regionally concentrated and highly loyal. The Zentrum won vote shares greater than 21 percent in 13 out of 35 electoral districts (37 percent), 11–20 percent shares in 4 districts (8 percent), and less than 10 percent shares in 18 districts (51 percent). In electoral terms, therefore, the Zentrum was less a swing party than it was either a dominant party in Catholic districts or a minor party in Protestant ones.

With the omission of the Zentrum, the book's first case configuration consists of pairing socialist, liberal, conservative, and fascist parties in both countries. This pairwise, cross-national comparison amounts to a most similar system design, since each set of parties shares many important historical and socioeconomic characteristics (Przeworski and Teune 1970, 32–35). These paired parties are not identical, but they are more similar than socialist, liberal, conservative, and fascist parties within each country. The most similar system design of chapters 3 to 6 controls the variance of socioeconomic and political factors and hence minimizes the bias from their omission.

The second case configuration pairs individual parties across the two time periods. Such a comparison is not possible for fascist movements, since they only emerged after 1918. Chapter 1 provides the historical baseline by describing the organizational trajectories of parties between 1870–71 and 1914. Against this baseline, chapters 3 to 5 identify continuities and discontinuities in the development of parties. This longitudinal comparison also can be considered a most similar research design because it pairs the same party in the same national context but varies their historical background conditions. It controls for time by investigating the possible bias created by different background conditions. The longitudinal comparison directly addresses criticisms from historians about underestimating the impact of unique historical legacies or contingencies. As indicated, time cannot be controlled for in the conventional sense of being dismissable if demonstrating no systematic effects. The longitudinal comparison only shows that important cross-national similarities existing during each period and cross-temporal similarities far outweighed any differences. It merely seeks to demonstrate to historians that the unique and distinct elements they frequently privilege in their explanations are insufficient to account for the significant differences in organizational trajectories and realignment patterns of French and German parties.

The third configuration involves pooling all the interwar cases for each country. This intranational and interwar comparison is carried out in the conclusion and primarily serves to analyze how the parties' very different contexts affect the effects of institutions. This case configuration amounts to a most different system design, since socialist, liberal, conservative, and fascist parties had rather distinct historical and socioeconomic background conditions. To the extent that institutional effects hold across such dissimilar national parties, it will again help us assess potential bias introduced by nonsystematic factors as well as omitted variables.

The research design largely dictates the sequencing and structure of chapters. Chapter 1 highlights how slowly and reluctantly French and German politicians adapted themselves to the entrepreneurial exigencies of mass politics before 1914. It argues that this shared risk aversion constitutes a key similarity in late-nineteenth-century France and Germany making their histories comparable. The chapter contrasts this historical interpretation with traditional and more exceptionalist ones. Finally, it is meant to provide a historical baseline against which we can more clearly see the divergent trajectories of French and German parties during the interwar period. Chapter 2 steps back from history and outlines the theoretical argument for the growing risk aversion of German parties after 1918 and the continued entrepreneurialism of their French counterparts. It spells out the causal mechanism linking historical contingencies with the actions of parties. It does so by drawing on rational choice institutionalism to elaborate how institutions constrain the recruitment, resource mobilization, and vote getting of politicians. Chapters 3 to 6 empirically substantiate the theoretical argument. Their structure is dictated by the aforementioned methodological considerations. They are organized as pairwise, cross-national comparisons of socialists, liberals, conservatives, and fascists. Chapter 6 departs somewhat from earlier ones by shifting attention from established parties to newly emerging fascist movements. This shift entails a slight change in the issues under consideration. As political newcomers, fascists had to be highly entrepreneurial and far less prone to the inertia and ossification of established parties. Their principal challenge instead consisted in making the transition from an extra-institutional social movement to an institutionalized political party. To explain how electoral institutions structured this transformation, chapter 6 adds a brief modification of the theoretical argument laid out in chapter 2.

Finally, the conclusion addresses two outstanding issues. It looks more closely at the interaction between transhistorical institutions and historical contingencies and draws tentative conclusions about the circumstances under which their respective importance varies. It also clarifies what inferences can be drawn for French and German overall political development from a study mostly focusing on the electoral and pre-electoral activities of politicians.

Chapter 1

Reluctant Entrepreneurs: Coping with Mass Politics before 1914

Entrepreneurial politicians and the innovation they breed are as central for the working of democracy as business entrepreneurs are for the functioning of a free-market economy. In the late nineteenth century, however, few politicians considered politics a vocation in which they could make a career out of their organizational, oratorical, and strategic skills. Most still considered politics a gentlemanly avocation confined to polite debates in exclusive clubs (Weber 1946). The driving force pushing politicians to become reluctant entrepreneurs was mass politics. Mass politics denotes various socioeconomic and legal changes shifting political decision making from a few powerful individuals to the anonymous dynamics of the electoral market. The first and arguably most important change leading to this shift was the introduction of universal male suffrage in France in 1870 and in Germany in 1871.[1] Subsequent reforms of electoral administration and balloting further strengthened this political groundswell by limiting possibilities to manipulate electoral outcomes. By the late 1880s, industrialization transformed the technological and social basis of electoral politics. New railways and roads, expanding public education, cheaper mass newspapers, growing state intervention in social and economic policymaking, urbanization, and changing class structures all nationalized and collectivized electoral politics. These socioeconomic and institutional changes unleashed new and powerful political forces from below. They inserted mass politics into the existing liberal constitutional order, whose rule of law, independent judiciary, and political representation had by 1870 largely supplanted the seignorial, ecclesiastical, and royal prerogatives of the ancien régime.

This chapter analyzes how mass politics turned French and German politicians into reluctant entrepreneurs before the First World War. It provides the historical backdrop for the subsequent chapters' analysis of how much latitude institutional factors gave these same politicians during the interwar period to remain risk-averse and resist innovation. The chapter analyzes the effects of mass politics separately for socialists, liberals, and conservatives, since each resisted it in different ways and degrees. In the socialist camp, revolutionaries frowned upon electoralism because it allegedly undermined their long-term goal of forming a revolutionary collective identity. Liberals rejected electioneering and strategizing as political agitation that was irreconcilable with rational deliberation. And conservatives condemned vote getting for inciting public expectations and undermining the status quo.

The different political groups, therefore, were reluctant to accept the entrepreneurial exigencies of mass politics and preferred to cling to their old conceptions of politics. This chapter analyzes the actors' reluctance to acquire three sets of entrepreneurial skills. First, the importance of campaigning skills increased as the deference of voters waned. Politicians needed to exploit technological opportunities, hone their oratory, and become tactically sophisticated. Second, the growing politicization and organization of societal groups demanded the crafting of delicately balanced and regularly changing political platforms. Politicians were required to combine substantive promises with personal appeal in order to accommodate the hopes and fears of voters and differentiate themselves from their opponents. Third, with the need to campaign and formulate programs ultimately came the need to organize. A political observer noted in 1910 that "the word *party,* which signified yesterday an opinion, now suggests an organization founded to sustain this opinion" (Albertini 1961, 566). Political actors needed collective governance structures to articulate policies and logistical infrastructure to implement them.

Besides setting the historical stage for the subsequent analysis, this chapter also pursues an important methodological objective. It provides an ex ante perspective by looking at French and German party development from their starting points in the 1870s. In doing so, it self-consciously departs from the ex post perspective employed by many traditional accounts. Many of these accounts have in recent years been revised, but they still shape the exceptionalist understanding of French and German history so strongly that their interpretations have to be critically evaluated. By employing an ex ante perspective, this chapter demonstrates that similarities in pre-1914 French and German party development far outweighed any differences. It argues that existing explanations overlook these similarities by committing the post hoc fallacy of reasoning backward from distinct outcomes to distinct antecedent causes as well as the static fallacy of treating intervening history as inconsequential. And to the extent that differences existed, this chapter's conclusion will show that they contributed to the greater entrepreneurialism of German politicians before 1914.

Mass Politics and Socialist Parties

Of all political groups, socialists were the least reluctant entrepreneurs. As political outsiders and newcomers, the Section française de l'internationale ouvrière (French Socialist Party, SFIO)[2] and the Sozialdemokratische Partei Deutschlands (German Social Democratic Party, SPD)[3] had to compensate for their lack of resources and initial repression with organizational ingenuity. Yet mass politics still confronted the two parties with new challenges to which they were reluctant to adapt themselves. At the core of this challenge was the debate over whether liberal democracy, and the mass politics it engendered, facilitated or hindered working-class emancipation. This debate was particularly lively in the SFIO and SPD since the early introduction of universal male suffrage engaged the two parties in mass politics far earlier than other European socialist parties. The possibility of electoral participation encouraged reformists to work toward socialism through incremental reforms and by maximizing the left's electoral potential. Revolutionaries, by contrast, viewed universal suffrage as a false gift that changed little about the legacies of repression, the church's unbroken power, and continuing economic inequalities. This debate defined the issues of innovation in the working-class movement. Revolutionaries rejected the entrepreneurial exigencies of mass politics. They argued instead for a centrally organized, highly mass-based, and ideologically principled party that would remain immune to short-term electoralist temptations. Conversely, reformists challenged the doctrinaire thinking of revolutionaries. They argued for a more participatory, pragmatic, and voter-oriented political party willing to respond to exigencies of the electoral marketplace.

The historiography of the SFIO and SPD pays insufficient attention to the debate between reformists and revolutionaries that mass politics set in motion. Many existing historical accounts do not view the two parties' characteristics in the 1930s as outcomes of possible alternatives in the late nineteenth century but consider them instead as foregone historical conclusions. Explanations of the SPD, for example, concentrate on its repression and political exclusion in Imperial Germany. They argue that this legacy contributed to the SPD's negative integration in the existing political order and its formation as a social ghetto party. They further contend that the SPD's negative integration before 1914 explains its organizational and ideological ossification during the Weimar Republic (Lipset 1983; Roth 1963; Groh 1974; Lepsius 1973; Mommsen 1974). Conversely, many accounts of the SFIO highlight the early opportunities for political participation and contestation in France. They argue that these opportunities contributed to the SFIO's positive integration within the existing political order and its development as a pragmatic and electoralist party. They maintain that the SFIO's positive integration accounts for its participatory organization, strategic flexibility, and ideological pluralism during the interwar period (Lipset 1983; Bergounioux and Grunberg 1992; Ziebura 1967).

While neither argument is incorrect, they both are incomplete. The negative integration thesis focuses too exclusively on Germany's (antisocialist) Socialist Law (1878–90), the restrictive association law (in place until 1900 in Prussia and until 1908 in the Reich), and police harassment. German socialists certainly were repressed, and this experience shaped their development before 1914. But they also operated within an increasingly less partisan Rechtsstaat, a partially sovereign parliament, and universal (male) and free elections.[4] The negative integration thesis also ignores that the necessity of forming electoral alliances under Germany's double ballot system led to political cooperation among virtually all parties, including the SPD (Anderson 2000, 397, 434–35). Conversely, the positive integration thesis concentrates too exclusively on France's democratic pedigrees. It overlooks the mass execution and exiling of Parisian Communards and the outlawing of socialist organizations by the Dufour Law (1872–76). France's police also were as cavalier as the Prussian police in interpreting the civil and political rights of socialists, thus largely negating any organizational advantages to be derived from France's somewhat more liberal association law (Haupt 1986, 244–45). Moreover, the late introduction of voting envelopes and booths in 1913 allowed conservative notables and the Catholic Church to unduly influence voters. In Germany, opponents of socialists lost this opportunity in 1903. Repression together with the insufficient protection of the secret ballot radicalized various French socialists in ways that the positive integration thesis ignores.

The negative and positive integration theses, then, are palatable for explaining post hoc the SPD's and SFIO's distinct qualities in the 1930s. But they are sorely inadequate for accounting ex ante for their organizational and behavioral development, particularly before 1914. An ex ante perspective provides a more differentiated and far less exceptionalist account. It particularly highlights two similarities. First, the SFIO and SPD only partly adapted themselves to the entrepreneurial exigencies of mass politics. By 1914, both parties were still divided into reformist and revolutionary factions and behaved at times like a vote-maximizing, tactic-driven entrepreneur and at other times like a revolutionary, ideology-driven movement. Their experiences with mass politics did not lead them to assess it in a uniformly favorable light. The strength of communists in both countries after 1918 illustrates this partial adaptation of socialists to mass politics.[5] Second, the SFIO and SPD's organizational growth did not lead to a level of bureaucratization that impeded their innovative capacity and prevented experimentation with new campaigning strategies. Their governance remained decentralized and participatory enough to preserve ideological diversity. The following analysis elaborates these two similarities further.

French Socialists

The easing of political repression in the 1880s gave rise to multiple and organizationally embryonic socialist parties (Judt 1986, 97–99). The Guesdists, Blanquists, and Allemanists were revolutionary, while the Independent Socialists and Possibilists had a reformist orientation. The electoral support of these parties was negligible since voters still were highly deferential and easily manipulated by political notables.

Despite their rudimentary organization, these parties held distinct organizational ideals. Guesdists, Blanquists, and Allemanists preferred a centralized and disciplined mass organization that was capable of forming a revolutionary working-class identity. They questioned the emancipatory potential of universal suffrage. In their eyes, it had done little to alter the existing distribution of power and in many ways facilitated bourgeois efforts to translate their economic power into political power. Little had changed since the Second Republic, when illiterate, devout, and deferential voters had elected a conservative rather than a socialist parliament (Agulhon 1983, 42–48). Independent Socialists and Possibilists, on the other hand, favored a decentralized, pluralistic, and election-oriented party. They believed that universal suffrage would facilitate the gradual emancipation of workers. Their organization reflected this belief by leaving most organizational and programmatic initiative to local organizations. In the eyes of reformists, local branches were best acquainted with the concerns of voters and thus most capable of maximizing votes (Noland [1953] 1970, 11–25, 79, 182–86).

The Dreyfus affair (1894–1906) and the general nationalization of electoral politics contributed to the left's organizational consolidation after 1900.[6] The reformists formed the Parti socialiste français in 1900, and the more revolutionary groups created the Parti socialiste de France in 1901. Efforts to unite the two faltered over disagreements on how centralized and disciplined the new party was to be (Noland [1953] 1970, 49–50, 93, 113–16, 137–38, 161–62). A compromise was finally reached in 1904 when the two parties formed the SFIO. The compromise consisted of a highly democratic governance structure that was meant to adjudicate between the factions' different organizational preferences. The SFIO also quickly established a nationwide administrative infrastructure through which it tried to coordinate its local and regional branches. The new party's organization proved very effective and increased the socialists' parliamentary size from 42 in 1898 to 101 in 1914 (Noland [1953] 1970, 144, 204–5).

The changing nature of politics also profoundly shaped the SFIO's programmatic and electioneering development. The republicanization of civil service, greater freedom of the press, and fewer restrictions on the right of assembly between the 1880s and early 1890s had leveled the political playing field and weakened the leverage of political notables (Goguel 1946, 50–52; Zeldin 1973, 209). The greater availability of cheap newspapers and improved means of communication by the 1890s had increasingly inserted national themes into local politics (Fitch 1992, 56–61, 79–82). And the growing labor unrest and politicization of social issues had led to a displacement of constitutional and clerical issues (Goguel 1946, 80–82). Both socialist parties had benefited from these changes, and their electoral strength had grown to 48 deputies by 1898 (Noland [1953] 1970, 68).

The winning of a disproportionate number of socialist seats in the 1890s by reformists induced the Guesdists, Blanquists, and Allemanists to moderate their programs (Noland [1953] 1970, 43–44; Magraw 1992, 88). The resulting ideological convergence led the two wings of the French left to formulate the joint Saint-Mandé program in 1896. It committed both camps to internationalism, economic nationalization, and conquest of power through the ballot (Noland [1953] 1970, 49–50). However, this convergence created new conflicts. The socialists' electoral growth increasingly tempted them to use their parliamentary strength and to cooperate more closely with bourgeois governments. Socialists accepted their first ministerial posts in the Waldeck-Rousseau government (1899–1902), which wanted to incorporate socialists into the anti-Dreyfusards alliance. This government participation split the socialists into a ministerial and an antiministerial camp. The latter claimed that governmental participation was irreconcilable with class struggle and would undermine the international solidarity of the working class (Noland [1953] 1970, 93–114). This division ended the tenuous electoral and programmatic rapprochement of the 1890s and contributed to the formation of the Parti socialiste français and the Parti socialiste de France.

The SFIO's first leader, Jean Jaurès, successfully mitigated the ideological divisions created by the ministerial question. He declared the SFIO a revolutionary party and committed it to abolishing capitalism. He also tried to firmly demarcate socialists from bourgeois parties by placing a moratorium on all government participation (Noland [1953] 1970, 177–80). Jaurès accommodated reformists by distinguishing between the short-term and pragmatic exercise of power, which was aimed at ameliorating the workers' daily life, and the revolutionary (and potentially violent) conquest of power through which the existing economic and political order would be fundamentally transformed (Judt 1986, 146).

This Jaurèsian synthesis moved the SFIO clearly to the left of the 1896 Saint-Mandé program. This leftward shift was a concession to the strength of the party's revolutionary factions, which remained influential because the most moderate socialists had stayed outside the new SFIO and coalesced by 1910 into the Parti républicain socialiste (Goguel 1946, 129; Noland [1953] 1970, 184). Furthermore, the Dreyfus affair underlined for many socialists the importance of forming a strong collective identity capable of inoculating workers against rightist demagoguery. The conflict around Dreyfus's guilt or innocence gave rise to various nationalist and antisemitic leagues whose emotionally charged politics readily swayed many potential socialist voters and shifted attention away from social issues (Fitch 1992; Magraw 1992, 88). The violent repression of strikes and police obstruction of unionization after 1900 further convinced many socialists that the existing political order was partial to bourgeois interests and therefore had to be overthrown (Judt 1986, 80–94; Haupt 1986; Magraw 1992, 50–51). In the eyes of many, the Third Republic remained a bourgeois democracy and the emancipatory potential of universal suffrage an empty promise. The organization and strategy of socialists thus should not orient itself so much to the exigencies of electoral competition but should follow more explicitly the demands of class conflict.

German Socialists

Even though the SPD unified earlier and became larger than the SFIO, its organizational and ideological development shared important characteristics with the SFIO. In the two decades following the unification of the Lassallian Universal German Worker's Association (1863) and Bebel's Social Democratic Worker's Party in 1875, the SPD's organization remained embryonic as elections had modest logistical requirements, notables firmly controlled many districts, voters were deferential, and the working class was still small (Nipperdey 1961, 36–38; Sheehan 1978, 143). Moreover, legal restrictions obstructed the SPD's organizational growth far more than in France. The Socialist Law in force between 1878 and 1890 had helped to limit the SPD's organization to a few elected deputies and a small net of party confidants. It also deterred prospective activists with financial penalties for supporting socialists (Craig 1978, 146). The lifting of the Socialist Law in 1890 facilitated the SPD's local organizing, but it still faced obstacles to coordination on a national level because association law prohibited the national integration of political associations across state lines until 1908 (Nipperdey 1961, 300–306). So until the turn of the century, the SPD was well organized locally but weakly institutionalized nationally.

The SPD quickly responded to the lifting of the association law in 1900 by expanding its national administrative and governance structures (Nipperdey 1961, 319; Suval 1985, 94). This new organization was formalized in 1905, one year after the founding of the SFIO, with a new party statute. It was built around the SPD's existing, strong local district organization. The SPD managed to increase its parliamentary representation from 56 seats (14.1 percent) in 1898 to 110 seats (27.7 percent) in 1912. This new organization placed little emphasis on increasing the SPD's capacity to form a revolutionary working-class identity (Nipperdey 1961, 323–25, 367, 373; Schorske 1955, 118, 127).

The SPD's organizational development before 1914 underscores two points missing in existing explanations. First, political repression between 1878 and 1900 inhibited more than it facilitated the SPD's constitution as a social ghetto party. In deterring activists and creating logistical obstacles, political repression severely impeded the development of the organizational infrastructure necessary to integrate workers into an isolated social milieu. And to the extent that it contributed to a negative integration, these effects were countered by the positively integrative effects of electoral competition (Suval 1985, 93–94; Nipperdey 1961, 391–92). Second, the SPD's organizational growth after 1900 was accompanied by a certain bureaucratization. Yet this bureaucratization did not undermine the SPD's democratic governance mechanisms. Party congresses experienced lively factional disputes, local party branches were crucial decision-making centers, and auxiliary organizations played a marginal role in shaping the political outlook of voters (Nipperdey 1961, 321, 334, 388–90; Buse 1990, 483–89).

The SPD's programmatic and strategic development shared important elements with that of the SFIO. The 1875 Gotha program had the same reformist emphasis as the SFIO's Saint-Mandé program. It made no reference to revolution or Marxism and demanded instead the strengthening of civil and political rights and implementing of social reforms by parliamentary means (Schorske 1955, 3). During the SPD's clandestine existence between 1878 and 1890, the limitations on party newspapers and the intermittent party congresses on foreign soil prevented any major revisions of the Gotha program (Craig 1978, 149). After 1890, however, new programmatic and strategic debates began, and culminated in the 1891 Erfurt program, which consisted of two parts. The first enshrined Marxism and outlined a theory of revolutionary class struggle. The second part enumerated various constitutional and social reforms that could be pursued within the existing capitalist order (Schorske 1955, 3–5).

As in France, the SPD's experience with mass politics from the 1890s onward led to a clear differentiation between its reformist and revolutionary factions, which the Erfurt program sought to carefully reconcile. The SPD's surprising electoral gains in the 1890s reassured leaders that workers were developing a stronger, revolutionary collective identity, and the leaders saw themselves validated for having pursued the more revolutionary path outlined in the new Erfurt program. These same electoral successes, however, convinced moderate socialists in central and southern Germany that the SPD now had sufficient political leverage to pursue their reforms through parliamentary means. These moderates consequently advocated a more incremental and nonrevolutionary road toward socialism and particularly clashed with the national leadership over participating as coalition partners in liberal state (Länder) governments. They generally advocated a pragmatic, activist, and electoralist strategy and criticized the present leadership for its revolutionary orthodoxy. After 1904, revisionists were strengthened by the increasing influence of the more cautious unions in the SPD (Craig 1978, 266–69; Schorske 1955,

7–25; Nipperdey 1993, 493). Yet, just as in the SFIO, the SPD's compromise with mass politics led to a backlash by radicals. The intensification of labor conflicts and the seduction of workers by nationalism gave rise to a new radical faction around Rosa Luxemburg and Karl Liebknecht. This group warned about the risks of a short-term electoral strategy and advocated using the political mass strike to strengthen the revolutionary consciousness of workers (Schorske 1955, 28–58).

Mass Politics and Liberals

The gradual insertion of mass politics into the liberal constitutional and economic order had major and frequently unanticipated consequences for its architects. Where liberals had long championed the rule of law, rationalism, and disinterested deliberation, they now faced growing popular sovereignty, emotionally charged nationalism, and partisan conflicts among collective actors. As Schorske observed in another instance, "the program liberals devised against the upper classes occasioned the explosion of the lower. The liberals succeeded in releasing the political energies of the masses but against themselves rather than against their ancient foes" (Schorske 1980, 117). As key architects of the existing order, liberals had less latitude than socialists or conservatives to extricate themselves from the adverse effects of mass politics seeking to lessen liberal democracy and exploring revolutionary or reactionary alternatives. Their political fate thus was closely linked to adapting themselves to this new political environment as quickly as possible.

Traditional explanations have long overlooked the importance that mass politics had for the development of French and German liberals. These explanations generally proceed at a macrohistorical level and relate the timing and degree of democratization to the success or failure of "bourgeois revolutions" in overthrowing the old feudal order. Such explanations then link the collapse of the Weimar Republic to Germany's delayed political modernization. The bourgeoisie's failure in 1848 to dislodge the ancien régime has been said to have burdened Germany with a feudalized bourgeoisie, an authoritarian political culture, and an insufficiently liberalized, let alone democratized, political order. The durability of the Third Republic, on the other hand, is related to France's early political modernization in 1789, when the French Revolution politically marginalized the ancien régime. The French Revolution is credited with giving rise to a thoroughly republicanized bourgeoisie, a civic culture, and a democratized political order.[7]

These explanations overlook the fact that the fortunes of French and German liberals, particularly in an epoch of electoral politics, were far more contingent on their success in coping with mass politics than on how revolutionary outcomes shaped the size and socioeconomic characteristics of the bourgeoisie. Mass politics also had a more significant impact on the development of French and German liberals than did differences in parliamentary sovereignty. We already saw that the parliament in the German Empire was not nearly as impotent as traditional arguments contend. Moreover, it is highly questionable that any lesser decision-making authority of the German parliament somehow made German liberals less entrepreneurial, as Wehler (1995, 864f., 1039f., 1287), for example, claims. Other institutional differences more than offset such alleged effects. Margaret Anderson (2000, 347–48) demonstrates that the unavailability of a parliamentary salary in Germany until 1906 imposed formidable financial burdens on prospective candidates that did not exist in France, where deputies received financial compensation (Kreuzer and Stephan 1999, 163). The resulting difficulties German liberals faced in recruiting candidates became a key incentive for developing their parties to the point where they could help defray some of the costs candidates faced in running for office (Anderson 2000, 347–48). Ultimately, in overlooking mass politics, traditional explanations become static and commit a post hoc fallacy. They selectively point to all those historical regularities or particularities that culminate in the outcome chosen to be explained. The historical process intervening between chosen outcomes and historical antecedents is ignored. Mass politics constitutes one such overlooked historical process. Its analysis reveals two very similar phases in the development of French and German liberal parties before 1914.

During the closing decades of the nineteenth century, the impact of mass politics on liberals was still limited. French and German liberal parties were locked with conservatives in constitutional, religious, and to a lesser extent economic conflicts. The substance of these conflicts and the means with which they were fought were familiar to liberals and consequently required few programmatic and organizational innovations. After 1890 in Germany and France, however, politics increasingly shifted away from this familiar political terrain. Liberals confronted a more multidimensional political environment in which a growing left, economic interest groups, and a nationalist right began to organize voters around partisan issues. Mass politics had arrived and trapped liberals between two increasingly organized and extremist flanks. French and German liberals slowly but reluctantly responded to the need for disciplined political action and a more partisan style of politics.

French Liberals

A liberal program and political organization long preceded the formal constitution of the Parti radical et radical-socialist (Radicals) in 1901.[8] Berstein (1980, 1:35) noted that "before there existed an organized Parti radical in the modern sense of the word, radicalism had been constituted. It possessed a program, a series of organizations . . . and an important electorate."[9] The Radicals' organization before 1900 rested on numerous local social clubs, cultural associations, and above all Masonic lodges (Agulhon 1983, 86–94; Bardonnet 1960, 228–44; Nord 1995). These civic groups first emerged in the Second Republic (1848–51) and reemerged after 1870 in response to the republicans' conflict with the Catholic Church and antirepublican forces. The republican leader Gambetta undertook in 1871 an unsuccessful attempt to unite these republican forces in his more disciplined Parti républicaine (Rebérioux 1975, 43–48).

The civic groups cooperated with radical notables and formed local election committees (Albertini 1961, 561–63). These committees had no formal members or organization but still provided candidates with important logistical and financial resources. They involved on a regular basis a sizable number of people in politics, which distinguished them from the family and friends committees of conservatives (Berstein 1980, 1:32–35). With the logistical support of these committees, plus the growing availability of patronage after 1877, Radicals managed to make important inroads in the rural strongholds of conservatives (Fitch 1992, 79–82, 92–94).

Before 1900, the Radicals' program and campaigning were shaped by their effort to curtail the influence of royalists and the church. The longstanding conflict with antirepublican forces had created distinct political alignments that readily mobilized voters. Radicals thus required little strategizing or entrepreneurial savvy. Furthermore, the conflict with conservatives pitted particularistic ecclesiastical, seignorial, and royalist prerogatives against the universal principles of secularism, rule of law, and republicanism. Radicals thus could credibly pose as representatives of the national interest and use its universalist themes to integrate their socially heterogeneous electoral base (Berstein 1980, 1:30–31).

In stressing universal issues, Radicals demonstrated that they, like socialists, saw electoral campaigns as transforming rather than accommodating public opinion. In their view, electoral strength was the by-product of enlightening citizens, demonstrating the merits of republicanism, and uncovering the sinister goals of monarchists and the church. Radicals viewed politics as rational deliberation rather than partisan group conflict.

By 1900, however, this conception of politics had become increasingly anachronistic. It had contributed to the Radicals' aloofness from tactical considerations and the social and economic interests that came to dominate electoral politics (Goguel 1946, 67). Radicals responded to the programmatic and tactical challenges of mass politics. After 1900, their program demonstrated a growing displacement of clerical and constitutional issues with economic and social ones. Activists succeeded by 1906 in including social reforms in the party's platform (Rebérioux 1975, 133–38). This social agenda, however, was quickly displaced by an economic agenda that reflected the Radicals' increasing financial dependence on economic interest groups. These groups proliferated by the late 1890s and gradually replaced civic associations as the Radicals' main organizational basis.[10] While their programmatic reorientation responded to changed political imperatives, it also complicated the Radicals' electoral strategizing. Before the turn of the century, Radicals could readily mobilize their heterogeneous electoral base around universal issues. Now, however, they had to form complex, short-term alliances that were necessary to accommodate particularistic and volatile economic and social issues.

Radicals also responded to the changing organizational and electioneering exigencies of mass politics that became more pressing from the late 1890s onward. The foundation of the Parti radical in 1901 was preceded by initiatives of local committees to expand the Radicals' electoral infrastructure beyond the existing local civic groups. In 1895, these committees, together with Masonic lodges, newspapers, and deputies, formed the loosely organized Comité d'action pour les réformes républicaines, from which in 1901 the actual Radical Party emerged.

In giving rise to rightist, nationalist mass movements, the so-called ligues, the Dreyfus affair further contributed to the Radicals' organizational consolidation (Rebérioux 1975, 51–52; Bardonnet 1960, 23–24; Berstein 1980, 1:38–40). These ligues capitalized on the nationalist, antirepublican, and antisemitic themes that surfaced during the Dreyfus affair (Goguel 1946, 92–99). The increased availability of inexpensive local newspapers and a more literate electorate facilitated such new forms of nationwide and inflammatory political agitation.[11] Furthermore, the growing strength of socialists and of economic interest groups from the 1890s onward politicized social and economic issues, requiring that Radicals build governance mechanisms capable of formulating more explicit and national policies.

The Radical Party responded to the organizational exigencies of mass politics with partial success. It quickly institutionalized effective governance mechanisms that permitted lively and spirited party debates. It created a Commission for Propaganda and Organization and set up the Ligue de propagande radicale socialiste (Bardonnet 1960, 55n, 25). The Radical Party also sought to increase its electoral and legislative cohesion by prohibiting in 1910 dual party memberships, merging in 1912 its two parliamentary groups, and requiring in 1913 its deputies to formally affiliate themselves with the national executive (Berstein 1980, 1:67–73; Bardonnet 1960, 145–46). Radicals required greater parliamentary cohesion because after 1910 legislative committees were staffed in proportion to each party's strength rather than by lottery (Albertini 1961, 568–69). While many of these organizational initiatives were not overly effective, they still constituted an important first step in the Radicals' institutionalization (Bardonnet 1960, 25, 55n, 64–65). The Radical Party remained highly confederative and placed most authority with local committees rather than with the national leadership. The increasing reliance on patronage after 1900 partially compensated for this weak national organization because it allowed Radicals to tap into the logistical resources of nationally established interest groups (Goguel 1946, 118–19).

German Liberals

Before 1890, the Nationaliberale Partei (the National Liberals) was a party in the loosest sense of the word. It only existed as an informal parliamentary faction and national electoral committee. It did not have a formal organization, and many of its deputies could not identify their affiliations (Nipperdey 1961, 120–21; Sheehan 1978, 137–38). From 1880 on, the Fortschrittspartei (the Progressives, or Left Liberals) had a somewhat more elaborate organization (Nipperdey 1961, 176–80). Outside parliament, social and civic groups made up the organizational fiber of both parties' local electoral committees. These committees coalesced around liberal notables but for a long time were not linked to any national organization (Sheehan 1978, 13–16, 149–52; Nipperdey 1961, 36–38). The logistical support these committees provided was adequate for a period with deferential voters, low voter turnout, and occasional campaigning events. The civic associations saw themselves, not unlike their French counterparts, as pushing back reactionary forces by instilling rational thinking and civic values in individuals. They intended to create the moral preconditions for a liberal and eventually democratic order (Blackbourn and Eley 1984, 195–204). Civic groups also frowned on organizing specific interests for partisan ends. For some liberals, the very idea of a political party as a disciplined and national organization consequently was rejected because it fostered partisanship rather than rational deliberation among disinterested deputies.

The programmatic emphasis of German liberals differed somewhat during the 1870s and 1880s from that of French Radicals. Where Radicals sought to consolidate liberal democracy, German liberals tried to democratize the constitutional monarchy and liberalize the economy. However, in both France and Germany, liberals fought conservatives on constitutional and cultural issues. German liberals sought to liberalize the economic and political order as well as to curtail the influence of the Catholic Church. As in France, these issues had a long lineage and were sufficiently politicized to mobilize bourgeois Protestant voters against the old order. These issues also were sufficiently universal for integrating the socially heterogeneous electoral support of Germany's liberals and eschewing the formulation of specific policies (Sheehan 1978, 172–74).

National Liberals and Progressives, however, did not employ universalist issues as successfully as did French Radicals. Arguably, these issues had a lesser mobilization potential because of Germany's deep confessional divide. The availability of a non-Catholic (i.e., Protestant), rural, and monarchist constituency allowed Liberals to win their political support by trading off concessions on their republicanism and economic liberalization for a more uncompromising pursuit of their anticlericalism. In short, the religious divide permitted liberals just as much as it did Bismarck to displace economic and constitutional issues with cultural ones. The resulting cooperation between liberals and Protestant conservatives blurred the very cleavage that French Radicals used so effectively to mobilize voters (Sheehan 1978, 137, 158, 181–88). Bismarck also successfully exploited divisions within the liberal camp. In 1880, a group called the Sezession broke away from the National Liberals because its leadership accepted Bismarck's offer to make cultural and economic concessions, which National Liberals desired, in return for their acquiescence to new restrictions of civil and political rights (Sheehan 1978, 153, 181–88). The Sezession merged in 1884 with the Progressives and formed the Deutsche Freisinnige Partei.[12]

From the 1890s onward, the Progressives and National Liberals increasingly responded to the challenges of mass politics. They adapted their organizations to deal with the growing nationalization of elections. The National Liberal party built its administrative structure around existing local committees, which themselves had grown and no longer constituted loose confederations of civic groups (Sheehan 1978, 232). It also formalized its governance mechanisms. The National Liberal party held its first party congress in 1892 and was pressured in 1905 by its Young Liberal faction (Jungliberale) to adopt a party statute (Nipperdey 1961, 99). Despite these changes, the National Liberal party remained highly confederative, relatively undisciplined, and without an organized mass membership. The National Liberals' most significant organizational innovation took place outside the party. They began to cooperate more closely with the newly emerging economic interest groups like the Bund der Landwirte, Centralverband Deutscher Industrieller, or the Hansabund. The generous financial contributions and logistical support of these groups partially compensated for the inadequacies of the National Liberals' confederative organization, which employed in 1902 only four paid functionaries (Eley 1993, 220–25; Sheehan 1978, 232; Suval 1985, 130–32; Nipperdey 1961, 153–54).

Eugen Richter, the energetic leader of the Progressives, had already expanded his party's organization during the 1880s. He managed to establish a surprisingly extensive network of local committees and integrate them in a well-institutionalized and fairly participatory governance structure (Anderson 2000, 349–50; Nipperdey 1961, 176–80). After 1903, Friedrich Nauman worked to expand the Progressives' mass membership, to win over economic interest groups, and even to move closer to the SPD.[13] After 1900, it can be said that both Progressives and National Liberals successfully expanded their logistical infrastructure and established national governance structures capable of aggregating interests. It is important to underline that while Progressives and National Liberals became more dependent on economic interest groups after 1890, they never were dominated by them to the same extent as they were during the

Weimar Republic. "The existence of 397 geographically bounded, single-member constituencies gave parties considerable protection, allowing them to fob off impossible demands by citing the necessity of integrating diverse interests" (Anderson 2000, 390).

As with the Radical Party, the programmatic development of German liberals after 1900 proved more difficult than their organizational one. What complicated this shift was their reluctance to abandon old beliefs in the rational and deliberative nature of politics and to adopt a more strategic and entrepreneurial behavior (Blackbourn and Eley 1984, 524–26). Such a shift was required because of liberals' changing organizational basis. Economic pressure groups and nationalist movements increasingly displaced civic associations and established new collective identities. These identities reached across traditional party lines and complicated the liberals' efforts to form a stable electoral basis. These new nationalist, economic, or social welfare constituencies also had to be appealed to through specific policies or bought off through backroom deals. In such a political climate, appeals to universalist economic, cultural, or constitutional principles became increasingly anachronistic (Nipperdey 1993, 524–26; Sheehan 1978, 235–37, 248–50).

National Liberals compensated for the decreasing integrative capacity of universal issues by moving to the left but also continued to espouse nationalist themes of a strong army, colonialism, or monarchism. This move proved only partially successful (Kühne 1993, 278; Sheehan 1978, 274–78). Progressives, on the other hand, moved to the left by making overtures to the SPD. Their repositioning also failed, because they were unwilling to relax their liberal economic principles and hedged on democratic reforms, fearing that they might undermine their political strength (Sheehan 1978, 265–70).

In sum, French and German liberals found themselves besieged on their left by the growing socialist parties, on their right by nationalist and antisemitic groups, and from within their own camp by economic pressure groups. Both undertook important, albeit reluctant, organizational and programmatic reforms that partially adapted their old notable politics to the exigencies of mass politics. Ultimately, these reforms were never far-reaching enough, and the political fortunes of French and German liberals remained precarious. French and German liberals continued to respond to the challenges of mass politics after the First World War, but the changed institutional contexts constrained their efforts in very different ways.

Mass Politics and Conservatives

Of all political actors, conservatives were the most reluctant entrepreneurs. They saw themselves as natural stewards of a preexisting and largely static national interest. Consequently, anything having to do with wooing public opinion seemed an anathema. Conservatives associated electoral activities with factionalism or opportunism and saw them as violating their moral obligation to represent the national interest (Anderson 1993, 1454). However, not all conservatives resisted mass politics so categorically. Intrigued by Louis-Napoléon's reign, a growing number of conservatives (including Bismarck) recognized that, given a deferential electorate and a modicum of demagoguery, mass politics could actually serve as an effective social defense mechanism that provided conservatives with new possibilities for defending their old prerogatives. The development of French and German conservative parties was very much shaped by the conflict between thoroughbred reactionaries and more entrepreneurial Bonapartists over how to cope with mass politics.

Traditional explanations have treated conservatives as single unitary actors, overlooking internal divisions between intransigent reactionaries and pragmatic Bonapartists. They have paid little attention to the similar ways in which these two factions responded to mass politics before 1914. They have used as their starting point the striking triumph of fascism in Germany and its alleged marginality in France. From this historical observation, they have inferred a less reactionary, more pragmatic right in France than in Germany. To explain these different political outlooks, traditional accounts have linked them to distinct historical antecedents. In the German case, the power of the right has been related to its failed 1848 "bourgeois revolution." This failure is said to have contributed to Germany's insufficient liberalization and democratization, feudalized bourgeoisie, and the unbroken dominance of old landed interests. The success of the French bourgeoisie in 1789, on the other hand, fatally weakened feudal interests and their resistance to liberalizing and democratizing the political order (Rueschemeyer, Stephens, and Stephens 1992; Gerschenkron 1962; Luebbert 1991; Moore 1966; Lepsius 1973; Kehr 1970; Wehler 1971; Dahrendorf 1967).

These explanations again commit the post hoc fallacy of ignoring the historical process that intervenes between historical outcomes and their alleged causal antecedents. The resulting historical determinism assumes that there is a single path to liberal democracy whose course has been determined by the direction taken at the very first juncture. The ex ante perspective offered below qualifies this determinism. It will highlight two very similar phases in their development.

During the 1870s and 1880s, the possibility of electoral manipulation and a deferential electorate permitted conservatives to use elections to defend the status quo. Conservatives dominated most administrative and governmental positions and employed them to interfere with the secrecy of balloting or redirect government resources for partisan electoral ends. These forms of electoral malfeasance became all the more effective because voters were still deferential to the church and old social elite. Few innovations were required of conservatives during this period of classical notable politics.

From roughly 1890 onward, however, the increasing juridification, politicization, and collectivization of elections eroded the basis of conservative notable politics. Conservatives responded in different ways. Some became ideologically more pragmatic and built a more voter-oriented party. Others tried to extricate themselves from the emancipatory pull of universal suffrage by developing new defensive strategies. This new right politicized national and antisemitic themes to deflect voters from the growing demands for social and political reforms. It also harnessed the emotional appeal of these themes to mobilize voters. After 1900, these themes became part of a new populist and demagogic strategy that served to defend the status quo. Despite this defensive use of universal suffrage, many conservatives remained unmitigated opponents of it. To them universal suffrage simply was "the great dupery of the century which rarely says anything intelligent in reply" and which fostered a "permissive climate" and false voter expectations (Irvine 1989, 50).

Ultimately, populism did little to lessen the right's lack of discipline and fragmentation. It reflected a continued reluctance of French and German conservatives to genuinely innovate and symbolized a larger authoritarian reflex that blamed their waning political preeminence and fragmentation on too much democracy and too little social and political hierarchy (Retallack 1988). During the interwar years, this authoritarian reflex grew into calls for a National Revolution. Populism, in turn, was co-opted and updated by various proto-fascist organizations, which increasingly began to outflank traditional conservatives.

The German Right

The term *party* has to be used loosely for German conservatives particularly during the 1870s and 1880s and even during the remaining decades before the First World War. The Deutsch-Konservative Partei (Conservative party, or the Conservatives) was the major conservative party during the imperial period. It was flanked to its left by the smaller, less rural, and less Prusso-centric Deutsche Reichspartei (Free Conservatives). The Conservative party itself was relatively small, winning around 15 percent of the seats, mostly in the rural districts to the east of the Elbe River. Outside Prussia, most conservatives belonged to the Zentrum or the National Liberals (Nipperdey 1993, 332–38). Conservatives faced weak pressures to expand their organization because their East Elbian districts were economically backward, were controlled by powerful Junkers, and had deferential electorates (Suval 1985, 102–5).

The Conservative party was a classical conservative notable party until the turn of the century and even beyond. At the national level, it consisted of an informal personal network, the so-called Wahlverein der Deutsch-Konservativen (Electoral Committee of the Conservatives), and locally it rested on equally loose friends and family committees. The electoral expenses at the time were so low that individuals could readily cover them without requiring an elaborate fund-raising infrastructure. Most importantly, Conservatives controlled governmental offices and social institutions which they employed for political organizing (Nipperdey 1961, 41, 242, 250–52). Moreover, with voters still coerced, little electioneering was required. Many conservative districts were so safe that they were nicknamed Riviera districts because their incumbents could be safely reelected while sunning themselves at the French Riviera (Nipperdey 1958, 561–62, 581).

Electoral malfeasance also helped many Conservatives, since they were likely to administer elections in rural districts. The absence of uniform official ballots, for example, facilitated illicit electoral monitoring. Voters received preprinted ballots by candidates that intentionally varied in thickness or coloration. These distinct qualities allowed election officials to report to conservative notables how individuals voted. Such forms of electoral manipulation remained uncontested in the backward East Elbian districts and allowed Conservatives to do without a formal party organization during the 1870s and 1880s. Preprinted ballots also helped to reduce the number of wasted votes. By containing a candidate's name, they lessened grounds for invalidating ballots that misspelled a candidate's name. In order to avoid the use of official blank ballots, candidates spent in the 1870s and 1880s much of their time and resources distributing preprinted ballots (Anderson 1993, 1456; Suval 1985, 41–42).

Nipperdey quotes the programmatic outlook of Conservatives before 1900 as "authority instead of majority" (1993, 334). Through authority, social, economic, and political privileges would be protected and reforms opposed. The Conservatives' political platform also was particularistic. They defended specific seignorial, ecclesiastical, or royal prerogatives that belonged to a vanishing political order without articulating a general and future-oriented political program.

The electoral campaigning of Conservatives also lacked any sense of strategizing and entrepreneurship. Conservatives saw office holding as an onerous obligation that brought no personal benefits and only was assumed out of a sense of public duty. Hence they considered elections to be ceremonial confirmations of their social status rather than as public endorsements of their policies. The political fate of Adolf Stoecker, the founder of the Christlich-Soziale Partei (1879), underlines this static conception of politics. He was the first conservative political entrepreneur who combined fiery and antisemitically laced oratory to actively woo voters and expand the Conservatives' electoral base outside their East Elbian strongholds. Stoecker joined the Conservative party in 1881, but widespread opposition to his innovative, aggressive, and voter-oriented campaigning contributed to his ouster in 1895 (Nipperdey 1993, 334–37).

From 1890 onward, the social and institutional basis of the conservative notable politics began to erode. The (antisocialist) Socialist Law was lifted in 1890, the restrictive association law was abolished in 1900, and the introduction of voting envelopes in 1903 protected more effectively the secrecy of ballots (Nipperdey 1993, 241). Voters also became less deferential, economic interest groups better organized, and the government increasingly involved in economic and social policy-making. Two visible signs of this politicization were the growing voter participation, from 51 percent in 1871 to 85 percent in 1912, and the rise in runoff elections, from 45 in 1871 to 147 in 1903 and 190 in 1912 (Nipperdey 1993, 471–76, 502–10). The growing size of the electorate required a more entrepreneurial campaigning style, while the increased number of runoff elections necessitated more national governance mechanisms to effectively coordinate second ballot contests with other parties.

The Conservatives' organizational innovations originated outside the party. They were initiated by the newly founded Bund der Landwirte (BdL, 1893), which emerged during the economic crisis of the early 1890s. The BdL was quite independent from the rural conservative elites and consequently had few hesitations about creating a national, centralized, disciplined mass organization through which it could lobby the national government for agricultural tariffs. The BdL offered the Conservative party important logistical and financial support during elections. Its 300,000-strong membership also provided the Conservative party for the first time with an organized mass base. The BdL and the Conservatives never were formally linked, but they established close relations through the overlapping membership of their leaders. The cooperation between the two organizations cooled off in 1903 when the BdL demanded greater discipline within the Conservative party and fielded for the first time its own candidates (Eley 1993, 219–25; Nipperdey 1993, 339; 1961, 249).

The Conservatives' own efforts to improve their organization failed. Party congresses were not much more than periodic meetings of elected deputies. The national leadership had so little control over local constituency organizations that it could not even arrange safe by-elections for major party leaders who lost their seat in regular elections (Nipperdey 1961, 254, 262–64). Nevertheless, the close cooperation between the Conservatives and the BdL until 1903 signified an important departure from the traditional programmatic orientation and campaigning style. The BdL's logistical resources and emphasis on agricultural issues meant that conservative voters were for the first time organized and wooed by appeals to their own self-interest. Their vote was increasingly won by influencing their individual decision making rather than manipulating the technicalities of the electoral decision-making process (Nipperdey 1993, 337–38). Notable politics thus began to change as some Conservatives started to compete and behave like political entrepreneurs.

The organizational and programmatic reforms that the Conservatives undertook with the help of various external mass movements ultimately were insufficient to transform them into an effective political party. If anything, these reforms divided the Conservatives in similar ways in which mass politics had polarized the SPD. One, albeit smaller, conservative faction accepted the existing political order and began to compete, while another one adopted a more conflictual, populist style of politics in order to fight a rearguard battle against social and political reforms. Unlike the SPD, this ideological differentiation took place inside an undisciplined and fragmented party with no strong organizational center. The gravitational pull of the Conservative party was too feeble to withstand the centrifugal pressures of mass politics. These pressures thus plunged the German right into a severe crisis that continued well into the interwar period. The Deutschnationale Volkspartei (German National People's Party,

DNVP) tried to address this crisis by reorganizing itself as a more prag-matic and voter-oriented *Volkspartei.* These reforms were temporarily successful, but under the changed institutional circumstances, this failure had more serious political consequences than it did before 1914.

French Conservatives

The 1870s and early 1880s constituted the heyday of conservative notable politics in the Third Republic. During these two decades, the French right was divided into three competing royalist camps: the legitimists, Orleanists, and Bonapartists. None of these royalist formations had any national organization; they were held together solely by the gravitational pull of no less than three pretenders (Levillain 1992, 276–86). The local committees of conservatives had no ties with civic associations and thus were even more embryonic and personality-centered than those of liberals. Candidates did not require extensive organizations because most of them drew on the notability of their aristocratic background, their personal wealth, and close church and government ties. Easy access to these levers of political manipulation and a deferential rural electorate gave conserva-tives few incentives to innovate (Fitch 1992, 79–82, 92–94; Goguel 1946, 80). Moreover, royalists intended to reestablish a monarchical regime in which elections would play at best a marginal, plebiscitarian role (Goguel 1946, 43–46).

The royalists' loss of their parliamentary majority in 1876 contributed to the first tentative organizational and electioneering reforms. After gain-ing political power, republicans purged throughout the 1880s conservatives from prefectures, courts, and schools. Now republicans, not conservatives, could avail themselves of electoral manipulation and government patronage for their candidacies the way the conservatives had been used to since the Second Empire (Irvine 1989, 53–54; Fitch 1992, 79–82). Republicans also tried to break the cultural hegemony of conservatives by restricting the activities of religious orders and the church's involvement in education.

In the mid-1880s, conservatives responded to these changes with cer-tain organizational initiatives. They formed in 1885 the loose Union des droites, which was led for the first time by political personalities other than one of the pretenders (Levillain 1992, 318–21, 330–32). The pretenders, particularly the Count of Paris, actively supported these new leaders by financing newspapers, electoral campaigns, and a national network of paid organizers (Irvine 1989, 52–57). These efforts proved ineffective.

Aristocratic notables frequently paid little attention to these organizers, as they often came from nonaristocratic backgrounds (Irvine 1989, 52–57). And continuing dynastic feuds among the three pretenders further undermined efforts to build a unified and disciplined party (Levillain 1992, 276–86).

Aristocratic notables dominated the French right during much of the 1870s and 1880s and thereby inhibited its programmatic development. Just as in Germany, the program of French conservatives was highly particularistic, concerning itself with the genealogical technicalities of royal succession, the constitutional specifics of the future monarchical order, or the defense of conservative prerogatives in the army, church, or schools (Levillain 1992, 276–86). French conservatives also had a highly static view of politics and little appreciation for electoral strategizing and campaigning. They regarded themselves as stewards of the national interest and considered office holding as a political responsibility with few personal rewards. The democratic notion that legislative office was to be won by competition among several candidates still was largely alien to conservatives. Conservatives thus did not strive "so much to promote political action that would justify their positions, as to prevent any political action that would upset it" (Agulhon 1983, 103).

The popular and maverick General Boulanger served French conservatives in 1888–89 as a quick fix for their unsuccessful organizational and programmatic reforms. Conservatives expected that the general's cross-sectional appeal and his fervent nationalism could win back their lost parliamentary majority. Then they hoped to co-opt him to establish a constitutional monarchy. This populist strategy failed. It only united republicans and contributed to the permanent decline of royalists within the conservative camp (Levillain 1992, 337, 352).

Between 1890 and 1914, mass politics penetrated the isolated and rural strongholds of conservatives and began to transform their style of notable politics. The growing inability of conservatives to rely on deferential voters, electoral malfeasance, or church support led them to gradually strengthen their own organizational basis. Moderate conservatives created, for example, the Association nationale républicaine (ANR) in 1888. It functioned as a national information and propaganda office that was loosely tied to local committees (Le Béguec 1992, 41–43). It also served as an agency for skilled public speakers or journalists who made themselves available to campaign with conservatives and compensate for their frequently lacking oratorical or campaigning skills. From the late 1880s on, these so-called publicists were, together with newspapers, the most important campaigning tool of conservatives and reflected their increasing realization that voters had to be wooed (Le Béguec 1992, 15–16, 33; Irvine 1989, 65).

During the 1890s, the Catholics also contributed to the organizational development of the French right. The church, at the prompting of Rome, tried to distance itself from the royalist right and adopted a more accommodationist stance toward the republic. This effort led in 1892 to the Ralliement, which committed the church to defending clerical issues through the ballot box. The Ralliement also spawned various Catholic defense organizations such as the Droite Constitutionelle (1890), the Comité catholique de défense réligieuse, or the Union de la France chrétienne (1891). These groups supported the candidacies of conservative candidates, particularly in the Action libérale populaire (Levillain 1992, 361–62, 374; Goguel 1946, 77–79).

The Dreyfus affair provided another important organizational stimulus for conservatives. It polarized politics to the point where conservatives coalesced into the Antibloc while republicans closed ranks in the Bloc de la défense républicaine. This increased cohesion of conservatives contributed to the creation of the first two conservative parties. Jacques Piou founded in 1902 the Action libérale populaire (ALP) in order to rally moderate Catholics in opposition to the renewed anticlerical initiatives. For a long time it was the best-organized party and won regularly around 30 seats (Le Béguec 1992, 43–45). In 1903, various center-right groups formed the Fédération républicaine, which won on average 100 seats and became the premier conservative party until the 1930s. Its organization was highly confederated and mostly coordinated the party's legislative matters and to a lesser extent its campaigning activities. The Fédération was organizationally too weak to prevent two major schisms in 1905 and 1911. Both times, around 30 deputies left to form a more centrist political organization (Le Béguec 1992, 16, 21–22).

The Fédération and the ALP also established an extensive but less visible organizational network with the newly emerging economic interest groups and nationalist mass movements. This network rested largely on joint members rather than on formal ties (Le Béguec 1992, 24). These interest groups and mass movements provided financial support, endorsed individual candidates, and used their national and mass-based organizations to lend logistical assistance to conservative candidates. As in Germany, they compensated for the continuing organizational weaknesses of conservative parties (Le Béguec and Prévotat 1992, 408–24).

The programmatic development of French conservatives was characterized by a similar ideological differentiation between a more moderate and voter-oriented right and a new, populist right. The political marginalization of monarchists by the 1890s had ended the conservatives' longstanding division over the nature of the regime. Many had come to accept the existing republic and now concentrated on winning elections (Le Béguec and Prévotat 1992, 385–86; Goguel 1946, 59–60). The increasing collaboration of conservatives with economic interest groups like the Société des agriculteurs de France (1867), the Ligues des contribuables (1889), or the Fédération des industriels et commerçants shifted their programmatic focus from the defense of old, particularistic prerogatives to advocating more general economic policies. This collaboration also marked the emergence of a new and more entrepreneurial type of notable whose influence depended less on his aristocratic lineage or local prominence and more on his contacts with national interest groups (Le Béguec 1992, 24).

French conservatives, however, also began after 1900 to cooperate more closely with nationalist and, to a lesser extent, antisemitic mass movements, which formed a new, more aggressive and conflictual right. The Ligue des patriotes, Action française, and Ligue antisémitique emerged during the antisemitic and antirepublican groundswell of the Dreyfus affair. These ligues employed a variant of the populist strategy that the French right had already used in the Boulanger affair. The ligues were better organized and centered less around a single charismatic personality than the Boulangists. The ligues inserted a new nationalist, antisemitic, and generally emotional dimension on which many conservatives felt more comfortable campaigning than on economic or social issues. Slogans like "France for the French," the politicization of old antisemitic prejudices, or attacks on the existing political or economic order readily tapped existing resentments (Le Béguec and Prévotat 1992, 401–8, 428–56; Fitch 1992, 93). The emotional appeal of these themes ultimately allowed conservatives to sway voters without having to build huge mass-based parties, which in turn would have limited their authority (Fitch 1992, 79–83).

The continued importance after 1900 of ligues for the ALP and the Fédération républicaine underscored the latter's continued organizational and programmatic shortcomings. The reforms of conservative parties went a considerable way toward transforming the old style of notable politics and toward making it more effective in an age of mass politics. Particularly the strategy of drawing on the organizational resources of external groups helped conservatives meet some of the logistical exigencies of mass politics. But their failure to establish a disciplined and nationally well-integrated party did little to reduce the right's traditional fragmentation, which mass politics increasingly accentuated. The political crisis of the French right thus continued during the interwar period, and with it a divided right that continued to advocate different solutions.

Conclusion

This historical survey demonstrated three points that are key for the subsequent analysis. First, it showed that mass politics reconfigured the opportunities and constraints for winning votes. It changed the political calculus so fundamentally that no political actor could continue with his traditional campaigning methods, organizational arrangements, and political programs. Mass politics, in short, made innovation a political imperative. How individual actors adapted to the new realities of mass politics differed. It was highly contingent on their distinct resources, historical experiences, and normative conceptions of politics. But the key here is that while different actors within each country responded to mass politics in distinct ways, similar actors across the two countries coped with mass politics in comparable manners. Second, all actors responded to the exigencies of mass politics with great reluctance. Unlike today's focus-group-obsessed politicians, their predecessors in France and Germany did not see demographic changes or technological innovations as political opportunities to be quickly exploited. It was more circumstances that partially tricked, lured, cajoled, and mostly forced political actors to innovate. Ultimately, the psychological, internal entrepreneurial deficit of French and German politicians meant that differences in external, institutionally created incentives for risk taking would have a particularly important impact on their political actions.

Third, this chapter's ex ante perspective revealed the centrality that mass politics assumed in French and German party development before 1914 and the similar effects it had. It underscored that the two cases are far more comparable than the exceptionalism of traditional explanations would lead one to believe. Arguing that France and Germany are comparable, of course, is not claiming that they were identical. Differences existed, undoubtedly, but do they matter for my argument? Can any of these differences be shown to make German politicians more risk-averse than French ones before electoral institutions did so in 1918? One frequently mentioned, albeit regularly overstated, difference pertains to differences in parliamentary sovereignty and its implications for politicians' ability to secure patronage. The Assemblée Nationale's powerful committees were providing deputies easy access to public works projects and other particularistic favors. Germany's weaker Reichstag and more autonomous bureaucrats, in turn, deprived its deputies of patronage opportunities (Anderson 2000, 402–4). This difference, however, cannot be said to have differently affected the innovativeness of French and German politicians. Patronage gave French politicians a substantial incumbent advantage and hence lessened their need for being entrepreneurial vote getters. To keep public works projects flowing, they needed to be parliamentary wheeler-dealers commanding the art of logrolling. The unavailability of patronage in Germany, in turn, limited the need for German politicians to be entrepreneurial legislators and might partly explain the high rate of absenteeism in the Reichstag (Butzer 1999, 153–56; Anderson 2000, 354–55). But in lacking this important incumbent advantage, German politicians had to be innovative in the electoral arena to establish an ideological affinity with voters and build effective vote-getting machines. In short, the differences in parliamentary sovereignty and availability of patronage did not translate into differences in political innovation.

Other differences were more consequential but primarily by making German rather than French politicians more entrepreneurial. Recent research suggests that French politics in various rural regions was until the turn of the century only weakly linked to national politics and still dominated by old-style notable politics (Weber 1976, 1991; Burns 1984). This persistence of notable politics was facilitated by the introduction of the secret ballot booth and voting envelope in 1913, a good decade later than in Germany. By contrast, the Kulturkampf significantly contributed to the nationalization of German politics by the late 1870s, while the unavailability of parliamentary salaries until 1906 accelerated the organizational growth of parties.[14] Finally, we saw that Germany's confessional cleavage cut across the economic and constitutional ones. It thereby provided the basis for changing political alliances rather than being the anchor for a pillarized and immutable party system. In short, to the extent that differences existed, they contributed to the greater entrepreneurialism of German politicians and made their inertia during the Weimar Republic all the more puzzling.[15]

Chapters 3 to 6 will show that the tumultuous economic and political circumstances of the interwar years added further pressures on French and German politicians to innovate. But, just like mass politics, the short-term historical circumstances were far too similar in both countries to explain the suddenly diverging rate at which French and German politicians innovated. Chapter 2, in turn, outlines the theoretical argument for why the institutional differences in interwar France and Germany help to explain the suddenly changing innovative capacity of French and German parties.

Chapter 2

Structuring Electoral Representation: Career Uncertainty, Electioneering Costs, and Strategic Voting

This chapter steps back from history and analyzes how institutions and political actors constitute two constants in the otherwise continuously changing political environments of France and Germany. It provides the stepping-stone for systematically explaining why after 1918 French and German politicians responded so differently to comparable historical background conditions. The chapter sets off from the earlier contention that political actors and institutions are characterized by unchanging, "transhistorical" and hence generalizable properties.

Throughout this analysis, politicians are assumed to be self-interested, single-minded seekers of public office and the salary, prestige, and influence it offers (J. Schlesinger 1975; Mayhew 1974). This assumption is made with reference to individual candidates rather than parties. Americanists convincingly argue that candidates have the analytical advantage of being genuinely single unitary actors and not, as in the case of parties, collective actors assumed to be single unitary actors. It therefore is easier to make motivational assumptions and specify preferences of candidates than for parties, since the latter consist of members, functionaries, leaders, and interest groups that frequently pursue diverse goals (Clark and Wilson 1961; J. Schlesinger 1975; Mayhew 1974; Cox and McCubbins 1993). The selection of individual candidates also is empirically realistic, since they shape a party's activities far more distinctly than any of its other constituent groups.

The chapter centrally focuses on how electoral mechanisms constrain the three principal activities faced by politicians in seeking public office: they have to be recruited to become candidates, they require the logistical wherewithal for election campaigns, and they need to sway voters with issues and vote-getting techniques. These three hurdles confront office seekers in every democracy, yet the obstacles posed by these hurdles differ a great deal across countries. These cross-national differences are attributable to the very distinct constraints that electoral mechanisms impose on politicians. This chapter consequently analyzes the hurdles that electoral procedures of the French Third Republic and the Weimar Republic posed for politicians. It discusses these constraining effects in terms of the *career uncertainty* prospective candidates encounter during the recruitment process; the *electioneering costs* of organizing election campaigns; and the level of *strategic voting* they confront in the electoral marketplace. Electoral mechanisms thus have a profound impact at the pre-electoral stage, when actors jockey for position within their parties and solicit resources from interest groups, as well as the electoral stage, when politicians finally interact with voters.

Career Uncertainty

By the turn of the century, French and German politicians had become professionals aspiring to long-term political careers. Some conservative notables decried this development and continued to view politics as selfless and disinterested public service. The conservatives' actions belied their noble rhetoric, and they were anyway a small and rapidly disappearing minority. Politicians thus viewed politics as a long-term career off which they hoped to live and through which they planned to advance professionally. Politicians consequently became concerned about reducing their career uncertainty. Epstein et al. noted that "with the advent of [political] careerism came the need to reduce career uncertainty" (1997, 966).

Politicians' concern for career uncertainty generally involves securing a candidacy, retaining legislative seats, moving up in parliamentary committees, becoming a minister, and occasionally securing post-electoral appointments. Since our analysis concentrates on the electoral politics, it focuses solely on career uncertainty during the candidate recruitment process. Prospective candidates face three potential hurdles: the *nomination* after an initial screening and short-listing of candidates; the *selection* from these nominees of an official candidate or candidates; and, in case of multiple candidates, their *ranking* on a party list.[1] Once candidates are selected and/or ranked, they will face additional uncertainty over their winning prospects on election day. I discuss this uncertainty in the section on strategic voting and narrowly confine the use of career uncertainty to the pre-electoral, party-internal candidate recruitment process.

The level of uncertainty a candidate faces at each of these three recruitment stages is directly influenced by electoral mechanisms and their effect on the capacity of parties to regularize electoral entry and reentry of candidates. Carey and Shugart correctly note that "allocating seats to parties is not all that an electoral formula must do; it must also allocate seats to specific candidates within parties" (1996, 417). Four electoral mechanisms affect the capacity of parties to regularize the candidate recruitment process and thereby reduce career uncertainty. They are the district magnitude (i.e., average number of seats available per district), vote-pooling mechanisms (e.g., apparentements, voter transferability, national adjustment seats), ballot structure (e.g., open list, closed list, runoff elections), and party laws (e.g., primaries, regulation of party governance). Party laws only have become important in Europe since the 1950s and therefore can be excluded from our analysis (Kreuzer, 2000; Tsatsos et al. 1990). The remaining three procedures differed considerably in the French Third Republic and the Weimar Republic and hence affected the career uncertainty of candidates in very distinct ways.

Determinants of Career Uncertainty

A crucial element of electoral systems is the average number of seats allocated in each electoral district. The literature refers to this element as district magnitude and calculates it by dividing the total number of elected representatives by the number of electoral districts (Rae 1967, 20). The district magnitude varied considerably in Weimar and the Third Republic. The latter had a low magnitude of 1 when it used single-member districts in 1928, 1932, and 1936 and a magnitude of 6.5 when it used a peculiar hybrid system in 1919 and 1924. This hybrid system can be thought of as a highly disproportional PR system with important majoritarian-like elements. It consequently was far closer to the double ballot system than Weimar's PR system. The specific features of this highly unusual electoral system are discussed below. Weimar's multimember districts in turn had a high magnitude of 18 throughout the interwar period (Mackie and Rose 1991; Lachapelle 1919, 1924).

District magnitude affected career uncertainty in two ways. First, Weimar's high magnitude reduced the number of recruitment sites, since the number of seats allocated per district is inversely related to the number of districts available for selecting candidates. Weimar's 18 districts centralized the recruitment process and allowed party leaders to control it more readily. In the Third Republic, by contrast, the low magnitude meant that candidates were selected in approximately 600 different sites between 1928 and 1936 and 100 sites between 1919 and 1924. Second, Weimar's large district magnitude created long electoral lists with more safe list positions. They made recruitment more hierarchical and permitted party leaders to use the high list rankings for reducing career uncertainty. The Third Republic's magnitude of 1, in turn, made it impossible to rank candidates, thus exposing each one equally to the whims of voters.

The effects of district magnitude were affected by two further electoral mechanisms: ballot structure and vote-pooling mechanism. The ballot structure refers to the type of choice that the electoral law offers voters in choosing their representative(s). Categorical ballots are the most common and restrict voters to a single, rigid (i.e., categorical) choice among individual candidates or fixed party lists. Ordinal ballots, on the other hand, are a feature of certain PR lists. They allow voters to fine-tune their choices by permitting the simultaneous expression of preferences for a particular party and the list ranking of its candidates (Katz 1986; Carey and Shugart 1996). Ballot structure thus determines whether the ranking of candidates belongs to the party-controlled recruitment process or whether it becomes part of the voter-controlled electoral process. Weimar's categoric ballot structure reduced career uncertainty by preventing voters from rearranging the list ranking of candidates. Technically, the French ballot structure between 1928 and 1936 was categoric since the availability of a single seat prevented voters from differentiating their choice. Since it had no effect independent of the district magnitude, it was inconsequential for career uncertainty. The ballot structure used in the 1919 and 1924 elections had an ordinal component by allowing voters to split their votes across candidates from different lists. The electoral law allocated one vote for each available seat and required voters to cast each vote for individual candidates. Voters thus could differentiate their preferences for individual candidates even though they could not rank them ordinally. The preference vote was so limited that it only marginally increased career uncertainty (Lachapelle 1920, 5–23).

Finally, vote-pooling mechanisms assure the most accurate possible translation of votes into seats. They involve provisions for the formation of electoral alliances—so-called apparentements—transferring excess votes among candidates, permitting prominent candidates to run in multiple districts, or having multiple-tiered seat allocations. Of these procedures, only the last two played a role in Germany.

Weimar's electoral law allowed the placement of candidates on multiple electoral lists. Party leaders shamelessly placed themselves on multiple lists, thus making their reelections a foregone conclusion (Pollock 1934, 60). Multiple candidates were illegal in France and deprived candidates of the opportunity to hedge their electoral prospects. Furthermore, Weimar's electoral law allocated seats on multiple tiers in order to award so-called adjustment seats for regular district votes that were insufficient for securing a full mandate. These adjustment seats reduced career uncertainty in two ways. They were awarded through national lists, which further centralized the allocation of seats and increased control over entry and reentry of candidates. Furthermore, their allocation depended on recycled votes, which made adjustment seats largely independent from overall electoral swings and provided virtually guaranteed seats. Adjustment seats were fairly important, constituting on average 26 percent of all seats (*Statistisches Jahrbuch für das deutsche Reich,* various years). They also were a highly controversial element of Weimar's electoral system and were unsuccessfully challenged in court for violating the constitutional right to *direct* elections (Pollock 1934, 59–60; Schanbacher 1982, chaps. 4, 8).

Effects of Career Uncertainty

The different uncertainty that French and German candidates faced over their recruitment had three distinct effects: it determined their autonomy vis-à-vis the party leadership; it affected their risk-taking and entrepreneurial skills; and it influenced their cooperation with external economic interest groups. Together, these three effects had significant repercussions for whose interests prospective candidates championed during their pre-electoral, party-internal career stage.

In the Third Republic, high career uncertainty protected the autonomy of candidates. It limited the party leaders' ability to regularize the recruitment of candidates. Party leaders consequently had little control over candidates' careers and lacked any effective leverage to maintain party discipline. In return for their autonomy, candidates had to be good entrepreneurs to reassure the quadrennial reselections. They had to be skillful tacticians to eliminate potential challengers and good at providing local supporters with particularistic benefits. Such entrepreneurial skills undoubtedly helped candidates to reduce career uncertainty by building a personal reputation, but such a reputation never matched the security of a safe list position. High career uncertainty thus contributed to a bottom-up, self-selecting, and competitive candidate recruitment process. Finally, this competitive recruitment process required candidates to maintain an arm's-length relationship with economic interest groups. The nature of such a relationship depended significantly on how easily economic interest groups could obtain credible policy commitments in return for the resources they provided candidates.[2] The high uncertainty candidates faced in their recruitment and the decentralized nature of their selection made it difficult for economic interest groups to secure such credible commitments. It complicated political quid pro quos and instead required interest groups to engage in more time-consuming and uncertain lobbying of numerous individual candidates.

In Weimar, on the other hand, low career uncertainty undermined the autonomy of candidates. It allowed party leaders to reduce the uncertainty over the entry and reentry of candidates and thereby gave them considerable control over this career stage. Party leaders thus could use de-selection as an effective lever to enforce party discipline. Moreover, they used their control over candidate recruitment to award themselves the safest list positions, which virtually guaranteed their reelection. The low career uncertainty powerfully reinforced the oligarchic tendency of parties. In exchange for their limited autonomy, candidates had to devote little attention to their recruitment. Their primary concern was to remain in the good graces of party leaders who reselected them and hide their political skills (if they had any) as best as possible, which political leaders would view as a political threat. Low career uncertainty thus led to a top-down, regularized, and noncompetitive candidate recruitment process that favored dull party bureaucrats over ambitious entrepreneurs. It also facilitated closer cooperation between candidates and economic interest groups. It allowed parties to make very credible policy commitments by selecting candidates that were either spokespersons for or direct appointees of economic interest groups. Interest groups hence could arrange corporatist-like quid pro quos with parties rather than having to lobby a multitude of candidates.

Electioneering Costs

Resources are an important ingredient for political success and hence influence a politician's actions just as much as career opportunities or voter preferences. The importance of resources grew with the shift from notable politics to mass politics and the concomitant increase in the cost of election campaigns. The costs of electioneering involve the time and resources required for advertising, traveling, hiring personnel, raising funds, mobilizing volunteers, or any other logistical means needed to solicit votes (Kreuzer, 2000). Electioneering costs can be thought of as the political equivalent to the legal, monitoring, and decision-making costs that firms face in their business transactions (Eggertsson 1990; North 1990).

As the first chapter demonstrated, electioneering costs are at one level influenced by large-scale, socioeconomic developments and new communications technologies (e.g., advertising techniques, mass newspapers). At another level, electioneering costs are shaped by generally five electoral procedures: the physical district size (i.e., the average number of registered voters per district), the frequency of nationwide electoral contests, ballot structure, campaigning regulations, and campaign financing laws. The first three mechanisms create distinct logistical requirements and concomitant demands for resources. The last two procedures deal more directly with the mobilization of resources. They reflect the view that electoral systems are not just about translating votes into seats but also about exchanging of money for political influence. Electioneering regulations and campaign finance regulations implicitly recognize that electioneering costs ought to be moderated to limit the distorting effects that money might have on political representation (Kreuzer 2000). Generally, though, electioneering regulations and campaign finance regulations played a far less significant role during the interwar period than they do in contemporary elections.

Determinants of Electioneering Costs

The Third Republic's electoral procedures kept electioneering costs very modest. It had an average district size of 18,000 registered voters for 1928–36 and 123,000 for 1919 and 1924.[3] These small districts contributed to a more personal interaction between parties and voters. They created a personal vote that was cemented through informal, private networks, emphasizing personal qualities (e.g., experience, independence) and taking credit for accomplishments benefiting the constituency (Black 1972, 147–48; Katz 1980, 30–31; Mayhew 1974, 49–65). Voters could use demographic factors or personal knowledge as "low cost shortcuts for estimating a candidate's policy preferences" or assessing his credibility (Popkin

1995, 19, 27–28). Such readily available cues lowered the voters' information costs and required fewer mobilizational efforts (Moe 1980, 39–47). French candidates thus rarely ever hired campaign workers. The central electioneering activity was to visit bistros and cafés and pay for a round of drinks. Such generosity, however, had to be handled delicately. Candidates could not simply pop in, give a short speech, and leave a few banknotes. Such crass drink-for-vote propositions would have violated norms of sociability and been construed as unacceptable bribery (Pollock 1932, 292). The only feature increasing the electioneering costs was the two election rounds. Otherwise, French voters faced no national electoral contests. Parliamentary terms were fixed ever since 1877, when French presidents de facto lost their right to dissolve parliament. The president was elected by parliament and the Senate by an electoral college. The constitution contained no provisions for referenda or initiatives. Direct popular participation was purposively curtailed because the founders of the Third Republic feared that a poorly educated electorate could succumb to the populist manipulation that Louis-Napoléon used to usurp the Second Republic (1848–52) and legitimize the Second Empire (1852–70). The Third Republic also contained electioneering costs through the rudimentary regulation of campaigning practices. It subsidized the printing and mailing of candidates' campaign material in return for restricting the amount and location of bill posting (Kheitmi 1964, 230–33; Huard 1991, 218; Pollock 1932, 290). In 1921, the National Assembly introduced a bill that prevented deputies from acting as business consultants and sitting on corporate boards of executives. The bill finally passed in 1928 (Pollock 1932, 318).

Electoral procedures in Weimar Germany, on the other hand, multiplied the logistical requirements for winning votes. The large physical district size most directly increased electioneering costs. German candidates faced a 33-fold enlargement of the physical district size, from 36,000 registered voters before 1914 to 1.2 million voters during the interwar period (*Statistisches Jahrbuch für das deutsche Reich,* various years). They also operated in districts that were 66 times larger than those in the Third Republic. These large districts contributed to a more impersonal interaction between parties and voters and made voters more dependent on opinion leaders, ideological cues, or media for their information. These sources of information increased voters' cost of becoming informed, since they were less readily accessible and verifiable than more personal sources of political information (Popkin 1995, 23–27). Candidates consequently required considerable resources to lower the informational costs of voters and assure their turnout (Aldrich 1995, 46–47; Black 1972, 147–48; Katz 1980, 30–31).

Large physical district sizes also created more capital-intensive campaigns. By nationalizing electoral contests, they limited the effectiveness of labor resources or personal reputations. They required instead more capital-intensive forms of mass communications (e.g., radio, mass rallies, bill posting) and a more professionalized campaign staff (i.e., party functionaries). Pollock observed that in Weimar "every modern instrument of electoral value is resorted to: the loudspeaker, vitaphone, the regular film, the airplane" (1931, 219). Moreover, German candidates had to absorb these high electioneering costs on multiple occasions. Weimar's nonrestrictive vote of no confidence cut short parliamentary terms and led to elections every 20 months. Parties also had to mobilize resources for septennial presidential elections and three referenda. The frequency of such national electoral contests reflects the deliberate effort by Weimar's constitution to correct the exclusionary old imperial constitution by maximizing direct voter participation. Weimar's electoral law also contained no campaigning regulations, conflict of interest restrictions, or campaign finance provisions that could have limited ever rising costs of elections (Pollock 1931, 220, 274).

Effects of Electioneering Costs

Electioneering costs have a significant impact on the closeness of the electoral connection that exists between voters and candidates. By determining the demand for resources, electioneering costs determine the distorting effect that large party bureaucracies and money have on political representation. More particularly, electioneering costs influence the leverage that the principal suppliers of resources—party leaders and economic interests—have over candidates in setting the party-internal agenda. They determine the extent to which voter-oriented preferences of candidates are constrained by the oligarchic, risk-averse disposition of party leaders or the rent-seeking concerns of economic interest groups.

The Third Republic's low electioneering costs minimized the leverage party leaders and economic interest groups exerted over the party-internal agenda setting. The modest costs did so in two ways. First, they preserved the effectiveness of candidates' personal reputations and permitted them to take credit for constituency-related services (e.g., administrative interventions, pork-barrel projects). They also enhanced the importance of informal vote-getting practices relative to more technology-intensive, mass-media-centered, and hence more expensive campaigning techniques. Candidates did become less dependent on the two ways in which parties could help them economize resources. Parties could defray electioneering costs by offering candidates a collective reputation or, in the language of merchandising, a brand name. Such a reputation significantly lowered electioneering costs by automatically mobilizing a large number of "inexpensive" partisan votes (Aldrich 1995, 49, 55; Downs 1957, 96–113; Cox and McCubbins 1993). Parties also helped to defray electioneering costs by offering enormous economies of scale. Such economies result from the fact that parties already had established administrative structures, fundraising networks, and frequently also dues-paying members (Scarrow 1995). Second, the low electioneering costs also lessened the dependence of French candidates on the logistical contributions from economic interest groups. These contributions involved endorsements, creating no-show jobs for activists, recruiting volunteers, and most importantly money. In short, the modest electioneering costs minimized candidates' logistical dependence on parties and economic interest groups. Candidates consequently had greater autonomy in choosing an agenda that accorded with the preferences of their voters rather than with the interests of their logistical backers.

Weimar's high electioneering costs, in turn, maximized the programmatic leverage of party leaders and economic interest groups. The significant electioneering costs undermined the logistical self-reliance of candidates. The organizational exigencies of communicating with 1.2 million voters simply exceeded the abilities of individual candidates. German candidates thus became dependent on the party brand name that could automatically mobilize partisan voters. They also came to rely on the economies of scale that parties offered in mobilizing resources. Weimar's high electioneering costs shifted the party-internal balance of power from candidates to party leaders. The ability of parties to economize resources is limited and ultimately cannot compensate for the need to externally mobilize resources. The high electioneering costs therefore made German candidates highly dependent on the various in-kind and financial contributions provided by unions and business groups. Overall, Weimar's high electioneering costs and the absence of any campaign finance regulations allowed economic interest groups and party leaders to exert a disproportionate influence over setting the party-internal agenda. In effect, these costs had a disenfranchising effect on the party-internal participation of candidates and the leverage voters exerted in the electoral marketplace.

Strategic Voting

Besides career prospects and electioneering costs, voters constitute the third and arguably most important determinant of a politician's behavior. At one level, voters matter because their preferences constrain a politician's programmatic choices. Yet, as Cain, Ferejohn, and Fiorina note, political representation cannot be viewed in purely sociological terms as "policy responsiveness, as the representative responding to and articulating the policy positions or ideologies of constituents in the legislature" (1987, 2). Cain, Ferejohn, and Fiorina cite the institutional constraints that voters face as a central factor for why their preferences alone are insufficient for explaining the conduct of politicians. The constraints that electoral mechanisms impose on voting choices thus become a crucial determinant for the actions of candidates.

The concept of strategic voting has been widely used to analyze how the institutionally constrained choices of voters affect the vote-getting strategies of office seekers. A strategic vote refers to a voting choice that evaluates a candidate's political platform *as well as* his winning prospects. A voter will act strategically by trading off his most preferred but unelectable choice for the next best alternative. What drives him to act strategically is the tendency of certain electoral mechanisms to inaccurately translate votes into seats and thereby create the risk of wasted ballots. The objective of strategic voting is to minimize this risk by voting for front-runners and deserting fledgling candidates (Sartori 1994, 32–33; Riker 1986, 33–41; Cox 1997).

To understand how strategic voting affects vote-getting strategies requires closer consideration of two points. An analysis is required of how accurately various electoral mechanisms translate votes into seats and thereby create incentives for strategic voting. Three procedures matter: the district magnitude, runoff ballot, and vote-pooling mechanisms. These mechanisms can be thought of as rationing representation; they regulate the exclusion and inclusion of interests and allocation of rewards (i.e., parliamentary seats) and punishments (i.e., exclusion). Furthermore, the level of strategic voting has important repercussions for the winning prospects of candidates. This link needs to be explored to understand more fully how strategic voting affects two aspects of a candidate's vote-getting efforts: his willingness to modernize campaigning technique and his programmatic choices.

Determinants of Strategic Voting

In the Third Republic, electoral systems created strong incentives for strategic voting by inaccurately translating votes into seats. In awarding a single seat per district, the small district magnitude made representation indivisible, allocated seats inequitably, and created a winner-takes-all situation. Voters consequently had to carefully assess the candidates' winning prospects and strongly discriminated in favor of front-runners.

The Third Republic's runoff ballot weakened the incentives that the small district magnitude created for strategic voting. It did so by creating two distinct but interdependent electoral contests. French electoral law required runoff elections in case no candidate obtained an absolute majority on the first ballot. It imposed no threshold requirements for eligibility on the runoff ballot. The runoff ballot weakened the strategic voting incentives of the district magnitude by making election outcomes contingent on the distribution of votes *and* intra-candidate bargaining. A fuller understanding of this point requires a look at the distinct and noncumulative effects of the first and second ballot.

Since relatively few candidates won an absolute majority, the first ballot assumed the quality of an exploratory, nonstrategic vote. It served voters to sincerely express their preferences and candidates to assess their bargaining strength. The double ballot made bargaining an important element in election outcomes because candidates negotiated over a variety of issues between the two election rounds. They included unconditional withdrawals, explicit withdrawals in favor of another candidate, trading-off withdrawals across districts, or threats of dividing the vote by not withdrawing.[4] First-round results played an important role in this bargaining process because they permitted front-runners to calculate how much and whose support they needed to win on the second ballot. Most importantly, however, the first-round results made it easier for candidates from different parties to cooperate and trade off withdrawals across electoral districts. Such trade-offs allowed them in effect to counter the strategic voting that occurred on the decisive second ballot, because the candidates' reciprocal withdrawals and endorsements improved their credibility with voters and helped them pool votes as best as possible. Such trade-offs were regularly but by no means universally used in the Third Republic. They consequently modified the effects of the small district magnitude without overriding it.

The peculiar hybrid system used in 1919 and 1924 created incentives for strategic voting that were comparable to the double ballot system. At first sight, though, three features of this electoral system would suggest a low level of strategic voting. The district magnitude of 6.5 made representation divisible (albeit far less than in Weimar) and allowed for semiaccurate translation of votes into seats. The electoral system also gave voters as many votes as there were seats and allowed vote splitting across lists (i.e., panache). It did not permit cumulating multiple votes on individual candidates. Multiple votes made strategic voting less likely because voters would have to assess on average the winning prospects of 6.5 candidates. Most likely, such a task would have overextended the voters' ability to process the necessary information. Finally, the electoral system allowed parties to nominate their candidates on joint lists. The possibility for such apparentements (i.e., electoral alliances) allowed the pooling of votes.[5]

On closer inspection, however, the proportional elements of the 1919 and 1924 electoral system were largely overridden by two majoritarian components. The electoral law allocated all the seats to any list winning an absolute majority. In 1919, 42 percent of lists benefited from this majority premium. The remaining seats were allocated through a two-tiered process. In the first tier, each list obtained as many seats as there were whole district quotas contained in the list quota. Seats went to list candidates with the highest-scoring personal vote. About one-third of seats were allocated through these quotas. The remaining seats were awarded in a highly disproportional manner to whichever list had the highest list quota. De facto, two-thirds of all seats were allocated on the basis of either a majority or plurality bonus, thus contributing to very inaccurate translation of votes into seats. As Lachapelle notes, the 1919 and 1924 electoral system was largely a Pyrrhic victory for advocates of PR. Voters consequently had to be very strategic and carefully assess the winning prospects of individual lists rather than individual candidates (Lachapelle 1920, 5–23; Wileman 1994).

Weimar's electoral system, on the other hand, made the accurate translation of votes into seats its paramount objective as its designers tried to rectify the distorting effects of the old imperial election law. As a result, it remains one of the purest forms of PR ever designed. The literature measures the accuracy with which seats are allocated by calculating a so-called disproportionality index. Weimar Germany had an extremely low index of 0.35 compared to the Third Republic's 2.97. Only Denmark's index of 0.44 came close, while Europe's interwar average was 1.6 (Bartolini and Mair 1990, app. 2). In awarding on average 18 seats per district, Weimar's large district magnitude made representation highly divisible and permitted an equitable allocation of seats. The large district magnitude only weakly constrained the voters' choices and encouraged sincere voting. The availability of multiple rewards significantly improved the winning prospects of candidates and made it easier for voters to choose their single most preferred choice without having to discount it by candidates' electability.

Weimar's two vote-pooling mechanisms further reduced the need for voters to act strategically. The availability of national adjustment seats allowed parties to pool votes from different electoral districts and assured highly accurate translation of votes into seats. National adjustment seats constituted a fifth of all seats allocated and played a particularly important role for small parties. Small parties won on average 60.1 percent of their seats as adjustment seats, compared to 25.1 percent for larger parties.[6] National adjustment seats thus were a major factor in reducing the risk of wasting ballots by casting them for small parties. The possibility of apparentements, in turn, allowed candidates from different parties to pool their votes both within the districts for the regular seat allocation and across districts for the awarding of national adjustment seats. Such electoral alliances were very common among Weimar's ever increasing number of small parties.

Effects of Strategic Voting

The defining characteristic of strategic voting is the concern for a candidate's electability and subsequent discounting of candidates with poor winning prospects. Strategic voting thus is intimately linked with the sort of winning and losing prospects faced by candidates. A high level of strategic voting induces voter defection from smaller parties and confronts the remaining front-runners with prospectively high gains and losses (i.e., winner-takes-all situation). A low level of strategic voting, in turn, will minimize the defections from small parties and lead to more marginal gains and losses for a wider range of candidates. In other words, the different levels of strategic voting can be understood as the type of losses and gains that voters can inflict on political actors and the type of leverage their votes have.

Strategic voting shapes candidates' behavior in two important ways: it affects their willingness to take risks and influences the general characteristics of their programmatic choices. Willingness to take risks depends not just on a mechanical cost-benefit calculus but also is contingent on the perception of prospective losses and gains faced by decision makers. This is the basic premise of work carried out by cognitive psychologists in the field of prospect theory. Through experiments, cognitive psychologists found that actors are risk-taking in facing losses and risk-averse when anticipating gains of the same magnitude. They maintain that "people do not make decisions based on absolute levels of utility (as conventional rational choice approaches assume) but in terms of relative gains and losses" (Weyland 1996, 33; Quattrone and Tversky 1988). Their most important finding is that people's aversion to losses outweighs their appreciation of gains of equal magnitude and therefore induces them to more risk-taking behavior. Applied to electoral politics, this finding explains why strategic voting creates strong incentives for political actors to take risks and quickly adapt themselves to two possible changes: innovations in campaigning technologies and shifts in voter preferences. Strategic voting thus will induce faster innovation of electioneering techniques and more immediate responses to new voter preferences. It accounts for the horse-race quality that frequently is attributed to plurality electoral systems (Katz 1980, 30–31; Amy 1993, 63–67). Nonstrategic, sincere voting, in turn, will not prevent campaigning and programmatic innovations, but it will make them less likely. It will permit greater inertia among politicians since their lack of innovation exposes them only to marginal rather than absolute losses.

Strategic voting also affects the general characteristics of candidates' political platforms. A high level of strategic voting increases candidates' concern about their electability and, more particularly, about being frontrunners. Their paramount objective, therefore, will be to maximize votes by targeting their platforms to the median voter. Candidates will have to make cross-sectoral, centrist appeals in their national campaigns and pay attention to the local concerns of their constituencies. This combination of cross-sectoral and localistic appeals requires candidates to eschew targeting narrow constituencies and pursuing principled, extremist policies (Schattschneider [1942] 1970, 85; Sartori 1994, 42; Katz 1980, 30–31). A low level of strategic voting, in turn, lessens candidates' concerns for maximizing votes. Facing prospectively marginal gains and losses, candidates have to pay less attention to voter preferences in choosing their issue positions. They can, for example, choose policies that closely accord with their personal ideological principles, please specific interest groups, or appeal to small extremist, fringe segments of the electorate (Schattschneider [1942] 1970, 85; Sartori 1994, 42; Katz 1980, 30–31; Cox 1990).

In the Third Republic, the high level of strategic voting allowed voters to impose prospectively high losses. It maximized the leverage of individual voters and turned elections into what Popper called "judgment days" (1988, 22). In doing so, strategic voting assured that the electoral market had an *amplifier effect* and contributed to the continuous translation of social into political change. It induced candidates to swiftly adopt newly available campaigning techniques. Strategic voting also made the rate of programmatic change contingent on shifts in voter preferences. The prospect of absolute losses provided a strong incentive for political actors to pay continuous and close attention to public opinion. Programmatic reforms thus did not depend on turnover in candidates or party leaders. Finally, strategic voting assured that the actual substantive agenda corresponded just as much with the diffuse preferences of a wide cross-section of the electorate as it did with the intense or well-organized preferences of party factions or economic interest groups.

In Weimar Germany, on the other hand, the low level of strategic voting turned absolute into marginal losses. Sincere voting permitted voters to express their preferences unconstrained by strategic considerations (hence the characterization of PR as being fair) at the expense of their ability to inflict effective punishment on politicians. Sartori (1976, 346) touches on this important difference when he notes that there is "a world of difference between the winner-takes-all and greater share notion of winning." Ultimately, sincere voting weakened the effectiveness of the electoral market mechanism by creating a significant *shielding effect* and by contributing to the delayed and discontinuous translation of social into political change. It created few incentives for established political actors to periodically capitalize on new vote-winning techniques made possible by innovations in advertising or mass communications. Similarly, facing no imminent electoral judgment day, political actors enjoyed a far greater slack in how immediately they had to adapt their policies to changes in public opinion. The rate of change instead became influenced less by voters than by the turnover in candidates and party leaders. Finally, sincere voting narrowed the scope of preferences candidates had to incorporate in their platforms and made agenda setting contingent more on the intensity or organizational clout of certain interests than on their sheer numbers after 1918.

In structuring careers, resources, and voting choices, electoral mechanisms had very distinct effects on how parties and electoral markets aggregated the societal preferences in France and Germany. Their effects constituted the systematic, mechanical dimension of political representation that turns out to be just as important as its historically contingent social basis. The preceding systematic explication of this mechanical dimension allows us now to return to the question of why France's and Germany's comparable historical contexts resulted in such different party developments.

Chapter 3

Organization and Ossification: Socialists, Keynesianism, and Catch-All Politics

In the late nineteenth century, the Section française de l'internationale ouvrière (SFIO) and the Sozialdemokratische Partei Deutschlands (SPD) were important driving forces of mass politics by organizing workers and demanding freer and fairer elections. Yet by 1900, it increasingly was mass politics that affected the development of the two parties. It led to the expansion of their bureaucracy and an accompanying atrophying of their party democracy. Mass politics also led to the SFIO's and SPD's growing ideological differentiation. Revolutionaries, impatient with the speed of change, wanted to use electoral contests to ferment revolutionary class consciousness, while reformists defended elections as an effective mechanism for emancipating workers. This rift was further deepened by the Great Depression and the rise of fascism, which led reformists to demand a less rigid, more catch-all campaigning style as well as a shift from Marxist economic orthodoxies to new proto-Keynesian policies.

The SFIO and SPD responded very distinctly to the threat of bureaucratization and the programmatic and tactical demands of reformists. After its bitter defeat in 1919 and breakup in 1920, the SFIO quickly rebuilt an ideologically diverse, democratically governed and electorally effective organization. It swiftly responded to the revisionists' proto-Keynesian demands and their lobbying to join the 1936 Popular Front that united communists, socialists, and liberals in an antifascist alliance. As a result of this innovativeness, the SFIO managed to maintain its electoral strength at around 20 percent even during the Depression, when radicalized voters were tempted by various extremist alternatives. The SPD's electoral support, on the other hand, stagnated after having decisively won the first interwar election in 1918. Its governance quickly became autocratic, its agenda unresponsive to new Keynesian initiatives, and its campaigning increasingly risk-averse. The SPD's overall ossification manifested itself in its 9 percent electoral loss during the depression-year elections, in its acquiescence to Brüning and von Papen's authoritarian rule, and in its tepid response to the Nazis' ascent to power.

The SFIO's and SPD's very different courses of action after 1918 reflect the very distinct ways in which electoral mechanisms structured their resource mobilization, career paths, and interaction with voters. Transhistorical, institutional factors played a far more significant role in shaping the SFIO's and SPD's interwar behavior than did either long-term socioeconomic legacies or short-term political contingencies.

Organizational and Programmatic Challenges and Responses

Reformist Challenge

Before the First World War, the revolutionary and reformist factions in the SFIO and the SPD had reached a tenuous ideological equilibrium. A growing number of revolutionaries came to accept the reformists' argument that liberal democracy, which after all had come to recognize workers' right to vote and unionize, provided a more effective venue for advancing socialism than revolution. Reformists, on the other hand, conceded to revolutionaries that there was no piecemeal, gradual transition from capitalism to socialism. Unlike liberal democracy, capitalism was not reformable and therefore had to be overthrown. In the 1930s, the Great Depression and fascism undermined this ideological equilibrium. It led reformists to challenge the revolutionaries on two fronts by espousing Keynesian ideas that departed from the established anticapitalist orthodoxy and by championing new, more entrepreneurial campaigning methods that deviated from the existing emphasis on politically educating workers.

The Great Depression profoundly challenged the SFIO's and SPD's prevailing economic thinking. The two parties' policies still followed Marx's economic determinism and thus rejected the usefulness of countercyclical, governmental economic programs. The principal challengers of the prevailing orthodoxy were the labor unions. The Confédération générale du travail (General Confederation of Labor, CGT) and the Allgemeiner Deutscher Gewerkschaftsbund (General Federation of German Trade Unions, ADGB) were the two countries' largest working-class unions. They were organizationally independent but politically closely affiliated with the SFIO and SPD. During the Great Depression, the two unions challenged the SFIO's and SPD's economic orthodoxies with renewed vigor since unemployment undermined their membership base and collective bargaining strength. The CGT borrowed much of its macro-economic program from the Belgian socialist Henri de Man. In 1934, it published the "Plan de rénovation économique," which included demands for nationalizing key industries and financial institutions as well as for an expansionary fiscal policy to stimulate demand (Jackson 1985, 140–41, 156–57). Conversely, the ADGB published in 1931 the WTB-Plan, whose initials stood for its three principal authors. The plan's central demands were almost identical to the CGT's proposal and reflected its principal author's close familiarity with Keynes's early writings (Harsch 1993, 159; Berman 1998, 190). The CGT and ADGB's proto-Keynesian plans were opposed by the SFIO's and SPD's party elders. Following their chief economic theorists, Lucien Laurat and Rudolf Hilferding, party leaders rejected the unions' plans for deviating too far from prevailing Marxist economic thinking. They dismissed proposed reflationary measures as futile and viewed the Great Depression as the final and hence welcomed collapse of capitalism (Jackson 1985, 38–39; Gates 1974, 349–51; Berman 1998, 185).

The rapid growth of fascism reinforced the reformist pressures created by the Depression. It did so in two ways. First, the fascists' talk about a national revolution that would overthrow liberal democracy was directly aimed at cutting the power that unions had gained in the labor market and socialists in the electoral arena. Reformists argued that the most effective way to counter this political threat was for the SFIO and SPD to moderate their strict anticapitalism and espouse Keynesianism. Reformists argued that such a shift in economic thinking would alleviate bourgeois concerns about socialists' respect for property rights and thereby make them more likely to participate in an antifascist alliance. Moreover, Keynesianism held the promise to limit the appeal of fascists by alleviating the economic hardship endured by workers and middle-class voters alike.

Second, the fascists' pioneering use of modern propaganda techniques challenged the SFIO's and SPD's pedagogical, identity-forming vote-getting techniques. Socialists were highly reluctant to copy these new campaigning methods because they viewed politics as a moral enterprise rather than a purely strategic game in which winning was the only goal. In their eyes, politics served to foster working-class solidarity around a key set of ideological precepts. Political strength would grow as a result of converting an ever increasing number of voters into partisans rather than scoring short-term tactical victories. Fascists jettisoned this moral conception of politics largely out of necessity. As political newcomers, they lacked a firm voting constituency and solid organizational base. They tried to compensate for this disadvantage by adopting the latest campaigning and propaganda techniques more quickly than their adversaries. Fascists assiduously borrowed ideas from commercial advertising, pioneered the use of emotional messages, exploited new technological possibilities offered by film and radio, and developed extensive political intelligence gathering systems. More than anybody else, they recognized that public opinion was no longer the static mirror image of preexisting socioeconomic structures but the psychological and hence highly manipulative amalgam of individual fears and desires.

The SFIO and SPD responded to the reformists' challenges in very different ways. Where the SFIO quickly espoused Keynesianism and modernized its campaigning, the SPD persevered in its prewar economic orthodoxies and inflexible, outdated electioneering practices.

During the interwar years, the SPD barely modernized its campaigning practices and persisted in transforming rather than accommodating voter preferences. It distributed long (often 10–20 pages) and tightly argued pamphlets rather than catchy and visually effective leaflets (Schaefer 1990, 238–48; Harsch 1993, 85). Its candidates were well known for giving lengthy, jargon-ridden lectures rather than spirited stump speeches. One party functionary captured the party's entrepreneurial deficit well when he declared that "our basic conviction is after all that the progress of socialism depends on the enlightenment and intellectual capacity of the masses. We cannot adapt ourselves to their unwillingness to reflect, but we have to overcome it" (Schaefer 1990, 256). While not entirely abandoning a pedagogical campaigning style, the SFIO at least complemented it with more entrepreneurial electioneering practices. Its centrist factions saw how effectively the ligues and foreign fascist movements exploited personal charisma, prejudices, and symbols. They consequently pushed the party to adopt a more modern campaigning style (Bergounioux 1983/84, 1164; Greene 1969, 4–5). The SFIO's more radical factions, in turn, continued to argue that the goal of elections was not to maximize votes but to strengthen revolutionary working-class identity (Greene 1969, 721).

The Keynesian plans proposed by the CGT and ADGB also experienced very different fates. The SFIO quickly adopted the "Plan de rénovation économique." The plan was first introduced at the 1934 Toulouse Congress but was defeated by Léon Blum's argument that there was no third way between capitalism and socialism. One year later, sufficient grassroots support had been generated to overcome Blum's opposition and to incorporate the plan into the party's platform (Jackson 1985, 148–49). The SPD, on the other hand, rejected the WTB-Plan even though it had been heavily promoted by the ADGB and was well received by regional party branches. The national executive decisively rejected it as un-Marxist (Harsch 1993, 209–10; Berman 1998, 185; Gates 1974, 352–53).

The different fates of these proto-Keynesian proposals cannot be easily explained by short-term historical contingencies. The fact that the Depression hit Germany harder and earlier than France would lead one to assume that the SPD should have been more attracted to Keynesianism's promise of full employment than the SFIO. Furthermore, it could be argued that the SFIO moved toward Keynesianism in 1934–35 only after it saw how the SPD's intransigence contributed to Weimar's collapse in 1933. Yet the SPD's fate had no decisive impact on the outcome of the SFIO's programmatic debates. Its moderate factions used the SPD as evidence that a centrist Keynesian-like policy was required. Its radical factions, in turn, saw the SPD's fate as proof that an intensification of the working-class struggle was needed (Marcus 1958, 22–23). Finally, if the political clout of labor unions were to have been decisive, then the SPD should have adopted Keynesianism rather than the SFIO, since the ADGB was far larger than the CGT. Saposs (1931, 120, 136) estimates the CGT's membership in 1927 at 800,000, or 10 percent of the male workforce, while the ADGB had 4.8 million members in 1928, which accounted for roughly 20 percent of the male employees (Braunthal 1978, 80). The ADGB also was organizationally more closely linked to the SPD than the CGT to the SFIO. The CGT, for example, prohibited overlapping membership in the executive organs of the union and party, which was common in Germany (Saposs 1931, 469–70; Braunthal 1978). Ultimately, historical contingencies fail to account for the SFIO's espousal and the SPD's rejection of new Keynesian ideas.

Bureaucratization Threat

The SFIO's and SPD's organizational development constituted a delicate balancing act between maintaining party democracy and enhancing administrative efficiency. In this balancing act, party democracy is symbolized by local grassroots activists involved in a sovereign national party congress, and administrative efficiency is represented by the central party

bureaucracy and professional politicians. The SFIO's and SPD's commitment to party democracy reflected their egalitarianism and belief that
effective membership participation was essential for strengthening working-class identity. Conversely, their striving for administrative efficiency
was necessitated by the logistical demands of mass politics as well as the
need to compensate for logistical resources that bourgeois politicians
could mobilize through their control of the church, corporations, and state
bureaucracy.

Before the First World War, the SFIO's and SPD's administrative
efficiency grew without much jeopardizing party democracy. This organizational equilibrium was most clearly evident in the SFIO. After its creation in 1904, the SFIO quickly established an effective party administration capable of coordinating local branches and organizing a growing
membership. But its logistical infrastructure remained highly decentralized, was run without salaried functionaries, and did not impede party
democracy (Ziebura 1967, 153–54). The SPD's pre-1914 logistical infrastructure was more extensive than the SFIO's, but it was not nearly as centralized and bureaucratized as is frequently argued.[1] Schorske (1955, 118)
noted, for example, that "before 1905, the national, hierarchical organization for which the SPD became famous existed only in embryo." A new
party statute in 1905 laid the groundwork for the SPD's subsequent organizational growth. It designated local district organizations as the party's
administrative anchor and delegated to them most important electioneering and logistical responsibilities (Schorske 1955, 118). In southwestern
Germany, the significance of these local committees was limited by the
growing importance of regional and *Länderorganizationen* (state-level
organizations). Nevertheless, before 1914 the SPD shared with the SFIO a
considerable degree of decentralization and grassroots involvement in its
logistical infrastructure.

After 1918, the SFIO was more successful than the SPD in preserving
the organizational equilibrium between administrative efficiency and
party democracy. The SFIO experienced only limited bureaucratization,
and party congresses continued to play a pivotal role. Its congresses represented a wide range of political views, formulated policies, kept leaders
and deputies accountable, and elected all important party officers
(Bergounioux and Grunberg 1992, 46–47, 11). Local party branches, in
turn, maintained their autonomy and became laboratories for new campaigning techniques and policy initiatives. By contrast, the SPD became
more and more autocratic after 1918. Its congresses turned into choreo-

graphed and largely symbolic events lacking the lively debates and contested votes of the prewar years (Buse 1990, 478–81; Nipperdey 1961, 358, 367). There also was hardly any turnover in the SPD's executive positions. Hunt (1964, 70) noted that the "election to the executive while formally democratic, amounted in practice to a disguised system of co-optation where leaders held their office indefinitely and hand-picked their successors." The demise of party democracy in the SPD increasingly left unimaginative functionaries in charge of elections that only tangentially affected their professional careers. These functionaries became one of the central obstacles to the adoption of new campaigning techniques introduced by fascists and Keynesian ideas formulated by the ADGB.

These different rates of bureaucratization are not easily attributable to differences in either long-standing cultural factors or short-term historical contingencies. Historians frequently attribute the SPD's democratic deficit to its ideological rigidity and repression during the late nineteenth century or to Germany's authoritarian political culture (Lipset 1983; Roth 1963; Lepsius 1973; Mommsen 1974). Ritter (1979, 109), for example, accounts for the SPD's ossification by arguing that it was "a party waiting for the system, following the historical laws formulated by Marx, to collapse by itself in order to assume its inheritance." Such explanations fail to account for why the SPD successfully maintained its organizational equilibrium before the First World War when similar historical and cultural factors were present. They also overlook that party democracy had local defenders among SPD activists. They demanded democratizing the selection of the party executive and widening access to party newspapers (Harsch 1993, 142–43). These demands aimed to "lead the party to political activism once again and rejuvenate its original characteristics as a movement. While the party executive isolated itself and tried to quell the resounding criticisms of the party's passivity, numerous dissenting Social Democrats left the party" (Mommsen 1973, 113–14, 131).

Conversely, party democracy inside the SFIO had its critics. The large neosocialist faction stressed the importance of restructuring the party along more hierarchical and disciplined lines. Many neosocialists believed that fascists and communists owed their political successes to greater organizational discipline. One neosocialist leader stated that "order and authority are the new foundations of the action we must take to win over the masses" (Greene 1969, 72). After the SFIO's rank and file repeatedly defeated the neosocialists, 46 of its deputies left the SFIO in 1933 and formed the Parti socialiste de France—Union Jean Jaurès (Marcus 1958,

6–29; Bergounioux 1985, 1170). This split signified a considerable loss for the SFIO but a loss it willingly accepted to preserve its party democracy.

Historical and cultural factors therefore are as insufficient in explaining the different fortunes of party democracy after 1918 as they were in accounting for the different outcomes of the reformist challenges. A more complete explanation has to consider how electoral mechanisms affected the rate of bureaucratization, the control over political careers, and the degree of centralization.

Electioneering Costs

Before 1914, the number of functionaries was still small enough to preserve the equilibrium between the national party organization and local party branches and to protect party democracy. After 1918, France's unchanged electioneering costs preserved the organizational equilibrium in the SFIO while the sudden rise of these costs in Weimar Germany tilted the balance of power in the SPD in favor of functionaries and national leaders.

The Third Republic's low electioneering costs created few organizational exigencies beyond those demanded by mass politics and thereby lessened the pressures for the SFIO to build a centralized and professionally staffed logistical infrastructure. With an average of only 18,000 registered voters, the small physical district size considerably reduced the costs of procuring and disseminating information. The fixed parliamentary terms also limited the frequency of elections. Finally, the absence of an elected presidency and referenda restricted the need to build a costly national organization and permitted SFIO candidates to capitalize on their personal reputations, draw on local contacts, and mobilize party volunteers (Ziebura 1967, 169).

The SFIO's surprisingly quick recovery after its breakup attests to the Third Republic's modest electioneering costs. At the 1920 Tours Congress, the SFIO lost three-quarters of its 180,000 members, entire departmental organizations left, and even the party newspaper *L'Humanité* fell under communist control. The remaining rump SFIO consisted mostly of 55 deputies (out of 68). These deputies quickly rebuilt the logistical infrastructure and won 105 seats in 1924 (Judt 1986, 125–26). This recovery was possible because the SFIO could still draw on the local notability and personal networks of its remaining deputies. It would have taken the SFIO much longer to rebuild a more capital-intensive and professionalized organization.

The low electioneering costs also limited bureaucratization, which was one of the major threats to grassroots participation. The small size of the SFIO's national organization left party members and independent entrepreneurial politicians in charge of local party organizations. As a result, local organizations rather than national leaders selected delegates to the annual party congresses and thus could actively participate in the SFIO's personnel and policy decisions (Greene 1969, 158–59; Ziebura 1967, 175–76; Graham 1994, 44–45, 95–100). This influence of local party branches was most clearly evident at the 1920 Tours Congress, which decided the SFIO's membership in the Third International. The party leadership objected to Lenin's stringent 21 demands. Yet they were defeated by party activists who were the central driving force behind the newly created Parti communist français (French Communist Party, PCF).[2] Party congresses also decided the party's participation in coalition governments in 1929 and 1933. In 1929 and 1933, they rejected tempting coalition offers made by the Radical Party (Ziebura 1967, 269; Greene 1969, 143–51; Winkler 1991, 195; Marcus 1958, 6–8, 19–20).

Furthermore, the independence of local party branches protected ideological diversity and thereby made it easier for the CGT to find party-internal allies for its Keynesian program. There were repeated instances where the national executive sought and failed to discipline renegade branches (Ziebura 1967, 169, 178; Graham 1994, 44–45). For example, in 1937 it tried to silence the Gauche révolutionnaire after it refused to stop publicly criticizing the congresses' decisions. After being formally expelled, the faction merely renamed itself and remained in the party. The leadership simply had too little control over the faction's stronghold in the Parisian departmental federation. The Gauche révolutionnaire finally left in 1938 after its ambitious leader F. Pivert decided to form his own party (Greene 1969, 215–16; Graham 1994, 95–100).

Ultimately, by preserving the organizational equilibrium, France's low electioneering costs facilitated the efforts of reformists to push for Keynesian policies and the modernization of campaigning strategies. SFIO candidates were directly in charge of their elections rather than relying on national functionaries. They consequently had a considerable incentive to adopt the latest campaigning techniques, since their career prospects were very directly tied to the effectiveness of their vote-getting strategies.

By contrast, Weimar's high electioneering costs contributed to the SPD's organizational ossification after 1918. With an average of 1.2 million registered voters, Weimar's physical district size was 66 times larger than that of the Third Republic. The large districts made interactions between parties and voters highly anonymous and limited the usefulness of volunteers and personal reputations. Weimar's presidential elections and referenda reinforced this effect. These enormous electioneering costs required the SPD to maintain a large-scale electoral machine and hire an increasing number of professional functionaries. To economize, the party also concentrated electioneering and administrative tasks in regional and national organizations even though before the war they had been carried out by local branches. By 1930, 20,000–30,000 functionaries had taken over the logistical tasks that party activists once carried out (Hunt 1964, 46–48; Harsch 1993, 29).[3] The national executive had to raise new funds to pay for this administrative expansion. It increased its share of party dues from 20 to 25 percent and levied a 20 percent tax on profits from party enterprises (e.g., newspapers, consumer cooperatives) (Hunt 1964, 46–48). Unlike the SFIO, the interwar SPD shifted many of its administrative responsibilities from the local activists to the national bureaucrats.[4] It consolidated its old 440 local organizations into 35 new regional ones (Hunt 1964, 46).

Unlike volunteering activists, functionaries were easily controlled by party leaders, who promoted and employed them. In 1920, for example, the SPD's national executive paid 20 percent of all regional party functionaries and decided all their promotions (Hunt 1964, 86; Ritter 1979, 123–34). Party functionaries also occupied unelected positions and consequently were not accountable to regular party members. They increasingly played an important role in selecting delegates to party congresses. Party leaders, in turn, would reward such interference with party democracy by promoting functionaries or even selecting them as candidates (Hunt 1964, 78; Mommsen 1974, 113–14).

This manipulation of the delegate selection process marked a distinct departure from the prewar period, when local party branches controlled it and when party congresses had more authority (Nipperdey 1961, 352; Schorske 1955). The SPD's increasingly autocratic selection of congressional candidates clearly tilted the organizational equilibrium in favor of party leaders. Between 1919 and 1930, only 21 individuals served in the party's top 18 executive positions. Party leaders were frequently criticized by their members for being too old, behaving like bourgeois politicians, or being autocratic (Hunt 1964, 70; Harsch 1993, 142–43). Twenty-five percent of congressional delegates were unelected, ex officio members (e.g., deputies or members of the party executive) (Harsch 1993, 25–26). Hunt (1964, 46) concludes that "the entire structure of the SPD's organization was altered to fit the electioneering demands of the Weimar [electoral] system, an alteration which incidentally encouraged the decline of intra-party democracy."

This decline in party democracy limited the ability of reformists to break with the SPD's economic orthodoxies and adopt more modern campaigning strategies. By weakening internal factions and ideological diversity, the decline in party democracy made it more difficult for the ADGB to find party-internal allies for its Keynesian WTB-Plan. Apart from the small but largely insignificant Klassenkampf-Gruppe (Class Struggle Faction), there were few distinct factions left in the SPD after 1918. Even the remainder of the more radical Unabhängige Sozialdemokratische Partei Deutschlands (Independent Social Democratic Party of Germany, USPD), which rejoined the SPD in 1922, failed to retain a distinct ideological and organizational profile (Heineman 1985, 505, 511; Schaefer 1990, 137; Harsch 1993, 97, 63).

The decline of party democracy also allowed the leadership to quell electioneering reforms that local activists proposed to counter the Nazis' appeal. Reformists suggested downplaying the party's didactic electoral message and placing greater emphasis on the candidates' personalities in the hope of imitating the success of Hitler's personal appeal. Party functionaries at various levels vehemently opposed such proposals. They feared that charismatic new upstarts could threaten the seniority they had accumulated over long years of loyal but unimaginative party service (Pyta 1989, 446–48). Harsch (1993, 63) notes a striking "contrast between the slow reaction at the top of the SPD and the relatively precocious response of provincial activists and lower functionaries who witnessed Nazis' extra-parliamentary activity at close hand and compared its quantity and innovations with SPD sluggishness and routine." The leadership's successful resistance to such reforms forced rank-and-file members to go outside the party's existing organizational structures. They participated in the SPD-affiliated Reichsbanner to stage large antifascist demonstrations. These efforts were received with considerable skepticism among party leaders, who were afraid to have their positions challenged by organizations they did not fully control (Harsch 1993, 169–90).

Parenthetically, it should be noted that electioneering costs affected the relationship between unions and socialist parties differently than they did the relationship between business organizations and bourgeois parties.

As the next chapter argues, Weimar's high electioneering costs gave business groups tremendous leverage over the internal affairs of the DDP and
DVP. Yet the large mass membership and high degree of self-financing of
socialist parties limited their dependence on external supporters and thus
mitigated the impact of electioneering costs. In other words, Weimar's
high electioneering costs did not provide the ADGB with nearly the same
leverage as it did economic interest groups with the DDP and DVP. Furthermore, the governance of socialist parties, to the extent that it remained
democratic, provided a check on external interest groups that did not exist
in bourgeois parties. It is important to keep organizational peculiarities
like this in mind to properly assess the effects of electoral mechanisms.

Career Uncertainty

According to socialist party statutes, the recruitment of candidates was the
prerogative of party members participating in local party branches. This
democratization of candidate recruitment was meant to keep candidates
sufficiently uncertain about their career prospects to prevent them from
becoming unimaginative, autocratic career politicians. In practice, the
intentions of party statutes conflicted with the organizational consequences of electoral mechanisms far more severely in Weimar Germany
than in the Third Republic.

Weimar's low career uncertainty gave SPD leaders a considerable
degree of control over the candidate recruitment process. Before 1914, the
SPD's local district organizations recruited electoral candidates. Their
autonomy was only limited in southwestern Germany, where regional and
Länderorganizationen (state-level organizations) informally sought to
influence the district branches (Nipperdey 1961, 325, 340–50). After 1918,
however, Weimar's large district magnitude reduced the number of
recruitment sites from 440 to 35 and thereby centralized the process by
which candidates were chosen. Together with the national adjustment
seats and categorical ballot, the district magnitude created longer, more
hierarchical electoral lists with more safe seats readily controlled by the
party executive. The effects of these electoral mechanisms clearly overrode
the democratic intentions of the SPD's party statutes. According to these
statutes, local branches could submit candidate recommendations to
regional party conventions, which would decide the final selection and
ranking of candidates. De jure, the national leadership had control only

over the selection of the national list. De facto, however, it nominated, selected, and ranked all candidates (Braunthal 1978, 132).

The low career uncertainty made career prospects highly dependent on party-internal politicking and loyalty. Candidates knew that career prospects primarily depended on their list ranking and therefore concentrated on pleasing party leaders (who ranked them) rather than voters. The low career uncertainty removed deputies so far from the actual electoral process that many had distinguished political careers without ever having shown much political initiative. It made loyalty rather than electability the criterion for candidate selection. The low career uncertainty literally divorced candidates from their task of representing voters and made them subservient to party functionaries and leaders who selected them. SPD leaders generally were disdainful of entrepreneurial colleagues, viewing them as unprincipled, personal careerists. Party leaders emphasized experience and seniority as grounds for justifying their repeated appointment to the safest list positions (Pyta 1989, 443). "The party reasoned that its leaders should have the majority of seats as a reward for their loyalty and for being the most capable spokesmen in the Reichstag" (Braunthal 1978, 136). Efforts by one district organization to promote new, more energetic candidates rather than reselect the longtime incumbent union candidates proved unsuccessful. Union candidates had been known as ineffective campaigners; their oratory was wooden and their availability for electioneering constrained by union responsibilities (Harsch 1993, 20–21, 213).

The low career uncertainty also limited the ADGB's capacity to lobby for its Keynesian WTB-Plan. We saw that the SPD leadership opposed the plan because it was inconsistent with existing Marxist economic doctrine and because it challenged its agenda-setting prerogatives. Traditionally, the SPD formulated policies and then cleared them with the unions (Harsch 1993, 166). A union-sponsored WTB-Plan threatened to reverse this division of labor. Party executives did not openly criticize the WTB-Plan, but they torpedoed it by making a vague counterproposal and having the party caucus vote down the original plan (Gates 1974, 352). This defeat was surprising given the ADGB's prominent role in the SPD. It provided the SPD with financial and logistical assistance that was substantial enough to regularly secure it 20–25 percent of candidate nominations and representation in important executive offices (Harsch 1993, 20–21, 213; Braunthal 1978, 121–23). Yet the ADGB's material assistance never was so decisive that it could dictate policies to the SPD the way economic interest groups did to Weimar's liberal parties. One source estimates that the ADGB contributed 10 percent of the SPD's campaigning expenses (Braunthal 1978, 127–29). The ADGB thus still had to lobby the SPD. But such lobbying was exceedingly difficult given the leadership's tight control over the career prospects of virtually all non-union candidates. The final vote over the WTB-Plan clearly reflected this difficulty. Except for the two union representatives on the national party executive, all others voted against the WTB-Plan (Braunthal 1978, 64).

The obstacles that Weimar's low career uncertainty posed for the WTB-Plan extended to other policy initiatives as well. Farmers, for example, were one non-working-class constituency that the SPD tried to mobilize after 1930. This initiative failed because the SPD only recruited a single farmer on its lists and because it did not meaningfully accommodate agricultural interests. It trained functionaries to become farm experts and only stressed those interests of farmers that were compatible with the existing working-class platform. The SPD's platform did not include any direct agricultural policies but simply stressed that the economic well-being of farmers depended on the purchasing power of urban workers (Pyta 1989, 393–94, 414). It is little surprise, then, that one rural party organizer complained, "How much we still lack the appropriate personalities and programs! How insensitively the mostly urban membership treats the rural problems!" (Pyta 1989, 428).

The Third Republic's high career uncertainty limited the capacity of the SFIO's leadership to control the entry and reentry of candidates. The small district magnitude devolved candidate recruitment to the roughly 600 local district branches. Such decentralization limited the influence of the national leaders and made candidates' political careers dependent on the support of local activists (Ziebura 1967, 169, 178). The low district magnitude further decreased job security by depriving candidates of safe, high list positions. SFIO candidates consequently had a much higher turnover than their SPD counterparts. On average, 50 percent of all SFIO deputies were newcomers as compared to 19 percent in the SPD.[5]

The high career uncertainty increased both incentives and opportunities for deputies to innovate. SFIO candidates lacked possibilities to shelter themselves from the pressures of the electoral marketplace by securing safe list positions. They consequently faced far greater incentives to adopt the new electioneering practices introduced by fascists. Lacking control over the recruitment process also constrained the SFIO leadership in pursuing its preferred campaigning style of transforming public opinion rather than accommodating it. Finally, the high career uncertainty enhanced the CGT's capacity to push its Keynesian program. By protecting the autonomy of individual candidates, it allowed the CGT to effectively lobby those receptive to its reflationary program even when the national party leadership opposed it (Jackson 1985, 145–50).

The double ballot added another element of uncertainty by making political careers partially contingent on the intra-candidate bargaining over withdrawal and endorsement that took place between the two election rounds. For example, the refusal of noncompetitive communists to bargain over withdrawal on the second round significantly added to the socialists' career uncertainty. The effects of the double ballot need to be qualified in two ways. First, the double ballot does not affect career uncertainty during the pre-electoral recruitment process like other electoral mechanisms. Yet it still warrants inclusion because it constitutes a nonelectoral, party-internal determinant of career uncertainty. Second, the career uncertainty resulting from the double ballot can potentially be reduced if parties form national alliances. The purpose of such alliances is to coordinate withdrawals among its members so that only the best-scoring first-round candidate goes on to the second ballot. Such coordination reduces uncertainty resulting from noncooperation. However, various political circumstances prevented the establishment and effective function of such national alliances in the Third Republic. In 1936, for example, 29.5 percent of SFIO candidates and 47 percent of Radical deputies refused to withdraw even though the Popular Front explicitly agreed that only the best-scoring of its members would go on to the second ballot.[6] Given that the 1936 Popular Front was the most formal interwar electoral alliance, it seems reasonable to assume the compliance rates for the 1928 and 1932 Cartel des gauches arrangements must have been far lower. The double ballot therefore constituted a genuine source of career uncertainty.

The SFIO's national executive repeatedly sought to form nationwide alliances with other parties. Yet, with the exception of the Popular Front in 1936, the complexity of local political conditions and the difficulty of enforcing such national agreements repeatedly led to their failure. Some local committees, for example, were reluctant to cooperate with Radicals if communists already had considerable support in their districts. They were afraid that such alliances would strengthen the communists' claim of being the only true working-class representative (Judt 1986, 146–47). On other occasions, the SFIO and its political allies had to agree on a joint first-round candidate to avoid the first-round victory of strong conservative opponents. The local particularities of 600 electoral districts were simply too complex to nationally coordinate the withdrawals and thereby reduce career uncertainty. The SFIO consequently left the intra-candidate bargaining to the local and regional party branches. The effect this had was to preserve their importance and autonomy vis-à-vis the national executive and functionaries (Judt 1976, 202, 207–10).

The greater centralization of the SFIO's alliance decisions during the 1919 and 1924 elections indirectly illustrates the decentralizing effects of the double ballot. These elections were held under a hybrid PR/plurality system whose apparentement mechanism required parties to form joint party lists, capable of winning 50 percent or more of seats, rather than coordinate their second-round withdrawals. Since the 1919/24 system only involved a single round, the SFIO had fewer difficulties in implementing a nationwide and uniform alliance strategy than it did under the double ballot system. In 1919, its party congress passed the famous Bracke motion, which forbade socialist candidates from participating in joint lists. The devastating results of this go-it-alone strategy led the party to relax the Bracke motion in 1923. It now permitted regional party branches to form joint lists with the liberal Parti radical. But such alliances had to fulfill three conditions: they had to contribute to the defeat of conservative Bloc national lists; the SFIO and its allies could not present joint programs; and the party's executive body, the Commission administrative permanente, had to approve every alliance (Judt 1976, 202, 207, 208–10). As these conditions indicate, the single-round hybrid system of 1919/24 facilitated the centralization and strict enforcement of decision making to a degree impossible under the double ballot. After its reintroduction in 1924, it was no longer feasible for the SFIO to implement nationwide alliances. It was once again the SFIO's regional and district branches that were in charge of forming local alliances.

Strategic Voting

As members of socialist parties and labor unions, workers had more possibilities to influence party-internal agendas than less organized middle-class voters. The electoral market provided an additional opportunity for workers to signal their economic and electioneering preferences and thereby act as silent adjudicators in the party-internal disputes over the adoption of Keynesianism and new vote-getting techniques. The clarity with which voters could send these signals depended on the incentives that electoral mechanisms created for strategic voting.

The Third Republic's high level of strategic voting induced risk taking by increasing prospective gains and particularly losses of electoral contests. It made the SFIO's electioneering highly contingent on the strategic moves of its opponents. It turned elections into horse races that required highly flexible electioneering strategies and left little room for jargon-ridden, didactic campaign messages. The SFIO consequently responded more promptly than the SPD to the tactical innovations of fascists. This prompt response is remarkable because the French right posed a smaller electoral threat than its German counterpart. France's conservative camp was highly fragmented, and the ligues failed to translate their considerable mass following into parliamentary seats. So even though the political context exerted less pressure on French socialists to innovate than on German socialists, the high level of strategic voting more than compensated for it.

Strategic voting also contributed to the SFIO's swift conversion to Keynesianism. By making representation indivisible, the Third Republic's small district magnitude required the sort of cross-sectoral programmatic appeal that Keynesianism offered. The CGT plan, for example, was specifically designed to appeal to workers and middle-class. In stressing reflationary macroeconomic policies, the plan offered benefits to workers and middle-class voters while at the same time leaving private property intact and respecting the managerial autonomy of firms. The plan expressly rejected nationalizations beyond a few sectors (banking and transportation) in order to assuage middle-class apprehensions about the left's traditional anticapitalism (Jackson 1985, 145–48). Strategic voting played a key role in hastening the SFIO's efforts to accommodate the interests of nonworkers. The exigencies it imposed on socialists to maximize votes were so strong that the SFIO never indulged in long theoretical debates about whether or not Keynesianism was consistent with Marxist doctrine (Bergounioux and Grunberg 1992, 105–6).

The pressure to adopt Keynesian and other centrist policies was particularly pronounced in electoral districts where the SFIO faced stiff competition. In such districts, candidates regularly preferred moderate platforms over orthodox ones. By contrast, in many rural districts, where socialists had poor electoral prospects, local committees more readily ignored the vote-maximizing exigencies imposed by strategic voting. They saw little prospect for advancing socialism through the ballot box and were hence more inclined to pursue a radical class warfare strategy. These different choices "reinforced the [SFIO's] equation of electoral success with moderation in party politics and conversely, the coincidence of electoral insignificance with a tendency towards radicalism" (Greene 1969, 165, 168, 183). This conclusion is largely borne out by Jackson's observation (1985, 145–48) that Keynesian planism was especially popular in the departments of Drome, Pyrénées-Orientales, Manche, and Seine. In all but the Manche department, the SFIO was highly competitive by either winning seats outright or being a strong runner-up (Lachapelle 1936).

The small district magnitude also induced programmatic innovation that was not directly related to strategic voting. It facilitated the evaluation of election outcomes since the 600 electoral districts provided a multiplicity of electoral contests from which inferences could be drawn about the effectiveness of the different campaigning strategies and political platforms. The large number of districts made it relatively easy for the SFIO to assess how its radical or centrist candidates performed and modify its platform accordingly. Weimar's PR did not provide the same transparency and frequently led to post-election accusations among SPD factions that the party's poor performance could have been avoided with the adoption of a more radical or moderate strategy. The lack of specific electoral outcomes complicated the assessment of such conflicting interpretations.

By contrast, Weimar's low level of strategic voting reduced the pressures that voters exerted on the SPD's leadership and functionaries. By limiting the punishment voters could inflict, the low level of strategic voting weakened incentives for the SPD to adopt the union's WTB-Plan. It meant that union members, who according to one estimate constituted one-third of the SPD's electorate, had insufficient leverage to change the leaders' orthodox economic views (Braunthal 1978, 120–21). Smaller voting constituencies had even less impact on the SPD's agenda. Party elders, for example, opposed making special appeals to workers defecting to the KPD and increasingly also to the NSDAP on the grounds that they were unreliable protest or swing voters (Mommsen 1974, 122; Harsch 1993, 97). The party executive also refused to woo lower-middle-class voters because it believed that the increasing concentration of wealth among capitalists would inevitably turn them into proletarians (Pyta 1989, 391).

Low levels of strategic voting contributed to the SPD's ideological ossification beyond the WTB-Plan. The party did little to attract young voters that had switched to the NSDAP. Party elders had a long-standing suspicion toward such voters whose radicalism and activism did not suit their staid and bureaucratic ways (Pyta 1989, 391). The center of the SPD's youth strategy was a paternalistic schooling campaign that instructed young voters on the virtues of socialism and the evils of fascism. The leader of the socialist youth organization, Ollenhauer, noted in typically schoolmaster fashion: "Our struggle for the youth . . . can only consist in performing even more political schooling than we already have." He further noted that this task might be "unpopular" with the youth, but "in the long run the strongest weapon in the fight [with the Nazis] will prove to be solely the growing insight" (Pyta 1989, 391).

The unemployed, the lower middle class, youth, and farmers all could have increased the SPD's vote share. But Weimar's large district magnitude exerted few pressures to woo these constituencies and instead allowed the SPD to concentrate on its working-class constituency. Indicative of the SPD's fixation on its working-class strength and disregard for its overall electoral support was the leadership's ritualistic pointing to its steady membership. This became its pat answer whenever it was criticized for ignoring nonworkers (Harsch 1993, 145). The SPD simply did not have to attract the new potential voters by modifying its platform; it could instead wait for socioeconomic circumstances that made interests of voters compatible with its ideological principles. Weimar's large district magnitude ultimately made cross-sectoral appeals less necessary and thereby freed the SPD from having to formulate a pragmatic and flexible program that accommodated conflicting interests. In short, it allowed programmatic choices to be made more in accordance with static ideological principles than with dynamic electoral expediencies.

The low level of strategic voting also imposed few constraints on the SPD's outdated campaigning style, which failed to exploit the appeal of personalities, ignored the latest mass communication technologies, and did not tap the emotional power of nationalism. The SPD, for example, responded to the NSDAP's electoral breakthrough in 1930 by intensifying its traditional mobilizational strategy of organizing and converting voters rather than wooing them. This pedagogical emphasis proved ineffective in responding to the electioneering innovations of the NSDAP. One party member complained that the SPD leaflets "assumed too much of the voters," that they were aimed at the "politically interested and trained" voters and did not appeal to the "ignorant" and "indifferent." He went on to draw the perceptive conclusion that the Nazis' success could be largely attributed to "the primitiveness of its message" (Schaefer 1990, 241).

Criticisms like this and the NSDAP's success led the SPD in 1932 to modify its didactic and schoolmasterly electioneering in favor of a more entrepreneurial strategy that aimed to reach those voters who were politically inactive and susceptible to emotional appeals (Pyta 1989, 479–80). The SPD finally used political symbols, discovered the virtues of negative advertising (e.g., publicizing the SA leader's homosexuality), and actively canvassed voters who were politically undecided. The party's new propaganda guidelines stated that electoral campaigns "had to incorporate all segments of society, and address each according to the particularity of its interests" (Pyta 1989, 479–80). The guideline's qualifying clause is interesting because it stands in stark contrast to the SPD's prior efforts to subsume the interests of new voters under the existing ideological principles.

The SPD also overcame its traditional reluctance to enter into political alliances. It responded positively to the Reichsbanner's appeal in November 1931 to unite all the republican forces in the so-called Eiserne Front to fight fascism.[7] It organized a variety of public mass events to convey the strength and determination of the antifascist forces and to counter the image of Hitler's unstoppable rise to power (Pyta 1989, 472). The SPD's participation in the Eiserne Front constituted an important departure from its previous suspicion toward cooperating with organizations it did not directly control and that could prove unreliable or threaten the leadership (Mommsen 1974, 123).

There is an irony that the SPD modernized its campaigning strategy at the very moment when the Nazis' rise and Brüning's rule by emergency decree constrained its political options just like a small district magnitude would have. The NSDAP's promises to eliminate democracy threatened not just the SPD's electoral strength but also its very survival. These promises therefore added the kind of zero-sum quality to Weimar's electoral contests that PR failed to provide. The absence of such competitive pressures allowed the SPD to ignore the Nazi threat until 14 months before Hitler assumed power.[8]

Chapter 4

Money and Votes: Liberals, Organized Business, and Disorganized Bourgeoisie

During the interwar period, the electoral performance of French and German Liberals diverged more dramatically than that of any other pair of parties. After winning 23 percent of the votes in 1919 and 22.4 percent in 1920, the electoral support of the Deutsche Demokratische Partei (German Democratic Party, DDP) and the Deutsche Volkspartei (German People's Party, DVP) dropped precipitously, to 16 percent in the mid-1920s and to 2.2 percent in 1932. The Parti radical (Radical Party), on the other hand, only marginally lost electoral support. Its prewar vote share of 20–25 percent gradually dropped during the interwar period, to 17–18 percent in the 1930s.

This striking divergence in the electoral performance of French and German Liberals reflects two different party-internal responses to fairly similar environmental challenges: the long-term shift from notable to mass politics and the short-term distributional conflicts created by postwar inflation. Unlike the DDP and DVP, the Parti radical successfully rebuilt its organization and adapted it to the ever quickening pace of mass politics. This responsiveness allowed the Radicals to compete more effectively than German Liberals in the increasingly polarized and professionalized interwar elections. Similarly, the Parti radical dealt more successfully with the distributional consequences that inflation inflicted on its political support base. Its economic platform responded far more equitably than those of German Liberals to the divergent preferences about when and how to deflate that existed among the three parties' wealthy, well-organized industrial backers and their vote-rich but unorganized middle-class voters. As a result, the Radicals better protected their middle-class electoral base than did the DDP and DVP.

Theoretically, three factors must be considered when explaining why

French and German Liberals made distinctly different programmatic and organizational choices in light of similar, albeit not identical, structural constraints. First, the changing socioeconomic context requires attention to see how it constrained the actions of parties and how its similarity across France and Germany allows it to be eliminated as a systematic variable. Second, political parties have to be treated as collective actors consisting of different groups with distinct preferences rather than as single unitary actors. What needs to be studied is how the political equilibria among these groups constrained the capacity of party leaders to respond to voter preferences. Third, French and German electoral mechanisms directly affected these equilibria and the incentives for liberal politicians to innovate their organizational and campaigning practices. Electioneering costs determined the capacity of liberal parties to modernize their logistical infrastructures and their financial dependence on economic interest groups. Career uncertainty affected the capacity of big business to leverage its financial contributions into actual policy outcomes. Finally, strategic voting influenced the readiness of Liberals to innovate in their electioneering practices and the ability of middle-class voters to translate their superior numbers in the electoral market into a sufficiently powerful leverage to offset the party-internal lobbying by economic interest groups.

Organizational and Programmatic Challenges and Choices

In claiming that the internal politics of liberal parties mattered electorally, it is presumed that their internal decision making was relatively autonomous from the socioeconomic circumstances to which it responded. This autonomy may be demonstrated by showing that the organizational and programmatic choices of French and German Liberals cannot be reduced to the constraints created by the two countries' mass politics and postwar economies. The first chapter discussed the similar challenges that mass politics posed for French and German Liberals before 1914. The following comments are limited to whether or not the First World War altered the organizational exigencies of mass politics in any significant way. The programmatic challenges posed by postwar inflation are then discussed more extensively, since they have not been previously elaborated.

    The First World War amplified the long-term effects of mass politics but did little to alter the organizational challenges faced by French and German Liberals. It contributed most immediately to the organizational collapse of the liberal parties, whose organization ceased to function during the war. The first task of Liberals therefore was to reestablish local party branches, revive party newspapers, and recruit new candidates. This was not an easy undertaking, since many former activists had died in the war, and most people were preoccupied with their economic survival.

The First World War also accelerated the long-term organizational challenges that mass politics posed for the Liberals' notable style of politics. The war economy had led to the rapid organizational consolidation of economic interest groups and to the establishment of corporatist arrangements. This changed political economy, in turn, required political parties to improve their organizational capacities by modernizing their logistical infrastructures and governance mechanisms (Maier 1975). Moreover, wartime propaganda, the front experience, and the Versailles Treaty ignited political emotions and nationalist sentiments that diminished the already limited prewar appeal of Liberals' free-market, cultural, and constitutional themes as well as the effectiveness of their rational, deliberative conception of politics. The First World War thus further undermined the personal electoral connection between liberal notables and their voters, requiring liberal parties to quickly expand their logistical infrastructure and modernize their electioneering practices if they were going to survive.

The logistical challenges of mass politics and the First World War produced very different responses by French and German Liberals. The Parti radical quickly rebuilt its organization and by the mid-1920s began to copy certain organizational features of socialist parties. It sought to demarcate itself from socialists by sharpening its ideological profile and adopting a more modern, partisan campaigning style. The DDP and DVP had some initial success in building up their logistical infrastructures. Very quickly, however, their organizations collapsed, and by the late twenties both parties "were hardly capable anymore of executing their most important tasks such as running campaigns, formulating programs, and recruiting young new members" (Albertin 1981, 57–58). The DDP and DVP did not try to adapt their antiquated style of notable politics to the more nationalized and partisan electoral contests of the interwar years.

Another divergent response to similar historical circumstances may be observed in the Liberals' postwar economic policies. These policies responded to three inflationary legacies left by the First World War. First, low income and corporate taxes required French and German governments to cover the costs of the war and reconstruction (which were particularly high in France) by issuing bonds, borrowing abroad, and printing money. The resulting budget deficits and increases in money supply eroded the domestic and foreign value of money (Schuker 1976, 36; Maier 1975). Second, the postwar electoral gains of socialist parties, and especially the membership increases of unions, created pressures for higher social welfare spending and made the old deflationary orthodoxies, with their emphasis on lowering taxes and cutting government spending, politically less feasible (Maier 1975). "For the first time in history, workers were more nearly the political match of holders of capital, setting the stage for a 'war of attrition', that is a prolonged conflict over economic policies that arguably contributed to inflation and currency depreciation" (Simmons 1994, 28). Third, the reparations required under the Versailles Treaty added to inflationary pressures. Germany's reparation payments contributed to its budgetary deficit. It also undermined the government's political will to control inflation, which permitted repaying the despised reparations with devalued money (Maier 1987, 203). In France, reparations contributed to budgetary ills because they induced the government to defer long-overdue expenditure cuts in anticipation of German reparations that never materialized (Schuker 1976, 41; Haig 1929, 101).

These inflationary legacies of the war had significant consequences on the electoral performance of French and German liberal parties. These consequences are most commonly analyzed by correlating the inflation rate with the defection rate of liberal voters. Weimar's hyperinflation thus becomes the sufficient condition for the collapse of the DDP and DVP while the Third Republic's lesser inflation is related to the Radicals' electoral continuity. This strictly economic, correlational line of inquiry is insufficient for three reasons. First, it does not explain why the loss of the franc's domestic and foreign value did not undermine the Radicals' electoral base. France's inflation never matched Germany's hyperinflation, but by 1922 it was high enough to become the central economic issue in the 1924 and 1928 elections. During this period, the French retail price index rose fivefold while the franc lost much of its value against the pound and the U.S. dollar (Schuker 1976, 73; Keiger 1997, 313–20; Paxton 1997, 33). Paxton (1997, 33) noted that "La vie chère [the high cost of living] recurs everywhere in the economic and political commentary of the interwar period." Furthermore, as early as 1922, Stresemann was "acutely aware of the disintegrative effect that the inflation had on his party's predominantly middle class base" (Jones 1988, 182). German inflation thus corroded the Liberals' electoral support long before it spiraled out of control in 1923–24. Second, inflation is not an objective economic indicator of voter preferences since it also has noneconomic, political antecedent causes that might be the more relevant voting determinants (Maier 1975, Simmons 1994). Third, inflation rates tell us little about the deflationary policies that parties ultimately adopted and by which voters most frequently evaluated their performance. In short, the electoral consequences of inflation cannot be inferred from its rate alone but also require analysis of how parties responded to it with their economic programs.

The deflationary programs of German and French Liberals were shaped by the party-internal political equilibria that existed between big business and the middle class. Inflation had created very different preferences among these two actors about when and how to deflate and thereby contributed to a distributional conflict among the Liberals' very own ranks just as much as it did in French and German society at large (Maier 1975, 510; Jones 1988, 163). As Jones notes, it "superimposed a pattern of social and economic conflict upon the political and ideological divisions that had already surfaced within the German liberal parties with the result that their integrative potential, already compromised by factors unrelated to the inflation, was further weakened" (1988, 163).

This party-internal distributional conflict had similar fault lines in all three parties, despite cross-national differences in the absolute rates of inflation. Each party had significant industrial backers. The Parti radical was supported by the Union des intérêts économiques (Association of Economic Interests, UIE) and the Comité Mascuraud, and the DDP and DVP were backed by the Kuratorium and the Commission for the Industrial Campaign Fund. These interest groups benefited in various ways from inflation and therefore were either indifferent or mildly opposed to deflationary policies. Inflation allowed governments to pay off wartime bonds, foreign debts, and, in Germany, reparations with devalued money and reduced the need to increase corporate taxes (Maier 1975, 490; 1987, 203). As Maier points out, "inflation itself became a method of taxation. It reduced the real earnings of households so that by means of newly printed money the government could claim a share of the national income" (1975, 358). Inflation also allowed business to use devalued money to pay off their debts and year-end taxes. It lowered labor costs, particularly in France, where workers were too weak to fight for wage indexation (Maier 1975, 361; 1987, 203–4). As long as inflation did not spin out of control, making economic transactions too unpredictable, business groups had few incentives to support deflationary policies that carried the risk of contracting the economy.

The middle-class sectors supporting the liberal parties had economic policy preferences diametrically opposed to those of business. They strongly supported deflation and revaluing the currency until it returned to prewar gold parity (Simmons 1994, 22–50). Support for deflation was particularly strong among rentiers, pensioners, government bondholders, or anyone deriving substantial portions of their income from liquid assets (Schuker 1976, 73; Maier 1975). White-collar and salaried employees also were insufficiently organized to force employers to index their wages. Nor did they receive the same tax discount as industry since they paid their taxes through monthly payroll deductions. Finally, inflation hurt small shopkeepers who paid wholesalers in cash but needed to extend credit to consumers (Maier 1975, 361).

In response to this similar distributional conflict, French and German liberal parties chose distinctly different economic programs. For this stage of the argument, it is sufficient to point out that these policies reflected the different political leverage that business could obtain from its financial contributions and the middle class from its votes in France and Germany. Further below, I will show how electoral institutions affected this leverage. The deflationary policies of the DDP and DVP responded far more closely to the preferences of big business than those of middle-class voters. The two parties lost their policy-making autonomy to business interests and became increasingly unable to respond to voter preferences. In France, on the other hand, the Parti radical succeeded in allocating the costs of stabilization more equitably. Maier concluded that the "French enterprises who benefited from . . . inflation could never impose the same policy of fiscal paralysis as in Germany" (1975, 509). Parenthetically, it should be noted that these different outcomes cannot be readily attributed to the greater organizational cohesion of business groups in Germany than in France, since the organizational advantage of the former was offset by the greater strength of white-collar unions and professional associations in Germany than in France (Jones 1988, 178–79).[1] The electoral implications of the different responses were straightforward. The DDP and DVP quickly became known as *Bonzenparteien* (parties of captains of industry), whose voters deserted them first for the various new special interest parties and then for the NSDAP (Jones 1985, 23–27). The Parti radical, on the other hand, avoided this predicament by remaining the party of the "little man." To explain these different electoral implications, we have to analyze how French and German electoral mechanisms affected the capacity of business and middle-class voters to translate their respective resources—money and votes—into political leverage.

Electioneering Costs and the Rate of Organizational Change

Organizational choices have significant electoral implications because they affect a party's ability to mobilize resources, coordinate local and national branches, and carry out election campaigns. The divergences of these choices reflect the dramatically different electioneering costs faced by French and German liberal parties after 1918. Weimar's large physical district size, presidential elections, referenda, and variable parliamentary terms increased electioneering costs. In multiplying the number of electoral contests and nationalizing their focus, these electoral mechanisms required greater financial resources and more professionalized logistical infrastructures and ultimately increased the dependence of the DDP and DVP on external financial contributors. Moreover, the suddenness with which these organizational exigencies changed dramatically increased the rate at which the DDP and DVP had to innovate. In France, by contrast, the small physical district size, the fixed parliamentary terms, nonelected presidency, and absence of referenda moderated electioneering costs and limited the rate of organizational innovation to that of mass politics. The personal and local electoral connection of radical politicians became obsolete at a much slower rate than in Germany and thereby facilitated the task of the Parti radical to upgrade its organization.

Weimar's high electioneering costs required an organizational quantum leap that left no opportunity for the DDP and DVP to gradually rebuild and modernize their organizations. The 33-fold enlargement of the physical district size from 36,000 to 1.2 million registered voters, the holding of legislative elections every 20 months, and septennial presidential elections suddenly increased the two parties' operating costs and campaigning expenses. Pollock recognized this effect: "More printed material is distributed in Germany than in any other country. More meetings are held than in any other country. Only an American presidential campaign surpasses a German Reichstag campaign in the expensiveness of its advertising material in the press and on the billboards" (1932, 219). These enormous costs led one DDP organizer to complain that it was impossible "without money, without party press, without organization to survive *in such an electoral system*" (Matthias and Morsey 1960, 58n; my emphasis).

Furthermore, the large physical district size and presidential elections required more modern electioneering techniques by further nationalizing and collectivizing electoral politics. They required that the DDP and DVP target specific groups with clear policies and use modern advertising and propaganda techniques. Altogether, the high electioneering costs diminished whatever effectiveness liberal politicians had derived from their personal reputations and local personal networks before the war.

The DDP and DVP's initial efforts to cope with high electioneering costs produced some results. In 1919, the DDP recruited 900,000 members (15 percent of its votes), hired 130 full-time functionaries, and built local committees. These local committees were capable of organizing regular social events for members and transporting old and sick supporters to the polling stations (Portner 1965, 52–54). The DVP was less enthusiastic than the DDP in building a mass organization. Nevertheless, between 1919 and 1920, it increased the number of local branches from 1,063 to 2,181, its full-time employees from 91 to 161, and its membership from 258,000 to 395,000 (Jones 1988, 75–76).

The DDP and DVP could not sustain these initial successes because they lacked the ability to internally mobilize the necessary resources. By the mid-1920s, the DDP had lost half its membership, and the national party executive fought with local committees over the allocation of the ever shrinking membership dues. By 1924, these dues accounted for only 5 percent of the party's budget (Schneider 1978, 70). The financial decline of the DVP was less steep because fewer of its funds came from dues. But, like the DDP, it soon had to cut back its administrative staff and forgo further organizational expansions (Jones 1988, 165–66; Schneider 1978, 227–28; Albertin 1981, 44–45). Despite these setbacks, both parties undertook repeated, but ultimately futile, efforts to strengthen their organizations and lessen their dependence on economic interest groups (Albertin 1981, 58–59; Jones 1988, 97; 1974, 814). Interestingly enough, one such initiative involved championing of a plurality electoral system with small, single-member districts (Schneider 1978, 147–49).

The most direct effect of the high electioneering costs was to increase the DDP's and DVP's financial dependence on industrial interest groups. The Kuratorium, the political umbrella organization of industry, made considerable contributions to both parties. But these contributions could not be used to strengthen the central logistical infrastructure since the Kuratorium regularly earmarked them for campaign expenditures or allocated them to regional organizations. Very little of the industrial funds consequently could be used by the national party executive to pay functionaries, finance newspapers, or cover operating expenses (Jones 1988, 189–90; Albertin 1972, 182–90).

Industrial interest groups used their financial leverage to gain direct influence over more and more aspects of the DDP's and DVP's organizations. In 1919, for example, the financial situation of six regional DVP associations (out of 35) grew so desperate that the industrialist Vogler, together with the Commission for the Industrial Campaign Fund, took full control of them (Jones 1988, 52). In 1920, financial difficulties forced the DDP to accept a special economic advisory body (Reichsausschuss für Handel, Industrie und Gewerbe) that united all industrial contributors and over which the party executive had no control (Jones 1988, 98; Albertin 1972, 192–93). Siemens, the head of the Kuratorium, complained to a DDP leader that his party did not, as he delicately put it, properly understand economic and trade matters and indicated that the Kuratorium was planning to "educate the party" by reducing its financial support (Albertin 1972, 185). This financial dependence severely constrained the liberal parties' policy-making autonomy. One DDP leader self-critically noted that "a party that is not financially self-supporting, that is not independent, cannot make good politics" (Albertin 1972, 187).

The Third Republic's low electioneering costs, on the other hand, considerably eased the Radicals' task of organizational rebuilding and modernizing while limiting their dependence on the UIE or Comité Mascuraud. France's low electioneering costs also explain the Radicals' quite modest and halfway successful reform efforts. During the early 1920s, the party chairman Edouard Herriot focused his political energies on rebuilding the party. He sought to resuscitate local branches and party newspapers that had become defunct during the war. He also tried to further integrate local committees in departmental organizations (Berstein 1980, 160–61, 182–83). This particular organizational initiative was a response to the new, hybrid electoral system whose physical district size of 123,000 registered voters was seven times larger than the prewar one. Ultimately, however, the logistical exigencies of this new electoral system were far more modest than those of Weimar's pure PR system. Its physical district size was still only one-tenth of Weimar's, and it was widely viewed as an awkward compromise solution that would not last. Partly because of its logistical implications, the Radicals despised the new electoral system and made a return to the old system one of their top political priorities (Berstein 1980, 163; 1982, 83, 90–91). Furthermore, the departmental committees set up by Herriot often remained semipermanent organizations, particularly in rural areas, that relied on the support of notables and local branches of civic associations like the Ligue des droits de l'homme or the Ligue de la république (Berstein 1980, 160–61, 182–83; Lachs 1927, 121–22).

The 1919/24 electoral system thus amounted to only a temporary, small-scale discontinuity in France's electoral institutions. Ultimately, the Parti radical did not experience dramatic increases in electioneering costs since its operating costs and campaigning expenses remained comparable to prewar levels. With 18,000 registered voters (after 1924), the French physical district size was 66 times smaller than the German, and its fixed parliamentary terms meant that Radicals faced elections only every four years and three months. These modest and unchanged electioneering costs limited the necessity of organizational innovation and slowed the rate at which notable politics was becoming obsolete. Radicals, for example, managed to preserve their electoral strength better in rural districts than in urban ones. Rural districts were less affected by the increasing nationalization and collectivization of electoral politics and permitted the continuing reliance on personal and local networks. In such districts, personal endorsements, old friendships, and a helping hand from the patronage-starved majors remained effective means for rallying voters (Florin 1974, 238–39; Berstein 1978, 77–88; 1980, 293–302). The Parti radical thus had to adapt its logistical infrastructure and electioneering practices only to mass politics and not to abruptly changing institutional exigencies.

Herriot's successful rebuilding of the Parti radical was followed by Daladier's effort to modernize it. In 1927, Daladier was elected party chairman with an explicit mandate from grassroots members to reorganize the party along the socialists' mass mobilization model. He consolidated the party's administrative structure by further strengthening departmental federations and integrating local committees more directly into regional branches. He also set up various ancillary organizations to widen the membership and improve the party's electioneering capacity (Berstein 1982, 83). By 1929, Daladier's organizational reforms led one deputy to declare, "Yesterday, many sections of the Parti radical were mere committees assembled around an elected deputy. . . . Since then, the party has become an organized party with statutes that were . . . applied and which were less flexible than their predecessors" (Berstein 1982, 92–93).

The modest electioneering costs became most visible in the limited resources the Parti radical had to mobilize. The party was never very aggressive in recruiting members. It consequently had a modest but stable membership of 100,000 (Bardonnet 1960, 51, 190). The dues paid by members were insufficient to sustain a large party administration or extensively subsidize newspapers. Radicals consequently could not do without industrial groups like the UIE and the Comité Mascuraud, which helped to cover their operating expenses and campaigning costs (Berstein 1980, 157–58). However, the modest electioneering costs limited the scale of these financial contributions. For example, one of the Radicals' more important contributors were brewers and distillers. Their contributions consisted of supplying cheap liquor during campaigns and pressuring local tavern owners to deny the Radicals' opponents the use of their establishments for political meetings (Bardonnet 1960, 258). Outright financial donations were less essential in the Third Republic since its low electioneering costs preserved the effectiveness of informal personal networks. Through such networks, local politicians could provide national politicians important nonfinancial resources by endorsing them, furnishing information about local issues, arranging free transportation, or facilitating the free use of public auditoriums.

Finally, it should be pointed out that the formation of electoral alliances between the two election rounds helped Radicals reduce the costs of the two electoral contests they faced. Usually, front-runners tried to convince candidates with low winning prospects to withdraw and possibly endorse them on the second ballot. The rationale of this strategy was to pool votes through relatively inexpensive extra-electoral bargaining. Such bargaining was inexpensive because local departments would trade off withdrawals across different districts. Occasionally, side-payments were required in the form of reimbursing candidates who stepped aside for their campaign expenses (Larmour 1964, 46–48). This vote-pooling strategy particularly benefited the Radicals, who used their centrist position to form alliances with socialists as well as various other bourgeois parties (Berstein 1980, 115–22; 1982, 67–69; Florin 1974, 238–60). The significance of such electoral alliances was to increase the Radicals' vote base without requiring any resources that would have increased the financial leverage of economic interest groups. After 1918, German Liberals lost the ability of vote pooling that had once provided them with a buffer against the influence of business groups (Nipperdey 1993, 502, 532).

Career Uncertainty and the Leverage of Money

The uncertainty that politicians faced over their recruitment played a crucial role in determining how readily big business could leverage its financial influence into actual policy outcomes. Financial contributions alone did not guarantee such outcomes since party congresses, legislative logrolling, or bargaining among coalition partners could easily overturn or compromise the informal policy promises that party leaders made to interest groups. The degree of uncertainty politicians faced over their recruitment had important implications for how credibly interest groups could commit parties to their policy promises. Low career uncertainty allowed industrial interest groups to make their financial contributions contingent on the selection of their candidates. This opportunity diminished as the candidate recruitment process became more uncertain. In short, career uncertainty determined how effectively big business could translate its money into direct control of the party-internal decision making. It consequently affected the policy-making autonomy of liberal parties and their ability to devise economic programs that equitably allocated the costs of deflation.

Weimar's low career uncertainty greatly facilitated the efforts of industrial interest groups to firmly commit the DDP and DVP to their promises. It was the result of three electoral mechanisms. Weimar's large district magnitude helped to centralize the candidate selection process and created long electoral lists with numerous safe list positions. It consequently gave party leaders considerable control over the entry and reentry of candidates. The categorical ballot structure and national adjustment list reinforced this effect. The former deprived voters of the ability to rearrange the ranking of candidates. National adjustment lists, in turn, virtually assured the election of anyone selected for one of its seats. These seats were so safe because they were allocated with remainder votes that were recycled from regular electoral districts and thus were unaffected by electoral swings. National adjustment seats particularly helped to reduce career uncertainty of small parties like the two liberal parties; 54.8 percent of the DDP's deputies and 40.5 percent of DVP legislators were elected through national adjustment seats (*Statistisches Jahrbuch für das deutsche Reich,* various years).

The leaders of the DDP and DVP quickly responded to the possibility of reducing their career uncertainty. The national executive and regional party leaders wrested control over candidate recruitment from local party branches. In doing so, they disregarded the provisions of their party statutes that sought to preserve the prewar practice of having local branches select candidates (Albertin 1972, 93–98, 151–52; Schneider 1978, 213–22). However, in attempting to reduce their own career uncertainty, liberal party leaders inadvertently tilted the party-internal political equilibrium from the middle class to industrial interest groups.

In centralizing the recruitment of candidates, the leaders of the DDP and DVP made it easier for economic interests to extend their financial leverage over party-internal personnel choices. Party leaders repeatedly complained that this influence of industrial interest groups undermined their ability to effectively respond to voter preferences. In 1924, a DDP internal memo noted that it "is unacceptable that a political party owes its existence to the coffers of a few interest groups that mercilessly exert their power in the nomination of candidates and abandon the party whenever it does not satisfy its smallest demand" (Schneider 1978, 73). In a similar vein, the leader of the DVP, Stresemann, warned against "capitalistic interests gaining an excessive influence on the formation of the Reichstag" and even went so far as to recommended public party financing to better protect the policy-making autonomy of parties (Pollock 1932, 253). Middle-class voters also were aware of the DDP's and DVP's infiltration by industrial interest groups, since it was widely reported in the press (Pollock 1931, 251).

Weimar's low career uncertainty thus amplified the already considerable financial leverage of big business by making it possible to estimate the value of candidate selections, which became the basis for arranging specific quid pro quos. Interest groups could peg their contributions to the specific worth of a list ranking, national adjustment seat, or multiple selections. Furthermore, assuring the election of their own representatives permitted big business to leverage its financial contributions into firmer policy commitments. These representatives could monitor the compliance of liberal party leaders with the initial policy promises. They also could serve in parliament as sanctioning devices by threatening to break with party discipline or switch to another party. Weimar's low career uncertainty thus clearly enhanced the political leverage of the interest groups' substantial financial contributions.

Party monographs provide ample evidence for this enhanced political leverage. Interest groups directly funneled financial contributions to those regional organizations that were most willing to select their candidates. They also made the amount of their contributions contingent on the number of candidates and the list positions they got to choose (Schneider 1978, 72; Albertin 1972, 189–90). In 1924, the Central Association of German Wholesalers pledged 250,000 reichsmarks to the DDP in exchange for the selection of their representative. The association, however, reduced its contribution to 50,000 reichsmarks after the DDP placed the candidate on the fifth rather than fourth place as was initially agreed (Jones 1988, 218).

The political leverage of industrial interest groups also made the DDP and DVP more risk-averse in selecting new or dissenting candidates. Both parties failed to select reformist candidates favored by activists as well as white-collar or lower-middle-class candidates who would have more effectively represented the two parties' major electoral constituencies (Albertin 1972, 165). They also refused demands of the major association representing victims of inflation, the Mortgagees' and Savers' Protective Association (Hypotheken-Gläubiger und Sparerschutzverband), to select some of their candidates (Jones 1988, 236). The low career uncertainty made liberal politicians risk-averse in another way. By virtually guaranteeing seats to members of the national executive, it severed the electoral connection between candidates and voters. This made candidates highly risk-averse and led them to concentrate their political energies on winning a good list position rather than trying to improve the party's overall electoral competitiveness. Liberal candidates, for example, were so disinterested in campaigning that the DDP required them in 1927 to give a minimum number of campaign speeches (Schneider 1978, 70).

The Third Republic's high career uncertainty severely limited the capacity of the Parti radical to control the entry and reentry of candidates. The small district magnitude decentralized the candidate recruitment process and deprived party leaders of safe list positions. Most importantly, the inability of party leaders to regularize electoral careers limited business's ability to extend its already limited financial leverage over personnel choices. Monographs of the Parti radical are striking for the limited references they make to the UIE's and Comité Mascuraud's involvement in the candidate recruitment process and economic policy-making. And in fact, these two interest groups could only use their financial leverage to lobby discreetly for candidates they favored and could not brazenly demand the selection of handpicked candidates (Larmour 1964, 178; M. Schlesinger 1974, 478–80). They abstained from influencing the actual recruitment process and concentrated their activities on lobbying incumbent candidates (Berstein 1980, 158). The UIE, for example, would formulate a fairly general economic program and make contributions to candidates promising to support it (Pollock 1932, 303–9). By being limited to such lobbying, the UIE and the Comité Mascuraud lacked the direct, party-internal political control of their German counterparts. They could not back their economic demands with threats of using their candidates to break party discipline or defect to another party. The influence of the UIE and the Comité Mascuraud therefore was limited to whatever lobbying pressure their financial contributions allowed.

The candidate recruitment in the 1924 election illustrates the limited political leverage the UIE and the Comité Mascuraud derived from their financial contributions. The prospect of an electoral alliance between the Radicals and the SFIO mobilized business groups as never before. Moreover, the hybrid 1919/24 electoral system facilitated the UIE's and Comité Mascuraud's task because the greater district magnitude (6.5) reduced career uncertainty and made it somewhat easier for the UIE and the Comité to oppose the impending formation of the Cartel des gauches. Yet despite these favorable circumstances, the effort of business to pressure candidates it financially supported not to join lists with the SFIO thoroughly failed (Berstein 1980, 158). In retaliation, the UIE set up a new party, the Fédération française des comités républicains et radicals socialistes, through which it hoped to nominate its own candidates in the future. The Fédération quickly folded and required the UIE to return to its traditional lobbying strategy (Berstein 1980, 377).

High career uncertainty preserved the Radicals' political equilibrium not just by limiting the influence of interest groups, but also by preserving the vitality of local organizations. By keeping the important task of recruiting candidates local, France's electoral mechanisms protected the autonomy of the Radicals' local branches, which frequently were the stronghold of factions whose political viewpoints closely reflected the concerns of middle-class voters (Bardonnet 1960, 148–49n; Berstein 1982, 129; Larmour 1964, 178). The "Young Turks" formed the most prominent dissenting faction. Their spokesmen E. Roche, Matinaud-Deplat, J. Zay, J. Kayser, E. Pfeiffer, P. Cot, P. Mendès-France, and B. de Jouvenel advocated close collaboration with the SFIO, criticized economic interest groups, and generally represented petite bourgeois interests (Burrin 1986, 33; Bouet 1996, 126–27; M. Schlesinger 1974, 478–84). Even though the Young Turks' political platform drew the ire of economic interest groups, the high career uncertainty made it difficult for these groups to oppose their selections.

The Young Turks were important in another way. They pushed for a modernization of the Radicals' campaigning strategies. They played an important role in shifting their party's platform from its universalist cultural and constitutional themes to embrace more fully sectional economic interests. One of their activists recognized that "the moment of the big anticlerical battles is past . . . the moment of the big social battles has arrived" (Berstein 1982, 99; see also Bardonnet 1960, 177–78).

Furthermore, the continued political significance of local district organizations helped mobilize activists who were attuned to preferences of middle-class voters and were less motivated by careerist interests. Compared to the DDP and DVP, their influence was far more visible and helped to preserve the Radicals' political equilibrium and political credibility. In 1926, for example, activists forced Herriot from the party's helm for having supported Poincaré's stabilization program, which was viewed as too pro-business. They shifted their support to Daladier, who campaigned in 1928 against Poincaré by accusing him of being a "tool of powerful economic interests" (M. Schlesinger 1974, 482). This is not meant to suggest that the Parti radical always favored the interests of the little man over those of business. Many deputies, for example, discreetly disassociated themselves from Daladier's antibusiness position after Poincaré's deflationary program proved successful and popular (M. Schlesinger 1974, 480–85). This episode, however, serves to illustrate that the Parti radical preserved its policy-making autonomy and represented the preferences of its middle-class as well as industrial constituencies. It clearly avoided the fate of becoming a *Bonzenpartei.*

Strategic Voting and the Leverage of Votes

Middle-class voters were silent bystanders to the party-internal wheeling and dealing between liberal leaders and economic interest groups. As consumers, bondholders, pensioners, or small businessmen, they lacked the organizational cohesion and financial leverage that permitted big business to directly lobby liberal party leaders. Moreover, liberal parties did not recruit a large mass membership that could offset the influence of business interests. Consequently, the ballot box provided the most important, albeit only an indirect and retroactive, opportunity for middle-class voters to influence the programmatic choices of liberal parties. It allowed middle-class voters to compensate for their organizational and financial disadvantages with their superiority in numbers.

The political leverage of the middle class's large numbers depended on the incentives that electoral mechanisms created for strategic voting. The more strategically voters could cast their ballots, the more impact each vote would have on the programmatic considerations of liberal parties. The fickleness and volatility of strategic votes translated into strong incentives for liberal party leaders to pay as much attention to voters in the electoral marketplace as they did to economic interest groups in their party-internal deliberations. Furthermore, strategic voting created important incentives for liberal politicians to innovate in their campaigning style. In the case of Liberals, this meant shifting from the old, personalistic notable style of politics with its emphasis on universalist cultural and constitutional issues to a more modern, entrepreneurial campaigning style that stressed partisan, economic issues.

The Third Republic's small district magnitude created strong incentives for strategic voting, as did the majoritarian element of the apparentement provisions used in the 1919/24 system. It maximized the leverage provided by the middle class's superior numbers and further weakened the already limited party-internal influence of economic interest groups. The clearest evidence for this leverage can be found in the deflationary measures that the radical-led Cartel government entertained between 1924 and 1926. These measures did not add up to a coherent and easily labeled economic program, but their incoherence reflects the Radicals' effort to distribute the costs of deflation as widely as possible. The radical finance minister M. Clémentel, for example, declared that his government "decided to demand entirely from acquired wealth and income the supplementary revenue necessary for balancing the budget" (Haig 1929, 108). A brief synopsis of the Radicals' economic policies illustrates how they sought to accomplish this objective.

The most significant and controversial measure of the Radicals' economic program was a planned capital levy. This new tax was to be imposed on property holders and industry to reduce the budget deficit and repay government bonds held by the middle class (Haig 1929, 123–25). Radicals also strongly pushed to democratize the tax system to spread the costs of deflation more widely and evenly. They tried to shift their revenue base from regressive, indirect taxes to the more progressive, direct taxes. They also advocated a more progressive tax rate (M. Schlesinger 1978, 220–23). In the Cartel's closing days, finance minister Caillaux, who belonged to the party's more conservative, pro-business faction, opposed the capital levy and democratizing the tax system. This exposed him to heavy criticism inside the party. At the 1925 Nice party congress, Caillaux was attacked by delegates for "having yielded to financial interests. Instead of frankly and forcefully asking from established wealth the necessary sacrifices, . . . he proposed an increase in taxes . . . which will weigh heavily on consumers, shopkeepers, and artisans" (Berstein 1980, 414). When the congress strongly reaffirmed the party's support for a capital levy and tax democratization, Caillaux resigned (Nogaro 1925, 292–93).

Radicals also tried to protect their support among civil servants by shielding them from the costs of deflation. The Cartel government, for example, resisted any governmental layoffs, which business demanded. It repealed measures passed by the preceding, conservative Poincaré government to eliminate the eight-hour day for civil servants and to cut administrative expenditures by one billion francs (M. Schlesinger 1978, 226; Haig 1929, 102–3). Until 1929, the Parti radical also opposed trade protections, which it believed benefited big business and hurt small consumers (Berstein 1978, 76–88).

These and other measures did not add up to an effective macroeconomic policy and ultimately contributed to the Cartel's collapse in 1926. As Maier notes, the inability of Radicals to formulate a coherent economic policy partly reflects the "close connection of deputy and constituency in France, even under the modified PR of 1919 and 1924, which made mediation of local interest a key function of the Chamber" (1975, 509). To the extent that radical economic policies reflected more narrow electoral considerations rather than sound economic management, they can at least be viewed as having effectively minimized the distributional conflict amidst the party's ranks.

Besides affecting programmatic choices, France's high level of strategic voting also created important incentives for Radicals to adopt modern campaigning techniques and place less emphasis on their traditional cultural and constitutional issues. These issues only briefly resurfaced during the opening months of the first Cartel government (June 1924–April 1925) when Herriot withdrew the newly appointed ambassador to the Vatican and sought to extend the separation of church and state to recently returned Alsace-Lorraine. These anticlerical issues, however, were quickly displaced by extensive party-internal debates about how to stabilize the economy (Berstein 1980, 407, 416). Furthermore, the Radicals' campaigning style became more entrepreneurial after 1918, especially when compared to the DDP and DVP. They were keenly aware that anticommunism, nationalism, and other emotionally charged issues were effective for mobilizing voters (Berstein 1980, 125–27). From the late 1920s onward, the Parti radical also began to establish ancillary organizations to rally voters more effectively. The party headquarters designated full-time functionaries for organizing national propaganda strategies and coordinating local election campaigns. It distributed to local committees a package that contained posters and party brochures listing past accomplishments and future plans, as well as a handbook with ready answers to the most commonly asked questions (M. Schlesinger 1974, 481; Berstein 1982, 83, 90–91).

Weimar's low level of strategic voting deprived German middle-class voters of the same electoral leverage their French counterparts enjoyed. They could not translate their superiority in numbers into a sufficiently effective sanctioning mechanism, and thereby offset the influence of big business. Weimar's large district magnitude and national adjustment seats all contributed to such an accurate translation of votes into seats that voters had virtually no reason to cast their ballots strategically. These electoral mechanisms in effect reduced the marginal value of votes by making them decisive only for relative gains and losses in seats rather than success or failure of individual candidates. They weakened the sanctioning leverage that the electoral market offered middle-class voters and consequently reduced the pressure on the DDP and DVP to allocate the costs of deflation more equitably and modernize their electioneering practices.

The effects of Weimar's weak strategic voting can be observed in the economic stabilization measures that the DDP and DVP considered in the early 1920s. Historical monographs point to a continuity in the DDP and DVP deflationary programs during this period and do not indicate any sharp change in response to the 1923–24 hyperinflation. It therefore is reasonable to use the two parties' economic policies in 1923–24, which monographs discuss most extensively, as being representative for the entirety of the early 1920s (Jones 1988, 182–83; Maier 1975).

These policies illustrated the limited leverage of middle-class voters. They closely reflected business's preferences for stabilizing the economy by drastically cutting government spending and lowering corporate taxes. In October 1923, the Stresemann government sought to reduce the budget deficit by laying off civil servants and freezing their wages. Approximately 750,000 civil servants lost their jobs as part of these subsequent stabilization measures (Jones 1988, 210; Brustein 1996, 77). He also acceded to business's long-standing demand of rolling back the eight-hour workday and exempted business from the tax increases levied on homeowners and small business (Jones 1988, 210, 218; Fritzsche 1990, 95–96). Furthermore, Stresemann introduced an elaborate price control system in an attempt to

check inflation even though such a system disproportionally punished artisans and small shopkeepers who could not pass on inflation to consumers
(Fritzsche 1990, 97). Finally, the DDP and DVP rejected demands from
the Mortgagees' and Savers' Protective Association and other middle-
class associations to fully revalue mortgages and other debts. The 1925
Revaluation of Mortgages Law revalorized debts only at 15 percent and
exempted all government debts until the settlement of reparations payments (Jones 1988, 211; Southern 1981, 66). Jones (1988, 208) therefore is
right to conclude that "in many essential respects, the stabilization of the
Mark . . . proved every bit as destructive as the runaway inflation in the
early 1920s . . . German liberal parties were compromised by their failure
to protect middle class economic interests during the stabilization
process."

The years between 1924 and 1930 provide further evidence for the
effects of Weimar's weak strategic voting. During this period, the leaders
of the DDP and DVP failed to respond to the quickening defection of middle-class voters that their earlier economic policies had alienated. The first
signs of this alienation had already surfaced in 1922 when the Mortgagees'
and Savers' Protective Association was formed. The association pushed
liberal parties to support revaluing debts and end the repayment of mortgages and loans in valueless currency. During its first two years, it functioned as a regular pressure group, but by 1924 some of its members had
become so disenchanted with the DDP and DVP that they founded their
own parties. Over the course of 1924, the Militant League of Beggars
(Kampfbund der Geusen), the German Revaluation and Recovery Party
(Deutsche Aufwertungs- und Aufbaupartei), and the Revaluation and
Reconstruction Party (Aufwertungs- und Wiederaufbaupartei) were
formed in time to run for the December election. Lacking effective organizations, these start-up parties won only a few hundred thousand votes. But
they were part of a large-scale voter defection to other parties like the Economic Party and the Bavarian Peasant League (Bayerische Bauernbund).
All these parties vociferously criticized the DDP and DVP as being
Bonzenparteien and for supporting economic policies that ignored the
interests of the little man (Jones 1988, 253–302). The initial success of these
special interest parties was, of course, also a by-product of Weimar's low
strategic voting, which made it easy for new, small, upstart parties to gain
an electoral foothold.

Weimar's weak strategic voting affected not just the DDP's and
DVP's programmatic choices but also their campaigning styles. The suc-

cess of the new special interest parties illustrated the potential of mobilizing voters around narrow, economic interests (Jones 1985, 31). Yet the two liberal parties failed to respond to this lesson. Both parties continued to present themselves as national interest parties (*Gesamtinteressenparteien*) and continued to describe politics in the old universalist and rationalist terms (Jones 1988, 252). In 1926, the DVP chairman Gustav Stresemann complained that "the most distressing thing about the present situation in Germany is the tendency to overemphasize the purely economic and vocational aspects of the political struggle. . . . But . . . the spiritual cement necessary to fuse these elements into a dynamic organic whole [is] sadly missing" (Jones 1988, 265). Stresemann and his counterparts in the DDP were slow to realize that mass politics and the distributive conflicts entailed by postwar inflation had pulverized this spiritual cement for good. Rather than accepting this fact, the DDP and DVP tried to shift the focus of the 1928 campaign away from partisan economic issues to issues like school reform, defense of the republican system, and reforming federal state structure (Jones 1988, 299; Fritzsche 1990, 139). These policies clearly failed to resonate. A local newspaper complained, "who in the provinces wants to hear about the question of the flag, about school policy, about the endangered Republic? First bread, then politics" (Fritzsche 1990, 110). Moreover, they failed to recognize how alienating this universalist rhetoric must have been to voters who were all too aware of the two parties' co-optation by big business.

The DDP and DVP also failed to modernize the most basic elements of their campaigning style. Their campaigns only started a week or two before the election, made little use of mass rallies, and relied more on the personality of their leaders than on emotionally charged or partisan issues. The DDP and DVP thus eschewed the continuous and partisan electioneering that sought to capitalize on changing political opportunities during and between elections. The propensity of German Liberals to meet in small and oftentimes closed circles and to commemorate important historical events rather than to take positions on current events or exploit mistakes of their opponents has been damningly labeled by Peter Fritzsche "a commemorative style of politics" (Fritzsche 1990, 137; see also Jones 1985, 31; Jones 1986, 204–6). Nothing could better illustrate these parties' inability to respond creatively to the present.

Chapter 5

Peasants versus Principles: Conservative Notables, Mass Politics, and Agricultural Crisis

The First World War provided French and German conservatives a modest reprieve from their prewar difficulties. It led to a nationalist upsurge, the suspension of domestic conflicts, and a renewed respect for military discipline and social hierarchies. The war temporarily brought back issues far more familiar to conservatives than the distributional, economic ones politicized by mass politics. Some of this reprieve carried over into the early 1920s. In Weimar, the reparations issue, the stab-in-the-back legend, and the war guilt clause incited sufficient nationalist sentiments to deflect attention from the right's loss of the war. In the Third Republic, postwar euphoria swept the conservative Bloc national to power. The war also had bolstered the reputation of conservative politicians like Poincaré and Clemenceau who could temporarily unite the fragmented right. And in both countries, the Russian Revolution contributed to the creation of domestic communist parties, which allowed the right to rally around anti-communism.

This reprieve was not to last. In 1927, one of the severest agricultural crises in memory hit the French and German countryside. This crisis accentuated the continuing organizational and programmatic difficulties that mass politics had posed for French and German conservatives. It became the catalyst for the rapid electoral decline of the Union républicaine démocratique (Republican Democratic Union, URD) and the Deutschnationale Volkspartei (German National People's Party, DNVP). Between 1927 and 1935, these two principal parties of the French and German right lost approximately half of their already modest 15–20 percent seat shares.[1] Much of this decline was the result of defecting deputies rather than disloyal voters. Between 1927 and 1932, 54 defections from the DNVP cost the party 52 percent of its original 1927 strength, while the

URD's 39 defections during the same period amounted to a 31 percent loss of its 1927 strength.[2]

While these defections were the most striking aspect of the URD's and DNVP's political performance, they are not readily explainable in terms of systematic institutional factors. The organizational particularities of conservative parties discussed below will explain why. Institutional factors, however, were not irrelevant. Rather than affecting the party-internal behavior leading to the defections, they influenced the actions of defectors and remaining party loyalists once the two parties broke apart. Additionally, institutional factors also structured the behavior of peasant movements and parties that emerged in the late 1920s to challenge the established right. This chapter thus focuses more on the party-external actions of defectors, loyalists, and peasant protest groups than on the party-internal actions of leaders, candidates, or interest groups that ultimately led to the defections. Defections themselves are explained by two noninstitutional, contextual factors: mass politics and the agricultural crisis.

Compared to previous chapters, this one focuses on multiple unitary actors rather than a single collective one. This changed focus simply reflects the right's fragmentation into multiple autocratic political organizations. The chapter explains the right's overall political performance by focusing on the cross-national differences of three principal actors: defectors, loyalists, and agricultural protest groups.

Defectors from the URD and DNVP differed in how they realigned themselves; URD defectors switched to already existing parties, while DNVP defectors formed new political organizations. In February 1928, DNVP defectors formed the Christlich-Nationale Bauern- und Landvolkpartei (Christian-National Peasants' and Farmers' Party, CNBLP) and in July 1930 another group of defectors formed the Konservative Volkspartei (Conservative People's Party, KVP) (Jones 1986, 212). In the URD, 21 out of 39 defectors switched to the more centrist Alliance démocratique. The remaining 18 (Groupe Pernot) remained electorally closely allied with the Alliance even though they formed a separate parliamentary group. In both parties, the schisms were caused by conflicts between defectors and loyalists over whether their agendas should emphasize short-term, agricultural benefits or long-term, reactionary principles.

DNVP loyalists did much better at the polls than URD loyalists even though there were few substantive differences in their reactionary and nationalist strategies. In 1932, the URD lost 21 of its remaining 61 seats and witnessed the defeat of 23 incumbents (Lachapelle 1932). The URD's principled strategy thus was doubly harmful because it cost votes and spurred the defection of moderate deputies. In Weimar, on the other hand, the DNVP stabilized its electoral support after it lost 36 seats in the 1928 election and experienced various post-electoral defections.[3] In 1930, the DNVP added nine seats to the 32 it had left prior to the election. It lost four seats in the July 1932 election and gained 15 seats in the November 1932 election. While the DNVP never returned to its 1927 strength, Hugenberg's nationalist strategy still mobilized a stable constituency. The DNVP's electoral recovery is all the more surprising because it occurred just when the NSDAP's support skyrocketed. By contrast, the URD's continued electoral decline took place in the absence of any serious electoral challenge from the proto-fascist ligues and rural protest movements.

In the late 1920s and early 1930s, rural insurgent movements mobilized a large number of peasants around narrowly defined protest activities. These movements consisted of rural and poorly organized peasant groups as well as more urban-based, better-organized proto-fascist paramilitary groups. As we will see, these rural and urban insurgency groups translated their extra-electoral protest support into actual votes more effectively in Weimar than in the Third Republic. Furthermore, Weimar's urban-based fascists outflanked in the long run rural peasant protesters far more successfully than the French ligues. The NSDAP became Weimar's largest party, while the French paramilitary ligues never captured more than a few seats.

Taken together, the actions of defectors, party loyalists, and peasant insurgencies reshaped the French and German right in very distinct ways. In Weimar, the DNVP's decline and the unsuccessful institutionalization of defectors led to a *centrifugal interbloc realignment* between the collapsing right and a surging extreme right. The parties formed by the defectors contributed to this interbloc realignment by transforming a fragmented German right into a segmented one. The segmentation of the German right obstructed the cooperation that would have been necessary to successfully fend off the electoral challenge emanating from the more radical peasant protest groups and, above all, the NSDAP. Collectively, the German right lost 55 percent of its strength between 1927 and 1932, while the NSDAP increased its support tenfold. In this interbloc realignment, the defectors "were destined to serve as little more than conduits for the transmissions of disaffected rural voters from more traditional bourgeois parties to the arch-enemy of the Weimar system itself, the NSDAP" (Jones 1986, 225). The Third Republic, on the other hand, witnessed a *centripetal intrabloc realignment* from the nationalist URD to the centrist Alliance démocratique. Party switching prevented the fragmentation of the French right from turning into a more rigid segmentation that would have restricted the right's capacity to fend off the challenges from various peasant insurgencies and proto-fascist leagues. Between 1927 and 1932, the URD and the Alliance démocratique lost only one-fourth of their strength, while the extreme right merely won a few seats.

In focusing on the actions of defectors, loyalists, and peasant protesters, this chapter explains why the French right preserved its political strength much better than the German right even though mass politics and the agricultural crisis created comparably adverse circumstances. The next section looks at these circumstances and shows how their similarity makes them insufficient to account for the different political outcomes of defectors, party loyalists, and peasant insurgencies. The remainder of the chapter is devoted to explaining how electoral institutions account for these different outcomes.

Agricultural Crisis

Beginning in 1927, French and German farmers were hit by one of their severest agricultural crises. In both countries, the drop in domestic wartime production allowed new overseas producers to conquer European markets with cheap agricultural imports, while the Great Depression undermined the purchasing power of urban consumers. As a result, between 1927 and 1935, agricultural prices dropped around 50–60 percent and indebtedness of farmers skyrocketed, leading to farm foreclosures (Abraham 1981, 87–88; Cleary 1989, 71–72; Paxton 1997, 14–15). However, it was not just the crisis's severity that posed a political challenge for the French and German right. The even bigger challenge resulted from the fact that the crisis accentuated the makeshift manner in which French and German conservatives had coped with the programmatic and organizational challenges of mass politics. This section demonstrates how the agricultural crisis aggravated the organizational and programmatic shortcomings of the French and German right in such similar ways that it is unable to account for their different political performances.

Agricultural Crisis and Agenda-Setting Conflicts

In deciding how to cope with mass politics, conservatives disagreed, not unlike socialists, on two issues. Centrist and reactionary conservatives argued over whether the existing democratic institutions provided a level playing field or gave the better-organized left a permanent advantage. They also differed over whether electoral participation was to focus on winning short-term material benefits or whether it should attempt to radicalize voters and transform their preferences over the long run. The agricultural crisis greatly accentuated these differences. It led centrist conservatives to advocate working within the existing institutions and to push for urgently needed agricultural relief programs. Reactionaries, in turn, saw the crisis as a unique opportunity to turn the fragmented right into a truly cohesive, reactionary bloc capable of transforming the political order along more autocratic lines. The agricultural crisis accentuated agenda-setting differences inside the URD and DNVP and thereby became the primary catalyst for the large number of defections.

In both parties, most defectors were centrist conservatives. Their time horizon was shorter than that of reactionaries and led them to prefer short-term economic benefits to long-term political principles. The agricultural crisis accentuated these different time horizons by making economic issues electorally more salient and increasing the urgency for agricultural relief programs. In the DNVP, pressure for such programs emanated most prominently from southern and western deputies who were closely affiliated with the regional branches of the Reichslandbund (Agrarian League). These regional branches commonly represented small independent farmers who were most severely hit by the crisis. Less is known about the precise policy preferences of URD defectors other than that they disagreed with the principled nationalist, clerical, and antiparliamentary course of their party leader, Louis Marin. This intransigent course kept the URD out of government and limited the ability of rural notables to secure their share of electorally crucial agricultural pork-barrel benefits (Gessner 1976, 219; Chanaday 1967, 71–72; Irvine 1979, 55; Pinol 1992, 309).

Reactionary conservatives, on the other hand, assessed the political opportunities created by the agricultural crisis very differently from their centrist colleagues. Reactionaries mostly were large landowners or industrialists who were less adversely affected by the collapse in farm prices. They also were loyal followers of their intransigent and highly nationalist party leaders, Louis Marin and Alfred Hugenberg. In the eyes of reactionaries, the agricultural crisis simply signaled the right's inability to defend peasant interests and the partiality of political institutions that favored urban and working-class interests. It simply was another reminder that the right could only overcome its own crisis by pursuing two goals above all others: building a more disciplined and cohesive party and decisively pushing for authoritarian institutional reforms. Compromising these long-term goals by supporting vote-winning relief programs seemed shortsighted and therefore needed to be resisted at all costs (Passmore 1997, 189; Gessner 1976, 225–26; Rousselier 1992, 322).

As one alternative to short-term electoralism, Marin and Hugenberg tried to politicize noneconomic issues like anticommunism, nationalism, and antisemitism. In France, the 1905 law separating church and state also gave the URD the opportunity to continuously politicize clerical issues (Delbreil 1990, 210–12). The rationale for politicizing noneconomic issues was to polarize public opinion and thereby increase the ideological, if not organizational, cohesion of the right in Germany. Hugenberg described this same goal with such a delightfully Teutonic touch that it is worth quoting him at length. In an article entitled "Bloc or Mash," he wrote: "There are two alternatives. Bebel [nineteenth-century socialist] once spoke of the great bourgeois mash in which everything that was left of the bourgeoisie would eventually gather in fear of Social Democrats. Such a mash is neither a protective dam nor a defensive weapon. What we need is not a mash but a block. . . . We shall be a block when the iron clamps of ideals unite us and in their grip solidify and weld everything soft and fluid into a rock" (Chanaday 1967, 82). For Hugenberg and Marin, nationalism, anticommunism, and clericalism were issues with a strong emotional appeal that could mobilize more voters than the right's traditional emphasis on stewarding the status-quo-biased national interest. The noneconomic emphasis of these issues also was thought to be capable of deflecting public opinion from growing demands for economic redistribution (Riker 1990; Mann 1995).

Another alternative to pure vote winning was implied in the oblique references to a National Revolution. This vaguely used term served as a shorthand for various institutional reform proposals that were thought to improve the right's political lot. Reactionaries simply wanted to substitute more authority for the waning deference that voters once accorded them and compensate for their diluted prerogatives with new hierarchical principles. Reactionary conservatives differed in the institutional alternatives they entertained. To some, the existing constitutional order could be fixed by introducing family suffrage, strengthening the executive, weakening parliament, or restricting the political access of economic interest groups. To others, constitutional tinkering was futile. They advocated corporatist, fascist, or technocratic alternatives to liberal democracy. The tacit goal of these proposals was to build more authoritarian institutions that would finally solve the right's perennial, internal fragmentation and eliminate the political advantage that the left allegedly gained from the existing institutional arrangements (Weinreis 1986, 63, 146–47; Passmore 1997, 197; Paxton 1972, 187–89).

Parenthetically, it should be pointed out that reactionary conservatives were not more extreme in the DNVP than the URD. Hugenberg certainly was more radical than Marin, but the larger constituencies for which they spoke were not all that different in both parties. Numerous URD members, albeit not Marin, belonged to the Jeunesses patriotes, Croix de feu, or even the Action française and became active supporters of Pétain's Vichy regime (Passmore 1997, 211–13; Irvine 1979, 102). In the DNVP, the most reactionary elements were expelled in 1922 for their involvement in the Kapp Putsch and formed the short-lived Deutschvölkische Freiheitspartei (Liebe 1956, 69–70). The influence of the remaining reactionaries was balanced until the late 1920s by centrist conservatives (Chanaday 1967, 71–72; Dörr 1964, 60–61).

Agricultural Crisis and Organizational Implications

The agricultural crisis underscored the tenuous nature of the URD's and DNVP's organizational responses to mass politics. Unlike liberals, conservatives never tried copying the mass party model of the left. Being accountable to the electoral masses already was troubling enough for conservatives, who consequently were loathe to place themselves at the mercy of activists or party leaders. As an alternative to the mass party model, French and German conservatives devised what Kalyvas aptly called a contracting-out model (1996, 48–50). They simply contracted out the central logistical tasks to organized societal groups and thereby avoided the need for centralized, mass organizations. Professional associations, nationalist societies, paramilitary movements, agricultural ligues, and, in France, clerical lay organizations commanded logistical resources and organized membership that could be placed at the disposal of conservatives. The most effective assistance these groups provided was to mobilize their organized members by endorsing particular parties. This endorsement mechanism was no match for the left's tightly integrated mass organizations, but it proved adequate as long as members of these groups remained sufficiently deferential to heed endorsements.

The agricultural crisis undermined the effectiveness of the URD's and DNVP's arguably most important subcontractor: agricultural associations. It did so in two interrelated ways. First, the agricultural crisis undermined the credibility of association leaders and limited their ability to make effective endorsements. It discredited agricultural leaders because they inadequately protected small, independent farmers from the collapsing agricultural prices. In both countries, agricultural associations were disproportionately led by conservative large landowners who either saw less urgency for agricultural relief programs or favored different policies than small independent farmers (Quellien 1986, 348–50; Cleary 1989, 51; Paxton 1997, 126; Gessner 1976, 104; Heberle [1932] 1963, 154–55). The most important agricultural association backing the URD was the Union national des syndicats agricoles. Its local affiliates were highly autonomous and had close ties with various Catholic lay organizations like the Ligue de défense catholique or the Fédération nationale catholique. Together these groups provided the URD with most of its logistical needs (Bergeron 1985, 97–98; Passmore 1997, 148–49; Pinol 1992, 303). The Reichslandbund, in turn, was the largest agricultural association in Weimar and the DNVP's central organizational base in the rural areas. It was very federally organized and left individual state associations considerable independence.

Second, agricultural crisis radicalized rural voters and reduced their readiness to comply with endorsements. It gave rise to various protest movements and parties that politicized rural voters and made them less deferential and undermined the usefulness of subcontractor services. In Weimar, the most significant agricultural protest was organized in northern Germany by the Landvolkbewegung, in southern Germany by the Deutsche Bauernpartei (German Peasant Party), which emerged from the Bayerische Bauern- und Mittelstandsbund (Bavarian Peasants' and Middle Class League, BBMB), and after 1930 by the NSDAP (Heberle [1932] 1963, 54–57; Pridham 1973, 69–70, 119–20). In the Third Republic, Dorgères's Greenshirts and Fleurant Agricola's Parti agraire et paysans français were the most prominent rural protest groups (Barral 1962, 237; Paxton 1997, 39). Ultimately, the radicalizing effect of these groups made rural voters less willing to comply with the endorsements made by agricultural associations. Moreover, in many instances, these groups became direct electoral competitors of conservatives.

The agricultural crisis was the central event causing the defections and thereby triggering the crisis of the French and German right. The agricultural crisis, however, was too similar in France and Germany to explain why the concomitant political crisis of conservatives unfolded in such different ways. To account for this requires closer attention to the effects that electoral mechanisms had on defectors, loyalists, and peasant protest groups.

Strategic Voting

In the absence of powerful party leaders and party members, voters affected the political fortunes of the URD and DNVP more directly than with other parties. The degree to which electoral mechanisms induced the casting of strategic ballots consequently had significant implications for the electoral performance of party loyalists, realignment patterns of defectors, and the electoral threat posed by peasant protesters.

For party loyalists, strategic voting determined the effectiveness of their principled, reactionary agenda. Weimar's low level of strategic voting minimized the political fallout of Hugenberg's extremist platform and allowed him to stabilize the DNVP's electoral strength. Hugenberg knew that his strategy would cost him votes in the short run. But he had good reasons to believe that these losses would be offset in the long run as his polarization strategy would enlarge the DNVP's voting pool by radicalizing more and more voters. According to one of Hugenberg's lieutenants, it was all right to "let 100,000 national workers [centrist members of one of the defected factions] leave the party; for that we will gain a million or more votes" (Fritzsche 1990, 125). Weimar's low level of strategic voting significantly reduced the risk of trading off short-term losses for potential long-term gains. It did so by minimizing defections of voters sympathetic with Hugenberg's nationalism and authoritarianism but concerned about wasting their votes on a party moving into untested electoral waters. The low level of strategic voting also reduced the need to maximize votes. Hugenberg could afford appealing to narrow, extremist constituencies and eschew the cross-sectional, centrist, catch-all strategy of his predecessors.

By contrast, the Third Republic's high level of strategic voting extracted a considerable electoral price from URD loyalists who adhered to Marin's principled course. In the 1932 election, the URD lost 21 seats of 61 remaining seats and saw the defeat of 23 of its incumbents (Bomier-Landowski 1951; Lachapelle 1928, 1932). Evidence from individual districts corroborates that the voters' concern about wasting their ballots ultimately undermined Marin's national strategy. URD candidates frequently did not campaign under the party's label to distance themselves from Marin's strident nationalism. Candidates in marginal districts "sometimes went to ingenious lengths to obscure, and even to deny, their affiliation with the URD" (Irvine 1979, 102–3). Local committees, when selecting a first-time candidate, regularly chose one who they believed would follow Marin's course. Yet, usually by the second election, such first-time candidates quickly moved to the political center to widen their electoral base and lessen their dependence on the committees (Irvine 1979, 45–47). This lack of ideological fervor was tellingly illustrated by the monthly bulletin of a local party branch. An article covering a quarter of the bulletin's front page announced that an umbrella had been forgotten at the last party meeting and kindly requested that the owner pick up his lost possession (Irvine 1979, 43).

The runoff ballot further constrained Marin's nationalist strategy. By inducing cross-district desistement alliances, the double ballot frequently led to the cross-endorsement of the two cooperating parties' policies. The resulting centrist platforms and ideological muddling ran counter to Marin's effort to present a nationwide and ideologically cohesive profile. In districts not subject to pre-electoral desistement arrangements, the runoff ballot generally preempted an overly adversarial strategy as candidates had to stay on good terms with prospective second ballot backers. Marin's decisions to give priority to political principles over the strategic exigencies of the runoff ballot led the Alliance démocratique and the Parti démocrate populaire (Democratic Popular Party, PDP)[4] to withhold their second ballot cooperation (Irvine 1979, 69; Delbreil 1990, 233).

The second ballot constrained the URD in even further ways. Being at the right end of the political spectrum, the URD could only find allies among centrist parties (Irvine 1979, 55–59). Marin tried to overcome this problem by proposing a nationalist cartel. In 1932, he suggested that all center-right parties agree on a strict desistement in favor of what he vaguely defined as nationalist candidates. This cartel initiative was meant to counter the centripetal constraints of the second ballot (Delbreil 1990, 231). Marin's initiative found few takers since it was a thinly veiled attempt by the URD to co-opt under the pretext of nationalism other center-right parties. Potential allies were all too aware of other center-right parties. The failure of this and similar initiatives led the URD varyingly to push for the adoption of a single-round plurality system or a PR system. One URD deputy, for example, noted that a single-round plurality system would eliminate "those run-off battles during which fatal and inavowable coalitions are formed" and that led parties "to concentrate their forces, to unite with their closest neighbors and agree with them on some common ideas" (Weinreis 1986, 62).

Strategic voting also constrained various new right-of-center parties trying to pursue a more principled course. The Parti démocrate populaire never managed to win more than 10 seats, while the Parti frontiste only elected two deputies.[5] The founders of these parties correctly concluded that the political strength of communists and fascists was directly the result of their ideological and organizational innovations. They were firmly convinced that communism and fascism constituted "historical trends from which France could not isolate itself" (Burrin 1986, 276). Yet these party founders thoroughly misread the institutional realities in which they operated. They simply ignored the high level of strategic voting that strongly handicapped small parties, especially those with narrow, principled political platforms. Ultimately, they made the same miscalculation as Marin.

Conservative defectors in both France and Germany felt the effects of strategic voting just as much as loyalists. Defectors faced highly uncertain electoral prospects, having lost access to logistical resources and well-established party brand names. They consequently paid close attention to strategic voting and how it affected the electoral viability of their two exit options: switching parties or forming new ones. For this argument, it is assumed that defectors were indifferent about whether to switch or form their own party and that their choice was solely determined by their reelection prospects.

The Third Republic's high levels of strategic voting provided powerful incentives for defectors to switch to established parties. And the ready affiliation of URD defectors with the Alliance démocratique testifies to the significance of this effect. Joining other parties enhanced the credibility of defectors sufficiently to reassure voters about their continued electoral viability. This endorsement effect of party switching may not have been centrally important given that defectors frequently enjoyed considerable personal reputations. Party switching was important for other reasons. It reduced the risk of strategic resource allocation by interest groups. Economic interest groups repeatedly threatened to withhold financial contributions to defectors seeking to form new parties because they wanted to restrict the right's fragmentation (Kuisel 1967, 81–84). Party switching also minimized the risk that the URD could punish its defectors by refusing cooperation on runoff ballots. Marin used this strategy to obstruct the electoral advances of the Parti démocrate populaire (Delbreil 1990, 233).

This strategy worked quite effectively because the PDP's small size limited its possibility to retaliate. Defectors could avoid this predicament by switching to another big party. This allowed them to more effectively coordinate re-retaliatory measures should Marin seek to split the votes of defectors by refusing to withdraw his marginal candidates. As members of the Alliance, defectors could more readily threaten to do the same thing to URD candidates and thereby deter Marin's electoral obstruction. Finally, party switching improved the governmental prospects of defectors and their capacity to secure electorally vital pork-barrel projects.

Weimar's low level of strategic voting, on the other hand, preserved the electoral viability of defectors and made party formation a feasible strategy. Defectors did not have to be concerned about voters bandwagoning around front-runners and deserting small parties without much of an electoral track record. Arguably, the most effective electoral procedures for preserving the electoral viability of defectors was Weimar's apparentement provision. It allowed the CNBLP and the KVP to pool votes in the 1930 election by forming an electoral alliance that also included other small parties (Falter, Lindenberger, and Schuman 1986, 52–59). Parenthetically, it should be noted that while Weimar's low strategic voting removed disincentives for party formation, it did not create disincentives for party switching. It therefore made both defection strategies equally feasible and cannot account for why one was chosen over the other. Explaining the latter ultimately requires analysis of career uncertainty, electioneering costs, and the effects that strategic voting had on the electoral potential of peasant protesters.

The surge of peasant protest in the late 1920s gave rise to insurgency movements tempted to enter electoral politics as well as peasant parties and fascist groups seeking to enlarge their small electoral base. These groups solicited support among peasants, by what could be labeled a product differentiation strategy. They narrowly focused on agricultural issues and criticized established parties for failing to do so. The ease with which these groups could pursue such a product differentiation strategy would determine how readily defectors, who were their most direct competitors, also had to differentiate themselves by forming a peasant party.

Weimar's low level of strategic voting greatly facilitated the product differentiation strategy of the Landvolkbewegung, the Deutsche Bauernpartei (German Peasant Party), and above all the NSDAP. It consequently pressured defectors to follow suit by establishing a separate peasant party. This was most clearly visible in the establishment of the CNBLP. Its founders decided to form their own party largely in response to the electoral inroads made by the more radical peasant protest groups (Heberle [1932] 1963, 156; Jones 1986, 204–5; 1988, 286–87). In the Third Republic, on the other hand, strategic voting limited the electoral threat posed by peasant protesters. Fleurant Agricola's Parti agraire et paysans français never posed a significant electoral challenge, and Dorgères's unsuccessful participation in a by-election marked the end of his Greenshirts' electoral involvements (Barral 1962, 237; Paxton 1997, 129–30). Defectors thus felt that they could more readily switch to other parties rather than having to differentiate themselves by also forming a peasant party.

The behavior of French peasant protesters directly reflected how strategic voting constrained them from choosing a product differentiation strategy. Frustrated by winning only one seat in 1932, Agricola launched the Front paysan (Peasant Front) in July 1934, which included rural notables, various local *syndicats agricoles* and Dorgères. The Front paysan was largely a sign of Agricola's and Dorgères's failure to win a sizable electoral support base with their product differentiation strategy. They hoped that cooperation with more conservative rural notables would improve electoral prospects by boosting their electoral viability among voters. Paxton (1997, 129) noted that for Dorgères, the "capacity to draw conservative agrarian notables into alliances was crucial to his progress from the margins to the center of political life." Strategic voting, however, undermined this strategy. It raised the electoral entry barriers so high that it made peasant protesters far more dependent on rural notables than vice versa. By 1937, when the agrarian crisis abated, rural notables defected from the Front paysan, while the Greenshirts and the Parti agraire quickly disintegrated (Paxton 1997, 140–41). In the end, rural notables managed to bolster their credibility with peasants by participating in and dominating the Front paysan rather than having to form separated, conservative peasant parties along the lines of the CNBLP.

Organizational Particularities and Institutional Indeterminacy

Career uncertainty and electioneering costs had none of the effects on conservative parties that we observed with other parties. We cannot, for example, demonstrate systematic institutional effects on the candidate recruitment process and observe any implications for the outcomes of party-internal agenda-setting conflicts. These conflicts led to similar rates of defections despite taking place in different institutional environments.

As pointed out earlier, the defections consequently had to be explained in terms of two contextual, noninstitutional factors: mass politics and agricultural crisis. Such institutional indeterminacy might be troubling for someone aspiring to predictions that hold irregardless of time and space. However, it poses a lesser problem for the mechanism-based explanations pursued here and even offers an opportunity to probe into the interaction between systematic institutional factors and historical contingencies. The historical contingencies of particular relevance for the URD and DNVP were their distinct party organizations. A brief look at the organizational peculiarities of the two parties will clarify how they overrode the effects of electoral mechanisms. This brief digression illustrates the larger theoretical point that institutions merely create incentives and constraints that inevitably interact with noninstitutional factors.

The URD and DNVP as well as the various smaller conservative parties had organizational characteristics setting them apart from other parties. The contracting-out model turned both parties into virtual interest group confederations. They were loose electoral alliances of primarily nonelectoral, organized societal groups. There was a considerable overlap between the leaders and logistical infrastructures of parties and interest groups. After the URD's and DNVP's breakups, the successor parties resembled electoral branch offices of different interest groups. Moreover, like most confederations, the URD and DNVP had very limited party administration and governance mechanisms. They became veritable umbrella organizations with no organizational and decision-making autonomy. The URD's and DNVP's national organizations remained highly underdeveloped. They had very small staffs and few financial means available to support candidates (Jeanneney 1976, 346). Marin, for example, never managed to transform the local family and friends committees into more permanent organizations that might attract a significant number of members or activists (Passmore 1997, 148–49). These committees remained what Irvine aptly described as "glorified corresponding societies" that went into organizational hibernation between elections (1979, 44). Both parties also were reluctant to institutionalize formalized and effective governance mechanisms. The URD's party executive had no authority, and party congresses mostly were symbolic events serving to at least rhetorically affirm party unity (Irvine 1979, 29–32; Jeanneney 1976, 29n). The DNVP's governance structure concentrated slightly more authority in the hands of the party leadership but otherwise was equally ad hoc and poorly institutionalized. It certainly was not able to withstand the conflicts that emerged among its various confederate members (Liebe 1956, 122–25).

These organizational particularities explain the indeterminacy of career uncertainty and electioneering costs in the URD and DNVP. They overrode institutional effects in two ways. First, we saw with other parties that career uncertainty affected how readily interest groups could use their logistical support to influence party-internal decision making. The URD's and DNVP's poorly institutionalized governance structures made it difficult for party leaders to credibly commit themselves to upholding their end of the bargain with interest groups. Interest groups in the URD, for example, faced double jeopardy. They were severely constrained in influencing candidate recruitment because of the high career uncertainty, and they lacked the possibility of influencing the political platform because the URD simply was too disorganized for any effective lobbying to take place. The high career uncertainty, for example, complicated the efforts of the *syndicats agricoles* to assure the reselection of agriculture-friendly candidates. The few candidates it managed to get reselected found it difficult to influence the party's agenda because there were no formalized agenda-setting procedures. For the DNVP, in turn, organizational uncertainty overrode the effects of Weimar's low career uncertainty. The missing governance structures negated whatever control electoral mechanisms gave party leaders over the candidate recruitment process. The Reichslandbund consequently could not engage in the co-optation strategy that industrial interest groups were able to pursue in the DDP and DVP. And since party leaders could not control the selection of candidates, the DNVP frequently faced a free-for-all between the agricultural associations and the interest groups over the distribution of candidacies. One candidate reported that "for somebody who participated in the preparation of electoral lists, the actual electoral contest cannot be any more difficult. Never before have the differences between the different economic interests clashed as much as this time" (Holzbach 1981, 221).

Second, we saw in our earlier discussion that electioneering costs made liberal parties dependent on interest groups. These interest groups, in turn, could leverage their logistical contributions for policy-making influence. The organizational makeup of the URD and DNVP, however, made such leveraging less feasible. Interest groups supporting the URD and DNVP were de facto constituent members of the two parties rather than external lobbyists. They consequently could not readily threaten to shift their support to other parties if their demands were not met. Constituting the party, they lacked a fulcrum for applying their logistical leverage. The URD's and DNVP's organizational uncertainty severed the link between electioneering costs and the leverage these costs conferred on interest groups. Interest groups faced a further constraint on readily switching their allegiances. Their primary contributions consisted of public endorsements rather than financial contributions. They consequently could not shift support too frequently without undermining their credibility that made such endorsements effective.

The URD's and DNVP's organizational particularities undermined the hypothesized effects of electoral mechanisms on the internal decision making of parties. This did not mean that career uncertainty and electioneering costs had no systematic effects on the party-external actions of loyalists, defectors, and party protesters.

Electioneering Costs and Career Uncertainty

Electioneering costs help explain why URD defectors were more likely to switch parties and why DNVP defectors preferred to create new political organizations. At first sight, we would expect defectors in both countries to chose party switching over party formation. Both parties' defectors heavily depended on rural voters. They consequently faced considerable difficulties mobilizing voters since the agricultural crisis limited the capacity of agricultural associations to make effective endorsements. Joining other parties would have provided a ready-made solution for this problem, yet only URD defectors followed this course of action. To understand why requires a closer look at how electioneering costs affected defectors' autonomy from agricultural associations. This autonomy mattered because French and German agricultural associations, unlike the defectors, had clear preferences for party formation over party switching. This preference directly reflected their disappointment about previous cooperation with the URD and DNVP. It also stemmed from the belief that separate peasant parties would better forestall electoral advances by peasant insurgency groups, which pose a direct threat to agricultural associations. In short, defectors and agricultural associations had different preferences about how to organize. The outcome of this conflict depended on how much leverage electioneering costs would give agricultural associations to prevent defectors from joining other bourgeois parties.

The Third Republic's low electioneering costs never made URD defectors as dependent on agricultural associations as DNVP defectors. The low cost of campaigning allowed URD defectors to maintain some autonomy from the *syndicats agricoles* and pro-church groups like the Ligues des patriotes or Fédération nationale catholique (Passmore 1997, 148–49; Pinol 1992, 303; Bergeron 1985, 97–98). Besides endorsing conservatives, these groups also provided campaign workers and mobilized audiences for their rallies (Quellien 1986, 304; Irvine 1979, 99). The Third Republic's small physical district sizes and limited number of election contests allowed defectors to maintain an arm's-length relation with these groups. Defectors could readily resist pressures from the *syndicats agricoles* to form an exclusive peasant party and could without much difficulty switch to the Alliance démocratique. The arm's-length relation between defectors and their logistical backers, which the low electioneering costs made possible, was most visible in rural districts. In such districts, defectors relied on their personal reputations to such an extent that they hardly needed to contract out logistical tasks to agricultural associations. In some instances, reputations were built on political services that candidates rendered to their constituencies. Such constituency services, however, were rare among URD deputies given that their party frequently was out of power. Their reputation therefore rested more often on social prestige, since "many deputies belonged to families which had traditionally dominated their region, both economically and politically. . . . these seats had become virtual fiefs that were passed down from one generation to the next" (Irvine 1979, 23; Passmore 1997, 148–49). Many URD deputies were titled and were elected in rural districts. The districting reinforced this benefit of low electioneering costs because it significantly overrepresented rural districts.

Weimar's large physical district size and multiple elections, on the other hand, increased electioneering costs. The impact of these costs was further amplified by the loss of the indirect logistical subsidies conservatives received before 1914. In Imperial Germany, conservatives could count on electoral assistance from the state bureaucracy and benefited in some state elections from restrictive *régimes censitaires* (Liebe 1956, 30; Nipperdey 1958, 581–86). The sudden loss of these benefits and the high electioneering costs turned defectors into virtual proxies of the regional branches of the Reichslandbund with which they were associated. These branches pressured defectors to pursue an exclusively agricultural agenda, which in their eyes would be most effectively achieved by creating a separate peasant party. Defectors were logistically so dependent on the regional Reichslandbund associations that they had little choice but to create the CNBLP (Jones 1986, 204–5).

Electioneering costs also permit insights into the electoral fortunes of peasant protest groups. The effect of electioneering costs hinged on the different organizational characteristics of these groups. Most of them, like Dorgères's Greenshirts, Agricola's Parti agraire, or the Landvolkbewegung, were amorphous, strictly rural protest movements. They coalesced around populist leaders and depended on high-profile issues capable of inciting protest. Others, like the NSDAP and the various French ligues, had entrepreneurial leaders who saw the agricultural crisis as a great opportunity to expand their mostly urban support base. These urban fascist groups had emerged from various paramilitary groups and managed, with varying success, to establish well-organized, disciplined, and national organizations. Urban fascist groups thus had a clear organizational advantage over the more rural protest movements. The electioneering costs help to explain why this organizational advantage turned into a greater electoral advantage for the NSDAP than for the French ligues.

Weimar's electioneering costs increased the NSDAP's comparative logistical advantage over the other peasant protest groups. The high campaigning expenses allowed the NSDAP to easily outperform the Landvolkbewegung and the Bauernbund in northern Germany or the Deutsche Bauernpartei in Bavaria[6] (Pridham 1973, 69–70, 119–20; Heberle [1932] 1963, 154–60). Weimar's large physical district size created such formidable logistical exigencies that it placed the strictly rural protest groups, with their small and poorly institutionalized organizations, at a comparative logistical disadvantage to the NSDAP. This disadvantage quickly became apparent to activists of peasant insurgent groups and led to their defection to the NSDAP. Moreover, the high electioneering costs allowed the NSDAP to capitalize on its organizational advantage vis-à-vis DNVP defectors. This advantage was most directly evident with respect to the Konservative Volkspartei. It had no organizational infrastructure and collapsed after only one election, leading many of its voters and some of its leaders to defect to the NSDAP. The CNBLP was organizationally better endowed than the KVP since it controlled various regional branches of the Reichslandbund. Yet it, too, could not resist the logistical bandwagoning effect around the much better organized NSDAP (Jones 1986, 225).

The Third Republic's low electioneering costs, in turn, limited the organizational advantage that French ligues enjoyed compared to other peasant protest groups and URD defectors. The Croix de Feu or Jeunesses patriotes never managed to capitalize electorally on the organizational shortcomings of the Parti agraire or the Greenshirts. These ligues also had no success leveraging their organizational resources against conservative notables. The small electioneering costs allowed conservative notables to capitalize on their personal reputations and limited the economies of scale that ligues derived from their national logistical infrastructures. The agricultural crisis, for example, had radicalized the rural Calvados region in northern France and made it one of Dorgères's strongholds. Yet despite trying, the Croix de Feu did not manage to electorally exploit this radicalized peasantry. Its national organization, urban image, and mostly national reputation proved to be obstacles in small districts, where personal connections and favors were most valued. To counter these obstacles, the Croix de Feu formed an alliance with the local Front paysan and backed traditional conservatives (Quellien 1986, 329–31). Generally, the Croix de Feu was most successful in those rural departments where the URD did not have local electoral committees and strong incumbent candidates (Jeanneney 1978, 344).

Just like electioneering costs, career uncertainty had no impact on the party-internal affairs of conservative parties. Its only noticeable effect was on whether defectors chose to switch parties or form their own. This effect was largely attributable to the fact that career uncertainty determined the career compatibilities between defectors and their new prospective parties.

The Third Republic's high career uncertainty contributed to party switching by minimizing the career incompatibilities between URD defectors and the Alliance démocratique. It did so in two ways. First, it limited the authority loss that leaders of the Alliance démocratique experienced by the influx of new members. The leaders' authority over candidate recruitment already was so minimal that the entry of new candidates with their own power base did little to alter this authority (Wileman 1988, 17). Second, URD defectors, by virtue of being incumbents, did not diminish the reselection and reelection prospects of Alliance incumbents. Weimar's low career uncertainty, on the other hand, posed a considerable obstacle for the merger of DNVP defectors with other parties like the CNBLP, Wirtschaftspartei, Volksrechtspartei, or Hannoversche Partei. Career control was a central authority lever for party leaders who could protect loyal incumbents or advance underlings by promoting from within the party. Party leaders thus had little interest in ceding some of this control by making room on scarce lists positions for defectors from the DNVP. Low career uncertainty thus created strong disincentives for parties to welcome defectors because they would have diminished the career prospects of incumbents and the authority of its leaders. It made parties less permeable and forced defectors to start their own.

Chapter 6

Mayhem or Majority?
Fascists and the Dilemma
of Electoral Participation

The interwar years provided unprecedented opportunities for right-wing extremists. In the early twenties, anticommunism became their rallying cry, returning soldiers their willing recruits, and disorganized conservative notables their immediate political prey. By the late 1920s, the agricultural crisis, the Great Depression, and antiparliamentarism further improved their political fortunes. The groups benefiting from this political and socioeconomic turmoil were numerous, since the far right was as fractionalized as the traditional right. Its spectrum extended from nationalist and paramilitary groups at the extremist fringe to establishment sympathizers in economic interest groups, professional associations, and bourgeois politicians. This chapter concentrates on the far right's paramilitary core by comparing the German Stahlhelme, Wehrwölfe, Jungdeutscher Orden, and Nationalsozialistische Deutsche Arbeiterpartei (National Socialist German Workers' Party, NSDAP) with the French Jeunesses patriotes, Croix de Feu, Faisceau, and Parti populaire français (French Popular Party, PPF). It varyingly refers to these paramilitary groups as the far right, nationalist movements, or simply fascists.

Comparing the political fortunes of French and German fascists is of twofold interest. First, it permits analysis of another mode of interest intermediation. So far, the focus has been on the representation of societal interests through party-internal agenda setting and market-driven electoral competition. By contrast, paramilitary groups began as social movements in the extra-institutional sphere of politics before ending up as regular parties. They consequently allow studying movement politics and party entry as additional modes of interest intermediation and permit insights into how readily societal polarization, on which these groups fed, is translated into political polarization. Second, the political fortunes of the French and German far right diverged during the interwar period. In the early twenties, paramilitary groups in both countries were comparably successful in mobilizing *as social movements* antiliberal, anticommunist, and antidemocratic sentiments in the extra-institutional sphere. By the early 1930s, however, only German fascist groups had managed to institutionalize themselves by shifting from a movement strategy to an institutional, electoral strategy.

This divergent development of French and German fascist groups is largely overlooked in their respective historiographies, as is the shift from an extra-institutional movement strategy to an institutional, electoral strategy. Many explanations attribute the strength of right-wing extremists either to long-term historical, cultural legacies like the strength of liberalism (Moore 1966; Luebbert 1991) or short-term factors like the severity of the Great Depression. Very rarely do these explanations recognize the difference between the movement and party phase of groups and specify the relevant factors accounting for the success during these distinct phases. This foreshortening of time may account for why it remains so controversial to compare the German far right. In many people's minds, Germany's far right is unique and hence incomparable. The NSDAP became Weimar's largest party, created the Third Reich, and plunged Europe into war and the Holocaust. By contrast, France's largest and most durable right-wing group, Colonel François de La Roque's Croix de Feu, won two by-elections and never came close to toppling the moribund Third Republic. These different historical characterizations are less historical facts than they are products of historical vantage points. They become far less stark if we shift the historical point of reference from the 1930s to the turn of the century. In the 1890s, both France and Germany experienced a very comparable first mobilization of right-wing movements around nationalist and antisemitic themes (Eley 1980; Irvine 1989; Sternhell, 1978). In the 1920s, anticommunism and the postwar crisis gave rise to a second wave. In short, the French and German far right seemed far less dissimilar before the 1920s than after.[1]

The development of the French and German far right is characterized by an interesting but largely overlooked tactical shift in the late 1920s. At that point, they began to consider whether to continue as movements by creating mayhem in the streets or whether to seek a parliamentary majority by entering electoral politics. The relative political stability of the late 1920s undermined the effectiveness of the extra-parliamentary movement strategy that right-wing groups employed in the early 1920s. As part of this strategy, paramilitary organizations acted as anticommunist militias and placed their activists at the disposal of the conservatives' anemic election machines. At certain points, following Mussolini's example, they also used their strength as movements to pressure governments into abdicating their power by creating political paralysis through strikes and street protests (Orlow 1969, 76–127; Passmore 1997, 228; Soucy 1986, 66–67). In Weimar, the tumultuous postwar years even created opportunities for right-wing groups to pursue an outright putschist strategy.

By the late 1920s, the return to political stability rapidly diminished the payoffs of this multifaceted movement strategy. Activists were more difficult to recruit, financial backers withdrew their support, and governments became more willing to repress extremist groups. Entering electoral politics and pursuing a parliamentary majority offered a possible solution to what Diehl aptly termed the fascists' "crisis of stability" (1977, 156). It promised stable parliamentary careers and clearly mapped advancement possibilities and firmer organizational institutionalization. Such benefits were not without risks, since electoral politics involved the danger of internal dissent from radical factions who could accuse leaders of compromising political principles for personal careerism. Not unlike socialists 30 years earlier, right-wing groups had to weigh the costs and benefits of entering electoral politics. As table 2 shows, this electoral calculus produced quite different results in France and Germany. German paramili-

TABLE 2. Movement to Party Conversion

	First Electoral Entry	Number of Seats
Weimar Republic		
Deutschvölkische Freiheitspartie (a)	1924	23 (4.8%)
NSDAP (b)	1928	12 (2.4%)
Völkisch-Nationaler Kampfblock (c)	1928	0
Jungdeutscher Orden (d)	1930	6 (1.2%)
Third Republic		
Jeunesses patriotes/PRNS (e)	1930	0
(Croix de Feu/Parti social français) (f)	1936	0
(Parti populaire français) (f)	1936	0

Source: Falter, Linderberger, and Schuman (1986, 43); Diehl (1977, 239–41, 270–74); Soucy (1986, 309).
Legend: (a) Was senior partner in alliance with NSDAP (only listed DVFP seat share); (b) the reasons for dating the NSDAP's electoral entry in 1928 rather than 1924 are explained further below in the text; (c) included the Wehrwolf, Vereinigte Vaterländische Verbände Deutschlands, and remainders of the DVFP; (d) had merged with DDP to form the Staatspartei (only listed seat share of Jungdeutscher Orden); (e) renamed in 1930 Parti républicaine national et social; (f) Croix de Feu renamed in 1936. Involuntary party conversions to circumvent 1936 government ban on paramilitary groups.

tary groups displayed a far greater willingness than their French counterparts to enter electoral politics.

Of the five largest German paramilitary groups, four entered electoral politics. Only the Stahlhelme abstained. In France, the Jeunesses patriotes alone were tempted by institutional politics. The Croix de Feu and Parti populaire français constituted themselves as electoral parties only in 1936 to comply with a ban on paramilitary organizations imposed by the Popular Front government. Table 2 shows further differences in the pattern of electoral entries. In Weimar, there is a surge of entries in the late 1920s, when fascist groups faced their "crisis of stability." With the exception of the Jeunesses patriotes, French groups responded to a similar crisis by staying out of electoral politics. French and German fascists consequently responded differently to the decline of opportunities for right-wing mobilization in the early 1920s. These different entry patterns also had important implications for the political success of fascists in the 1930s. As Bracher points out, the NSDAP's success in institutionalizing itself in the late 1920s meant that it controlled a well-organized logistical infrastructure through which it could fully capitalize on the Great Depression (1970, 137–50). French ligues, in turn, were organizationally less ready to benefit from the Great Depression. Instead, the political opportunities created by the Depression led to renewed proliferation of right-wing groups, which split their support and undermined their overall reactionary impact.

Two possible conclusions can be drawn from table 2. First, French ligues were more radical than German ones and hence valued a pure movement strategy more highly. There is little evidence to support this contention. If anything, the German far right was more vitriolic in its anticommunism, dislike for conservative parties, and contempt for liberal democracy. Moreover, its antisemitism, *völkisch* ideology, and expansionist foreign policy goals made it even more radical than its French counterpart.

Second, the greater electoral eagerness of German right-wing groups could be interpreted as a result of their larger size and hence better electoral prospects. Table 3 undermines this hypothesis. It lists the estimated membership of different paramilitary organizations for the closest available date to their electoral entry. It should be emphasized that these figures are in many cases estimates, since affiliations oftentimes were not very formalized. As a result, there are reasons to suspect that figures double-count members belonging to several groups.

Table 3 does not show a significant difference in the membership strength of German and French right-wing groups. It demonstrates that the choice to enter electoral politics cannot be readily attributed to the social support of the different right-wing groups. An alternative explanation therefore is needed. I contend that the electoral entry decision owes much to the different ways in which French and German electoral mechanisms structured the payoffs of an electoral strategy.

To fully explain how electoral mechanisms affect the overall payoff of an electoral strategy, I first need to specify the individual costs and benefits of an electoral calculus. Then, it will be possible to explain how institutional parameters affect the probability of obtaining the benefits or incurring the costs.

Costs and Benefits of an Electoral Strategy

Much of the literature on fascism or the Nazi vote inadequately differentiates between extra-institutional and institutional arenas of politics and consequently overlooks how these two arenas affect the organization and strategy of fascist movements (Childers 1976; Brustein and Falter 1994; Luebbert 1991; Soucy 1986, 1995). This literature views fascist movements as black boxes or simply conduits of long-term structural forces or short-

TABLE 3.   **Movement Strength before Electoral Entry**

	Membership Estimates	Percentage of Electorate	Year of Estimate
Weimar Republic			
Stahlhelme	300,000 (plus 100,000 young members < 21)	0.7 (0.96)	1925–29
Jungdeutscher Orden	80–100,000	0.19–0.23	Late-1920s
Wehrwolf	40,000	0.1	Mid-1920s
NSDAP	81,000	0.2	1927
Third Republic			
Faisceau	60,000	0.27	1926
Jeunesses patriotes	100,000	0.45	1929
Croix de Feu	100,000/750,000	0.45 (3.4)	1934/1937
Solidarité française	100,000	0.45	1934
Action française	40,000	0.18	1934
Parti populaire français	50–80,000	0.22–0.36	1936

Source: Mackie and Rose (1991); Bracher (1970, 133); Diehl (1977, 293–95); Soucy (1995, 36–38; 1986, 52, 87, 152, 198).

Note: Electorate size based on 1928 figures for France. I doubled the electoral size for calculating the percentage in order to control for the disenfranchisement of French women until 1945. German women were enfranchised in 1918.

term historical contingencies. Such environmental factors are adequate for explaining the ebbing and swelling of fascist mobilization potential in the extra-institutional sphere of politics; they are insufficient for explaining how such a potential is translated into actual parliamentary strength. Bracher recognizes this limitation of purely contextual explanations. He points out that strictly socioeconomic explanations cannot explain why Weimar's 1923 hyperinflation did not produce the same fascist grounds-well as the Great Depression. Similarly, Zimmerman argues that levels of unemployment in the 1930s did not correlate with strength of fascist parties (Bracher 1970, 169; Zimmerman 1987). Passmore (1997, 163, 185) correctly argues that "there is no automatic link between a particular type of crisis and the kinds of political movements it generates, let alone the chances of a particular movement winning power." I concur with these criticisms and would add that existing explanations overlook the electoral calculus that fascists faced before entering electoral politics. The entire French historiography on fascism entirely ignores this point.

Costs of Participation Strategy

Two potential costs weighed heavily in the electoral calculus of French and German fascist leaders. They were afraid that electoral politics required organizational modifications that would dilute their authority and create internal dissent.

   Losing of authority was the constant concern of fascist leaders. Many of them had founded the groups they led and thus considered them their personal property. They also organized them very hierarchically by adopting variants of the highly autocratic Führerprinzip. Electoral participation threatened this personal concentration of power in two ways. First, it required a more complex logistical infrastructure than movement politics that was less readily controlled (Kalyvas 1996, 82–108). As parties, fascists became more dependent on permanent and professional organizations because they did not control the scheduling of elections. They consequently had to build organizations that were capable of mobilizing large capital or labor resources within a short period of time. The mobilization of organization-intensive labor resources was particularly important during the interwar period, when electioneering depended on postering, pamphlet distribution, or mass rallies. Electoral politics also required a higher degree of professionalization. Legal expertise, for example, was important to incorporate local party branches, register candidates, or design governance procedures for selecting candidates. Second, electoral politics made it more likely that leaders would have to share credit with candidates and activists. Particularly successful local organizations could take credit for their victories and thereby build a local power base. As Kalyvas notes, with entry into electoral politics, the legitimacy of leaders shifts to voters (Kalyvas 1996, 43).

The concern over authority loss was very evident among fascist leaders. In Germany, this worry probably was most pronounced in the Stahlhelme, which were divided into two factions led by its two founders, Franz Seldte and Theodore Duesterberg. The Stahlhelme repeatedly discussed forming their own party, but most likely Seldte and Duesterberg decided against it, fearing that electoral politics might further dilute their already divided authority (Berghahn 1966, 103). In 1924, the NSDAP adopted the so-called urban plan, which sought to mobilize the urban working class. Hedging his bets, Hitler never fully endorsed the plan. He recognized that its success required the establishment of labor unions, which could undermine his authority. Not willing to take this risk, he abandoned the plan by 1926 (Orlow 1969, 67, 103; Diehl 1977, 279). The French ligues tried to preempt any loss of authority by severely restricting the autonomy of local branches. The Croix de Feu, for example, circulated a monthly bulletin that gave local leaders detailed instructions and strongly discouraged the publication of local newspapers (Passmore 1997, 259; Berstein 1992, 91). La Roque also was constantly worried that electoral involvement would strengthen ties between local branches and conservative politicians. He was particularly afraid that the latter might coopt the former and declared that "one does not annex the Croix de Feu, one follows it" (Irvine 1979, 124).

Having been keen students of socialist parties, fascist leaders were aware that an electoral strategy would lead to internal dissent and even possible schisms. The principal source of dissent was activists whose very short time horizon contributed to their radicalism. They generally were mobilized with the promise of immediate political action and thus had little patience for electoral politics and its emphasis on quadrennial elections, long-term organization building, and careful coalition formation. The long-term perspective required by elections was the antithesis of the emphasis on action and street protest that had mobilized activists in the first place. In short, radicals were very reluctant to join their leaders on the long march through the very institutions they sought to overthrow. Moreover, electoral entry tempted leaders to broaden their appeal by wooing voters outside the original core constituency of the movement. Such cross-sectoral appeals would require policy compromises and dilute the benefits the core constituency could expect (Przeworski and Sprague 1986, 57–95). This trade-off is nicely captured by Samuel Beer's (1982, 23) observation that if a modern party has policy, it will not have a majority, and if it has a majority, it will have no policy.

The internal dissent caused by prospective electoral participation was observable across all right-wing groups. The efforts by the Stahlhelme and Jungdeutscher Orden to have their candidates nominated by conservative parties or to nominate their own lists led to significant factional disputes (Diehl 1977, 170–71). In the NSDAP, opposition to the electoral strategy was concentrated in the Sturmabteilung (storm troopers, SA), "an organization destined to be less important in an election-centered party than in an activist group dealing with civil disobedience and terror" (Orlow 1969, 124). The SA's opposition posed the most serious threat to Hitler's authority and was not overcome until 1932. The situation was almost identical in France. When G. Valois wanted to adopt an electoral strategy in 1927, the congress declared, "The Faisceau, having as its goal a national revolution, which excludes parliamentary means, will present no lists or candidates for legislative elections" (Soucy 1983, 190). Even though La Roque railed against electoralism and solemnly declared elections "an exercise in collective decadence," he could not prevent the defection of the radical Volontiers nationaux faction after he entered electoral politics in 1936 (Soucy 1995, 159; Machefer 1970, 114–15; Burrin 1986, 191). In an identical fashion, Pierre Taittinger lost the more radical supporters of the Jeunesses patriotes (the Légion and Phalangeards factions) and various local branches after he began collaborating with conservative politicians (Irvine 1979, 109; Müller 1980, 489–90; Soucy 1983, 199; Passmore 1997, 215).

Benefits of Participation Strategy

The central benefit of electoral participation is the prospect of greater institutionalization and organizational stability. As strict movements, fascists faced considerable organizational uncertainty because political protest is, in Claus Offe's apt characterization, a "highly perishable resource." Offe further points out that movements "are extremely ill equipped to deal with problems of time. In their actions and protest, they respond to present dangers. . . . In their demands, new movements do not anticipate a lengthy process of transition, gradual reform or slow improvement but an immediate and sudden change" (Offe 1990, 227–32). This organizational uncertainty is a particular problem for leaders of movements, who often invest considerable time and occasionally personal money in the hope of advancing their political careers. Electoral politics helps to attenuate this organizational uncertainty by giving movements access to state resources, providing more stable career opportunities, and reducing the risk of state repression.

Fascist movements depended on contributions from industrial interest groups and wealthy individuals. Since these contributors saw their donations as an antisocialist insurance policy, they scaled their support back every time leftist strength ebbed (Diehl 1977, 153, 170–71; Soucy 1983, 197–98; 1995, 113, 124–25). Consequently, paramilitary organizations had a very ambivalent attitude toward their financial backers, whose politically highly contingent support greatly complicated building stable organizations (Passmore 1997, 278; Wolf 1967, 150–53). Electoral entry held the promise of reducing the dependence on external benefactors. Once elected, deputies would receive salaries, pensions, travel allowances, and legislative staffers. The NSDAP, for example, levied a tax on deputies' salaries to finance party activities and extensively used deputies as public speakers to economize on travel expenses (Orlow 1969, 123, 137). Hitler quite frankly admitted that the deputy's free train ticket "is the main thing. This makes it possible for us to send round agitators. . . . The men who represent us in the parliament do not travel to Berlin to cast their ballots but travel around uninterruptedly with their tickets. . . . It was through this that we were able to hold over 2370 mass meetings in the past year" (quoted in Pridham 1973, 79). A parliamentary presence permitted fascists to offer interest groups lobbying services and patronage favors in return for donations, thus creating a more equitable relationship. Finally, electoral strategy also allows "tapping of resources of those who are willing neither to act [i.e., protest] nor pay, but just to vote" (Offe 1990, 241).

The perishable nature of protest increased career uncertainty, making it difficult to recruit the skilled activists that were necessary to effectively run local branches. The prospect of fairly stable legislative positions and clearly defined advancement possibilities significantly reduced this problem. The announcement of electoral participation generally produced a surge of new supporters who were attracted by prospective parliamentary careers. Old-time members responded suspiciously to such newcomers, viewing them as opportunists. This suspicion clearly came through in La Roque's sarcastic account of the new fair-weather supporters he had to deal with after 1936. It is worth quoting him in full:

> First act, my guest is congratulatory. . . . Second act, my guest denounces parliamentarism. . . . Third act, my guest asks me what the Croix de Feu might do in the upcoming election. . . . Fourth act, struck by a sudden inspiration, my guest suggests a random list of . . . candidates. Casually, and merely as an example, he mentions that he himself has some well placed friends who have (fancy that!) offered him a constituency. At that, the rascal leaves, undoubtedly believing that he had laid some foundation. (Irvine 1979, 114–15)

The prospect of becoming a public office holder also appealed to Nazis. Despite all their antidemocratic tirades, the status-conscious political parvenus in the NSDAP were not unimpressed by the prestige of public office. "The parliamentarization of the party [NSDAP] held out the promise of legislative seats and the honoraria that went with speaking engagements" (Orlow 1969, 147). The prospect of more stable political careers also tied cadre members more firmly to their movements and reduced the poaching that frequently took place among different right-wing groups.

Finally, an electoral strategy reduced the risk of government repression. In France, we already saw how the ban on ligues in 1936 precipitated the transformation of the Croix de Feu into the Parti social français (French Social Party, PSF), and Doriot's Rayon majoritaire became the Parti populaire français (French Popular Party, PPF). The PPF's party statutes, for example, explicitly forbade any organizational features that the government could construe as paramilitary (Burrin 1986, 283). In Germany, the Stahlhelme were outlawed in 1922 and 1929 and needed to mobilize all their political contacts to have the bans lifted (Berghahn 1966, 35–37, 137, 152). Hitler's decisions in 1926 to abandon his putschist strategy and in 1927–28 to stop his movement strategy were directly related to governmental repression efforts. At various points, Hitler was prohibited from speaking in certain states, in addition to local and state governments banning Nazi rallies, public wearing of uniforms, or the SA (Brustein 1996, 169). Hitler repeatedly ordered the SA to refrain from paramilitary activities to avoid giving governments a pretext for such repressive measures (Orlow 1969, 106–7). Orlow observes that "the rewards for a successful [electoral] campaign were perhaps less immediately satisfying than the sight of a dozen enemies moaning on a beer hall floor, but they were socially far more acceptable" (1969, 122).

French and German fascists thus clearly differentiated the costs and benefits of an electoral strategy. This calculus, however, was largely indeterminate and did not produce a clear-cut payoff or optimal solution. This participation calculus by itself cannot explain why French fascists attached a lower value to electoral politics than their German counterparts. Accounting for these different evaluations requires an explanation of the probability that actors attached to realizing electoral payoffs (Tsebelis 1990, 26–27). I contend that once political events had shifted the fascists' preference from a movement to an electoral strategy, different electoral mechanisms account for why German fascists attached a greater probability of succeeding under an electoral strategy than their French counterparts.

The following sections formulate three auxiliary arguments to the ones elaborated in chapter 2. These modifications simply take into account that we are dealing with extra-institutional movements contemplating a major organizational transformation rather than established parties worrying about the next election. The three auxiliary arguments closely follow the theoretical rationale of the earlier argument and simply restate the effects that strategic voting, career uncertainty, and electioneering costs have on the electoral calculus.

Strategic Voting

As movements, French and German paramilitary groups stressed collective goals and targeted national audiences. They emphasized their principledness, iron determination, and disdain for compromise. To them, liberal democracy, with its endless deliberation and politically expedient compromises, was the antithesis of their movement strategy. Yet the feasibility of direct action heavily depended on economic crisis, political scandals, or international tensions that radicalized voters. In the absence of such circumstances, the tedium of institutional politics was the only alternative. How much electoral politics would compromise fascists' erstwhile radicalism depended on the extent to which voters would discount their ideological preferences with the risk of wasting their votes. In other words, the payoff of electoral participation was contingent on the level of strategic voting.

Generally, strategic voting reduces the payoff of electoral participation in two ways. First, it lowers the prospects of success. New parties by definition have not participated in prior elections and therefore are largely unknown to voters. They lack an electoral track record through which voters can assess their electoral viability. The absence of such a track record discourages voters from supporting new parties whose electoral prospects are highly uncertain. Prospective electoral entrants thus face the problem of how to overcome this bandwagoning effect around front-runners. The only way to counteract such bandwagoning is to move to the center, forming electoral alliances or seeking endorsements from interest groups. These measures boost the electoral viability of new electoral entrants and lessen voters' fear of wasting their ballots. Yet for fascists, such moves to counteract strategic voting increased the risk of party-internal dissent and defections. The more fascist leaders moved toward the center to improve their electoral viability, the more they jeopardized their party-internal standing by alienating ideologically highly committed grassroots activists. By pressuring political leaders toward the center, strategic voting increased the risk of internal dissent and defections.

Przeworski and Sprague (1986, 71–72) also point out that median voter strategies carry potential opportunity costs in the electoral arena. Such costs result from the fact that broadening the platform can only be achieved by diluting the benefits to the original core constituency. Such opportunity costs are relatively modest for right-wing extremists. Their magnitude depends on the presence of a rival party that woos voters alienated by political moderation. In the case of fascists, the emergence of such a rival party was highly unlikely. The only conceivable organizers of such a rival party were the radical activists who were most unlikely to create a party given their deeply felt antipathy toward electoral politics.

France's small district magnitude and runoff ballot significantly reduced the payoffs of an electoral strategy by inducing high levels of strategic voting. These effects are somewhat difficult to verify since no regular election was held after the electoral entry of the Croix de Feu and the Parti populaire français. We therefore have to make inferences from the 34 by-elections held between August 1936 and the outbreak of the war in September 1939 (Goguel 1977, 47–51). Unfortunately, I was not able to obtain detailed information about each by-election. But the by-elections analyzed in the various regional studies reveal the continued electoral hesitance of ligues. The Parti social français, for example, did not participate in two by-elections held in the Calvados and Allier departments even though it had a local party organization. In both instances, this reluctance can be attributed to its marginal winning prospects. In the Calvados, farmers radicalized by the agricultural crisis favored local peasant candidates, whereas the Allier department had been a solid socialist stronghold (Quellien 1986, 290–93; Viple 1967, 89, 241–44). A study that pooled the election returns of the 34 by-elections showed only a modest electoral strength of the ligues. In the 16 by-elections during the Popular Front government, when anticommunist hysteria peaked, the PPF received on the first ballot only 2.71 percent of the votes and the PSF 3.57 percent. On the second ballot, the PPF won 3.8 percent of the votes and the PSF 4.4 percent. Neither party won seats. During the first ballot of the remaining 18 by-elections, the PPF won 9.3 percent of the votes and the PSF 21.8 percent. This improvement, however, was not repeated on the second ballot, where the PPF only received 1.7 percent of the votes and the PSF 6.8 percent. Goguel attributes this second ballot drop-off to the conservatives' noncooperation with the ligues on withdrawing candidates. This strategy was largely successful and limited the PSF's electoral surge to only two parliamentary seats (Goguel 1977, 47–51). PSF candidates even did poorly in districts in which their party had formidable organizations. Barral reports that the PSF candidate in the Isère department received only 1,419 votes (13 percent) even though PSF rallies regularly attracted 6,000–10,000 people. This incongruence between popular and electoral support partly can be attributed to the unwillingness of voters to risk casting their votes for unproven candidates (Barral 1962, 335, 561). Goguel argues that the presence of ligue candidates on the second ballot also increased the cooperation among center and leftist parties. They became more disciplined in withdrawing their candidates and thereby pooled their votes to prevent the election of fascist candidates (Goguel 1977, 52). Fascists thus faced not only strategic voters but also strategic adversaries.

After 1936, the ligues went to great lengths to demonstrate their electability. They did so in two ways. First, they adopted a more moderate, median voter strategy to widen their electoral appeal. Police reports, for example, cite a marked moderation in the rhetoric of the Croix de Feu and the Parti social français after 1936. The reports indicate that the Croix toned down its propaganda, banned sorties into working-class neighborhoods, and reduced the number of paramilitary parades (Passmore 1997, 260; Machefer 1970, 114–15). Second, ligues sought to improve their electoral viability by forming alliances with conservative deputies. After entering electoral politics, Pierre Taittinger announced that his Jeunesses patriotes (by now the Parti républicain national et social) was seeking an electoral alliance with all center-right parties (Pinol 1992, 309). In 1937, Doriot launched the Front de la liberté, which encompassed all center-right parties except the Parti social français. Doriot's aim was to increase his party's credibility by coordinating the selection of only one conservative candidate per district (Burrin 1986, 282; Passmore 1997, 291). In 1937, the Parti social français formed an electoral alliance with conservative politicians for regional elections in the Rhône department. The results were a bitter disappointment. The Parti social français failed to win a single seat, in part because its candidates were selected in mostly working-class districts (Passmore 1997, 291).

The initial reluctance to enter electoral politics, subsequent ideological moderation, and alliance efforts demonstrate that high levels of strategic voting required a drastic break with the old movement strategy. Soucy astutely observed that "rather than democracy succumbing to the Jeunesses patriotes, the Jeunesses patriotes succumbed to democracy" (1986, 210). This observation holds for all ligues. In short, *strategic voting in France required the ligues to pool their policies to accommodate diverse but geographically concentrated interests.* Such pooling, in turn, exacted a high political price by increasing internal dissent and threatening organizational cohesion and collective discipline to a far greater extent than among German paramilitary groups.

France's runoff ballot further reduced the payoffs of an electoral strategy by giving conservative politicians an opportunity to obstruct the election of fascist candidates. Threatened by the better-organized ligues, conservatives commonly refused to cooperate with them in coordinating the withdrawal of their candidates. In the Third Republic, it was common for center-right candidates to withdraw in favor of their highest-scoring first-round candidate and openly endorse him. Conservatives intentionally did not extend such cooperation to fascist candidates in order to split their votes and obstruct their election prospects (Müller 1980, 482; Quellien 1986, 308; Irvine 1979, 139–42; Passmore 1997, 291). The ligues, in turn, sought to woo conservatives by making themselves politically less threatening. Taittinger, for example, claimed that his Jeunesses patriotes did not intend to challenge the Union républicain démocratique but simply aimed to recruit new members for the right. To underline his sincerity, he promised to field candidates only in constituencies where the URD had no effective organizations (Müller 1980, 482). The Union, however, was far from reassured and rejected Taittinger's all too transparent overture.

Weimar's large district magnitude, national adjustment seats, and apparentement minimized strategic voting and thereby increased the pay-off of an electoral strategy. Weimar voters consequently could vote their preferences without having to discount them with their choices' probability of winning. This possibility for sincere voting allowed right-wing groups to enter electoral politics without moderating their policies or forming alliances.

Unlike Taittinger or La Rocque, Hitler did not have to adopt a moderate median voter strategy or form electoral alliances after his 1928 electoral entry. Instead, he continued with his extremist niche strategy that targeted the same extremist constituency that had followed him during his movement days. The elements of this strategy hardly changed. He continued to emphasize extra-rational elements such as anticommunism, *völkisch* themes, antidemocracy, hypernationalism, and antisemitism. This emotionally charged platform had the dual purpose of mobilizing already radicalized voters as well as radicalizing new potential swing voters. Hitler used these issues for what electoral students nowadays call wedge issues or herestethical devices. The tactical objective of such issues was to politicize new issues that would drive a wedge into existing political loyalties and thereby create newly available swing voters. Put differently, wedge issues served to manipulate the issue space and move it closer to the Nazis' ideal point (Riker 1990). Furthermore, Hitler's defection from the Harzburg Front illustrates the viability of a go-it-alone strategy. The Front was the initiative of the Stahlhelme to coordinate in 1929 the nationalist opposition in a referendum against the Young Plan. Unlike in France, conservatives in the DNVP wanted to extend the Harzburg Front to the electoral arena. Yet the low level of strategic voting minimized Hitler's need to boost his electoral viability and therefore made it easy for him to terminate his cooperation with the Front.

The NSDAP's continued radicalism and uncompromising go-it-alone strategy were instrumental in minimizing internal dissent. The large district magnitude, national adjustment seats, and apparentement permitted pooling of geographically dispersed interests and reduced the number of groups to which the NSDAP had to appeal. And by pooling voters, it did not have to pool policies by adopting a moderate median voter strategy. Not having to comprise political principles in turn minimized the risk of internal dissent. As a result, critics of Hitler's electoral strategy found it difficult to accuse Hitler of selling out and did not pose a threat to the NSDAP's organizational cohesion (Orlow 1969, 204). The limited organizational costs the NSDAP paid for its electoral entry proved important in the long run because it permitted Hitler to capitalize on the new opportunities that arose with the onset of the Great Depression.

The NSDAP's emotionally charged, extremist issues defined its macrostrategy. This macrostrategy, however, did little to differentiate the NSDAP from other right-wing groups. Ultimately, what set the NSDAP apart from its nationalist competitors was a finely honed microstrategy that starting in 1930 directly targeted the material concerns of voters. Nazis, for example, appealed to small shopkeepers or farmers by opposing foreclosures or demanding higher taxes on department stores or agricultural imports (Richter 1986, 116; Brustein 1996). These appeals promised to each group whatever it wanted to hear regardless of whether the various promises were compatible. Frequently the promises that were part of the microstrategy conflicted, yet the NSDAP's credibility did not suffer from such contradictions. The NSDAP had such an unrivaled logistical capacity that it could compartmentalize the delivery of its microcampaign messages to the point where various constituencies were not aware of any overall contradictions (Richter 1986, 117). This accomplishment owed much to Goebbels's Reichspropagandaleitung, which could gather information about voters' specific concerns and then target campaign promises exclusively to its intended audience (Mühlberger 1986, 85; Childers 1985, 234–35). This logistical accomplishment might explain why Nazis could mobilize voters with divergent material interests and did not have to rely exclusively on shared extra-rational, extremist preferences. It sheds light on Brustein's finding that the NSDAP's electoral appeal cannot be reduced to the irrational issues but also rested on its responsiveness to voters' material self-interest (Brustein and Falter 1994; Brustein 1996).

A final but slightly different illustration of Weimar's permissive electoral procedures can be found in the 1924 alliance between the NSDAP and the Deutschvölkische Freiheitspartei. At the time, the NSDAP still was a Bavarian-based, little-known paramilitary group that was three years away from fully committing itself to electoral politics. The decision to form this alliance can be interpreted as an effort to stabilize an organization that was on the verge of disintegrating while Hitler was imprisoned. Unlike the Harzburg Front, the Freiheitspartei had little potential for co-opting the NSDAP. Its organization was concentrated in northern Germany, where the NSDAP had no presence, and its virulent nationalism and antisemitism made it ideologically highly compatible. Ultimately, the feasibility of this strategy largely rested on Weimar's apparentement provision and national adjustment seats (Falter, Lindenberger, and Schuman 1986, 43). Without these two electoral mechanisms, the NSDAP would have won 7 instead of 14 seats in the May election and 2 instead of 4 seats in the December election (*Statistisches Jahrbuch* 1924, 390–92). These two pooling mechanisms thus doubled the NSDAP's parliamentary representation without exacting any moderation in its electoral appeal and increased risk of internal dissent.

Career Uncertainty

Military adventurism, anticommunist hysteria, and, in Germany, irredentism sustained the early movement strategy of French and German fascists. Over the long run, however, the expressive benefits provided by the pursuit of such goals lost their mobilizing potential. Such psychological benefits also proved insufficient to attract people more adept in organizational matters than in street brawls. Orlow notes that by 1927 Hitler had "given up all hope of becoming the German Mussolini." What he now needed was "able administrators of election campaigns and membership activities, not organizers of terror" (1969, 120). An electoral strategy promised tangible career benefits that could help recruit more skilled political activists. The magnitude of these benefits depended on the career uncertainty faced by new prospective recruits. Party leaders could reduce career uncertainty by such coordination mechanisms as seniority, loyalty, or quotas to regularize the recruitment of candidates (Cox 1997, 151–72). But their capacity to do so depended on institutional constraints (Epstein et al. 1997, 969–71; Canon 1990, 6–8). The more electoral mechanisms could reduce career uncertainty, the stronger the career incentives became for cadre members and the less inclined they would be to criticize their leaders. In short, the more fascist leaders could do for the careers of their subalterns, the less likely the leaders would see their authority challenged. Three electoral mechanisms affected career uncertainty: the district magnitude, vote-pooling mechanisms, and ballot structure.

The Third Republic's small district magnitude provided ligues with little opportunity to reduce the career uncertainty and regularize the recruitment of prospective candidates. This lack of opportunity explains why cadres in the ligues had such weak incentives to support an electoral strategy. It also accounts for the limited capacity of movement leaders to discipline factions opposing any greater electoral involvement. Table 4 illustrates this limited disciplining capacity by summarizing the switching of factions between various ligues. It dates the exit and entry of such switches.

These numerous exits and entries of different factions underline the ligues' limited organizational cohesion. There even are reasons to believe that table 4 underestimates the fragmentation by only focusing on factions. The table does not report the actions of local branches which frequently broke away in protest over strategy changes undertaken by the national leadership (Passmore 1997, 215).

The ligues' limited ability to control candidate recruitment also permitted their parliamentary sympathizers to hedge their affiliations. Many conservative deputies were fully-paid-up members of ligues. In 1936, the Croix de Feu counted 8 to 12 conservative deputies as its members, while the Jeunesses patriotes had 12 of its members sitting with various center-right parliamentary groups (Irvine 1979, 129–30; Kergoat 1986, 181). These members used their dual memberships in conservative parties and ligues to secure the latter's electioneering services and to hedge their bets in case the ligues managed to become a large party. They treated the membership in the ligues merely as an insurance policy. The ligues could do little to change this hedging strategy as long as they had so little control over the recruitment of candidates. It therefore is hardly surprising that they frequently advocated the introduction of proportional representation even though it would have significantly increased the parliamentary strength of communists (Passmore 1997, 226).

TABLE 4.   Movement Switching in France

Movement (founding year)	Faction Exit (year)	Faction Entry (year)
Faisceau (Nov. 1925)[a]	AF (late 1926)	AF (1925), Légion (1925)
Croix de Feu (1928)	VN (1935)	—
Jeunesses patriotes (1924)	Légion (1925); L. d. P. (1926); Phalangeards (1929); SF (1933)	—
Parti populaire français (1936)	JP, AF, VN, Neo-socialistes, Francistes (1937–38)	JP, AF, VN, PSC, Neo-socialistes, Francistes (1936)

Source: Irvine (1979, 106); Burrin (1986, 283, 304–5); Machefer (1974, 15–16); Soucy (1986, 57, 92–101; 1995, 59–60); Jankowski (1989, 60); Goodfellow (1992, 162).

Legend: AF: Action française; L. d. P.: Ligue des patriotes; JP: Jeunesses patriotes, PSC: Parti socialist-communiste (Sabiani); SF: Solidarité française; VN: Volontiers nationaux.

[a]Founding year.

Weimar's large district magnitude, categoric ballot structure, and national adjustment seats, on the other hand, significantly reduced career uncertainty and gave party leaders considerable control over candidate recruitment. The NSDAP leadership masterfully used the centralizing and hierarchical effect created by these electoral mechanisms to minimize opposition to electoral strategy.

The NSDAP's executive organ, the Reichsleitung, deliberately employed the ranking and multiple listing of candidates to strategically reduce the career uncertainty of its upper-echelon cadres. Senior party leaders or *Gauleiter,* for example, all were placed on the national and regional lists that awarded adjustment seats. These lists virtually guaranteed election even during the party's limited popularity in the late 1920s. For good measure, upper-echelon cadres also were placed at the top of district lists. Middle-echelon cadres, in turn, received the remaining places on the district lists. Incumbents as a rule were automatically reselected (Orlow 1969, 126, 183, 266–67). This high career certainty provided a powerful incentive for the Nazis' cadres to support Hitler's adoption of an electoral strategy after 1928.

In a more selective manner, Hitler used candidate recruitment in two additional ways. In the late 1920s, when the NSDAP's electoral support was still weak, Hitler tried to form electoral alliances in some Länder elections. He tried to win the endorsements of the Stahlhelme and Wehrwölfe by offering their leaders safe list positions (Tracey 1975, 35–36). Furthermore, he tried to appease internal dissent coming from the SA by placing its leaders at the top of district lists (Orlow 1969, 126–27).

The ability to reduce career uncertainty also gave Hitler a formidable disciplining lever. He and his closest advisors personally controlled the nomination, selection, and ranking of candidates. Regional *Gauleiter* would compile lists according to strict criteria set by the Reichsleitung. One such criterion, for example, prohibited the selection of recent joiners of the NSDAP. The preliminary lists were then sent to Munich, where the Reichsleitung usually revised them. These revisions frequently concentrated on removing candidates who already held a paid party job. The objective of this exercise was to increase the number of individuals who were financially dependent on the Reichsleitung (Orlow 1969, 83, 123, 266–67). Given this ironclad control, the few complaints ever voiced over the candidate recruitment failed miserably. The leader of the SA, Pfeffer, wanted more safe seats for his storm troopers. As an ostensible reason, he cited the need for income and free travel so that the SA could more effectively carry out its propaganda activities. Hitler flatly refused his request and forced Pfeffer to resign (Orlow 1969, 210–11).

Electioneering Costs

The paramilitary origins of French and German fascists explain their preference for strong leaders, national and centralized logistical infrastructures, and disciplined mass memberships. The war experience led them to link hierarchy to efficiency and thereby increased their impatience with the deliberation and slowness of the democratic process (Machefer 1974, 6). "Fascists eschewed elite politics in favor of mass mobilization. They, like their Marxist enemies, formed genuinely popular movements adept at the politics in the streets, at home with mass rallies" (Irvine 1991, 295). The compatibility of this mass mobilizational and military-like organizational model with electoral politics constituted an important factor for the payoffs that right-wing groups could expect from an electoral strategy. An important element in determining this compatibility was the electioneering costs. Generally, high electioneering costs pose an entry barrier for new parties. In the case of fascists, however, high electioneering costs provided distinct benefits that encouraged the adoption of an electoral strategy. Paramilitary groups differed from most start-up parties because they already had a centralized logistical infrastructure and a large membership before entering electoral politics. With their high sunken organizational costs, they were less deterred by high electioneering costs than other new electoral entrants or contemporary social movements, which lacked an organizationally well integrated membership. Rather than being a deterrent for electoral entry, high electioneering costs allowed paramilitary groups to capitalize on their existing logistical infrastructure in two ways. First, high electioneering costs increase the benefits of an electoral strategy by giving fascists an organizational advantage over their principal competitor, conservative notables. Resource-intensive elections significantly reduce the effectiveness of the personal vote and private social networks on which conservative politicians traditionally relied. Second, high electioneering costs increase the compatibility between the movement's organization and the logistical exigencies of electoral politics. High electioneering costs consequently require few organizational changes and preserve the authority of fascist leaders. The electoral mechanism most directly affecting electioneering costs is the physical district size. It creates distinct logistical exigencies that determine how readily right-wing groups can capitalize on their existing organizational resources.

France's modest electioneering costs limited the payoffs that ligues could expect from their organizational infrastructure. Their national and centralized organizations were not readily compatible with the logistical exigencies of 600 very small and diverse electoral districts. The ligues' repeated tirades against the existing electoral system reflect this incompatibility. For the most part, however, the ligues tried to mask this difficulty with organizational bravado. At his party's first congress, Doriot declared that "the only thing that counted was that the men of the Parti populaire française spread the same position at exactly the same moment, in every corner of France" (Wolf 1967, 143). Not to be outdone, the Croix de Feu referred to its activists as "apostles" advancing the party's "crusade" (Irvine 1991, 283). Such brave pronouncements, however, did little to alter the existing institutional constraints. The ligues' leaders refused to adapt their national organizations to the electoral exigencies of France's small districts because the costs in loss of discipline and organizational cohesion would simply have been too high. La Roque, for example, discouraged too much local activism and initiative out of fear that this would lead to the establishment of autonomous local power centers (Passmore 1997, 259). Quellien also reports that in the Calvados department, ligues had a weak organizational presence. They instead relied on the Centre de la propagande to put them in contact with local party branches seeking their electioneering services (Quellien 1986, 301). In the Parti populaire français, the only two functioning local party branches were Doriot's own political bases in St. Denis and Sabiani's political machine in Marseilles (Jankowski 1989, 44–60; Wolf 1967, 100–101).

Furthermore, the Third Republic's low electioneering costs protected the effectiveness of the old-style notable politics and thereby diminished the ligues' logistical advantage over conservative politicians. The Calvados region, for example, experienced a severe agricultural crisis in the 1930s that radicalized the peasantry. Because of its national organization, the Croix de Feu was constrained from politically exploiting this situation. To counter its "urban" and national image, it had to form an alliance with the local Front paysan and yield the district to local candidates, who had a much better chance of winning than national ones belonging to the Croix (Quellien 1986, 329–31). The small district magnitude, in other words, required ligues to adopt the very notable style of politics that they despised so much.

Weimar's large physical district size, on the other hand, created logistical exigencies that were highly compatible with the NSDAP's paramilitary organization. It allowed the NSDAP to capitalize on the existing organization by entering electoral politics. The NSDAP required only minor organizational modifications after 1928. The most visible change was the redrawing of the *Gau* boundaries along those of electoral districts, which required a doubling of *Gau* organizations. In France, a similar restructuring would have involved a far greater degree of decentralization (Orlow 1969, 121). The NSDAP's electoral machine also required few changes. The SA continued to provide the foot soldiers for protecting rallies, distributing leaflets, and keeping the upper hand in the postering wars with the left. While maintaining its own organization, the SA received its instructions from the newly created Reichspropagandaleitung. The Reichspropagandaleitung with Goebbels at the helm established a formidable information-gathering network and was in charge of devising political campaigns (Mühlberger 1986, 72–74; Orlow 1969, 82; Childers 1986b, 234–35).

Furthermore, Weimar's high electioneering costs increased the economies of scale the NSDAP's national organization could provide. The NSDAP managed to centralize many of the resources required for campaigning. It established a central speaking school, leadership training camp, office for procuring and distributing campaign material, and national film service. The film center distributed straightforward propaganda as well as *Heimatfilme,* whose *völkisch* kitsch was a favorite at more informal party soirees (Orlow 1969, 159–60). The NSDAP's centralized organization also facilitated the raising of money through sales of party paraphernalia like armbands, boots, brass knuckles, and, not surprisingly, first-aid kits. The NSDAP even arranged franchise agreements for the sale of "Sturm" (charge) cigarettes and margarine with the incongruous name "Kampf" (battle) (Turner 1984, 116–18).

These economies of scale and organizational compatibility minimized the need for organizational adjustments. Hitler hardly paid an organizational price for his electoral strategy and kept tight control over the NSDAP. He personally appointed and dismissed each *Gauleiter* as well as a business manager who ran the local branches' finances on behalf of the national Reichsleitung (Orlow 1969, 82).

The high electioneering costs also amplified the logistical advantage the NSDAP had over conservative politicians. By 1928, this advantage was no longer so striking, as the DNVP had managed to build a fairly effective party organization. It played, however, an important role in the

NSDAP's successful mobilization of rural voters. These voters were organizationally far less firmly integrated than urban voters and thus more readily available. Weimar's large physical district size had undermined the personal reputations through which notables once could lay claim to farmers' political loyalties. The agricultural groups like the Vereinigung der deutsch-christlichen Bauernvereine (Association of German-Christian Farmers' Organizations), Deutsche Bauernschaft (German Peasantry), and above all the Reichslandbund (Agrarian League) lost considerable credibility staying above party politics and doing little to protect farmers from the collapse of agricultural prices in the early 1930s (Gies 1967, 357–58). The political support of farmers therefore was available to whichever party could solve the logistical difficulties of campaigning in the countryside. The geographic isolation and poor transportation made it difficult for farmers to attend political rallies. The NSDAP used its extensive cadre of disciplined activists to mobilize farm voters (Orlow 1969, 130; Gies 1967, 352–53).

Conclusion: The Capacity and Limitations of Institutions

The previous chapters demonstrated the far-reaching impact that electoral mechanisms have on the risk taking and entrepreneurialism of politicians. The constraints that these mechanisms create for the recruitment process, resource mobilization, and electioneering played a crucial role in determining how swiftly French and German politicians responded to their ever changing political environments. In short, the preceding pages concentrated on the capacity of institutions to shape party politics and consequently insufficiently addressed their limitations. More particularly, two questions have received inadequate attention. First, the analysis so far primarily underscored the systematic effects of institutions and consequently placed less emphasis on history, how it limits institutional effects and how it interacts with institutions. This issue requires attention since the introduction argued for an interdisciplinary approach that combines institutional theory with political history. Second, the previous chapters remained focused on electoral institutions and how they shaped electoral and pre-electoral activities of individual parties. They consequently did not fully specify how these specific electoral institutions and activities are related to the two countries' overall democratic performance. These concluding remarks address these two issues in order to get a fuller understanding about the capacity and limitations of institutions.

Institutions and History

The chapters on the individual parties were biased in favor of institutional factors. Being arranged as cross-national, pairwise comparisons, they varied institutions and held contextual factors constant. This may have given the impression that historical contingencies did not matter and provided few opportunities to analyze how these contingencies interact with institutions. The arrangement of the previous chapters, therefore, left unaddressed the stated theoretical objective of following especially historical institutionalists in reflecting more self-consciously about the interaction between institutional and contextual factors (Thelen and Steinmo 1992; Pierson 1996). I pursue this objective in two ways. First, I shift the analysis from the previous cross-national, ideological pairing of parties to two national, cross-party comparisons. Such a reconfiguration of cases amounts to a most different research design in which contextual factors vary while institutional ones remain constant. Second, I parse the explanatory variable into its three principal institutional effects—strategic voting, career uncertainty, and electioneering costs—to see whether they varied across the distinct contexts of national parties.[1]

National, Cross-Party Comparison

Previous chapters already referred to the importance of historical, noninstitutional factors. The chapter on conservative parties, for example, pointed out that the defections from the URD and DNVP solely were the combined result of long-standing factional disputes and the agricultural crisis. Similarly, the tremendous innovativeness of the NSDAP and the French ligues primarily was attributable to their status as political latecomers lacking a well-established voting constituency. In neither of these examples did institutions play an important role.

One way to assess the impact of such contextual factors relative to institutional ones is to compare parties within each country and see whether their political support varied significantly over time. The idea is to use the variance of parties' support as a proxy measure for assessing whether highly variable factors (i.e., history) or invariant ones (i.e., institutions) determine their electoral performance. Considerable variance in the continuity of parties' electoral support would indicate that changeable, historical circumstances were the principal determinant of political success. Specifically, it would mean that postwar inflation, mass unemployment, or agricultural crises were three very distinct sets of historical circumstances that determined the electoral support of liberals, socialists, and conservatives at very different rates. Conversely, little variance across the parties' electoral support or a gradual decline would serve as evidence that electoral institutions constitute the principal determinant of political success. Specifically, it would indicate that electoral mechanisms requiring a high degree of entrepreneurialism induce politicians to adapt so quickly to whatever political circumstances exist that their political strength will fluctuate only marginally over time. Electoral mechanisms, in turn, that fail to induce political innovation should make all parties equally inert and contribute to comparable rates in electoral decline.

Table 5 measures the variance of parties' political strength by comparing their first and last interwar election results. It supports the contention that history matters since neither did *all* French parties retain their level of support nor did *all* German parties lose votes at the same rate. In the Third Republic, the SFIO and the Parti radical performed well, the former gaining 13.6 percent of the legislative seats and the latter keeping its seat share constant. The URD, in turn, lost 15 percent of its parliamentary strength, and the ligues failed in translating their mass support into legislative representation. In Weimar, the SPD maintained its strength. Its 18 percent loss largely turns out to be an artifact of a one-time electoral surge in 1919 and obscures the SPD's otherwise very stable support after 1920. The DNVP experienced losses that were even bigger than the 1.6 percent indicated in table 5. The losses rise to 14 percent if we compare the DNVP's best election results in the mid-1920s with its electoral strength at the end of the Weimar Republic. The DDP and DVP experienced massive voter defections from the mid-1920s onward, which eventually benefited the NSDAP. The varying rates at which French parties retained support and German parties lost votes cannot be explained in institutional terms since these various national parties operated under identical electoral procedures. It thus strongly suggests that contextual, historical factors must have played a key role.

We can only speculate about which specific historical contingencies had an impact and how strong it was. The poor showing of the URD and

TABLE 5.   **Stability of Parliamentary Strength**

	First Election	Last Election	Difference
SFIO	10.9%	24.5%	+13.6%
Radicals	17.2%	17.9%	−0.7%
URD	27.9%	12.9%	−15%
Ligues	0%	0%	0%
SPD	38.7%	20.7%	−18%
DDP	17.8%	0.3%	−17.5%
DVP	4.5%	1.9%	−2.6%
DNVP	10.5%	8.9%	−1.6%
NSDAP	0%	33.6%	+33.6%

Note: Figures for Germany's last election based on 1932 election.

DNVP, for example, can be attributed to their origins as notable parties and the resulting organizational deficit. This made them more vulnerable to the logistical challenges of mass politics regardless of what institutional framework they operated under. Or it is conceivable that the agricultural crisis affected conservatives more adversely than the Great Depression did socialists. One possible reason would be that the agricultural crisis not only alienated traditional rural voters but also decimated agricultural associations that provided conservatives with crucial logistical support. Communist parties provide another example for the importance of contextual factors. As members of the Third International, both the PCF and KPD based their actions almost exclusively on the directives they received from Moscow. This highly particularistic historical characteristic of Communists made them equally impervious to national contextual factors as well as institutional constraints.

Similar conjectures could be undertaken for other parties. But they would be pointless, since our objective is not to estimate how much historical contingencies affected party performance. The goal instead is to show that the systematic institutional effects are too weak to displace the non-systematic, contextual effects. The national differences in party performance serve as a useful reminder that institutions shape rather than cause political behavior and therefore have to be configured with noninstitutional factors. Duverger put it more elegantly when he pointed out that institutions are not the engine of politics but merely its brakes and accelerators (Duverger 1951, 292).

Parsing the Explanatory Variable

If the previous section underscored the importance of history, the parsing of the institutional variable is meant to shed light on how institutions interact with history. Electoral institutions can be parsed into their three principal effects—strategic voting, career uncertainty, and electioneering costs. Such parsing permits varying of both national contextual factors and electoral procedures. It allows us to evaluate the constancy of various institutional effects and thus assess whether different electoral mechanisms vary in their susceptibility to historical circumstances.[2] Comparing the constancy of institutional effects ultimately permits a few general insights into the conditions under which institutions and context interact more or less closely.

Strategic voting had a consistent effect across parties in both countries. Regardless of their different contexts, all French parties responded very similarly to the high level of strategic voting, just as German parties did to the low level of strategic voting. Strategic voting seemed barely affected by the historical background conditions that varied across national parties. The effects of career uncertainty were almost as consistent as those of strategic voting. It had clearly discernible effects on socialist, liberal, and fascist parties since they all had an institutionalized candidate recruitment process. Career uncertainty had no discernible effect on conservative parties because they lacked formalized candidate recruitment. Finally, electioneering costs had the most inconsistent effect, reflecting the very different logistical endowments of parties. Again, it had no discernible effect on conservative parties, which is not surprising given their ready access to wealthy donors and distinct contracting-out model. Electioneering costs had a limited effect on socialist and fascist parties, whose extensive mass mobilizational organization partly shielded them from the costs imposed by electoral mechanisms. It had the most dramatic effect on liberal parties, which lacked the capacity to mobilize either a large number of activists or wealthy contributors.

The parsing of the explanatory variable not only reconfirms that history matters but adds the insight that the influence of historical contingencies varies with different institutions. This raises the question of what differences among institutions could account for the stronger or weaker influence of history. One answer that I find highly suggestive has been provided by Douglas Rae and Maurice Duverger, who differentiate between institutions that have proximate, psychological effects and others that have distal, sociological ones (Duverger 1951, 315–16; Rae 1967, 134–45). They argue that the latter have effects that are far more indeterminate than the former. In our analysis, strategic voting provides the clearest example of institutions with proximate effects. In framing the winning prospects of parties, it creates opportunities and constraints with clear costs and benefits that actors can readily and unambiguously calculate ex ante. The effects of strategic voting are discrete, direct, and therefore more consistent across parties than those of career uncertainty and especially of electioneering costs. What warrants characterizing these proximate effects as psychological is that they are unfiltered by socioeconomic or historical factors and impact directly on actors' decision making. There is a causal and chronological proximity between the district magnitude's mechanical/mathematical property (i.e., number of available seats) and the psychological dimension of actors' decision making (i.e., avoidance of vote wasting). More generally, such causal proximity increases the confidence that observed institutional effects are nonspurious and hence reduces the need to consider historically contingent factors.

By contrast, electioneering costs and to a lesser extent career uncertainty furnish illustrations of institutions with distal effects. Their consequences are indeterminate, diffuse, and difficult to assess ex ante. For example, it is not easy for parties to differentiate the organizational costs created by the physical district size from those imposed by mass politics. Moreover, the consequences of the organizational costs depend on how readily parties can mobilize resources. In short, historical and sociological factors intercede between the mechanical properties of the physical district size (i.e., costs of electioneering and ongoing operating expenses) and the organizational choices of parties. This causal distance increases the level of institutional indeterminacy. It also explains why the effects of electioneering costs were far less consistent across parties than the other two institutional effects.

This difference between proximate/psychological and distal/sociological effects of electoral institutions sheds interesting light on debates among different institutional approaches. These debates frequently seem more driven by a priori philosophical convictions about the power and limitations of theory than by reflection about how much theory might be appropriate for a particular subject matter. Yet if we look more closely at the different institutional approaches, we can see that their theoretical rigor is more a reflection of the type of institutions they study than the epistemological positions they espouse. The more positivist approaches are rational choice institutionalism, social choice theory, and economic (transaction-cost) institutionalism. They tend to focus on institutions with arguably proximate effects such as voting procedures, legislatures, courts, bureaucracies, regulatory agencies, or any other set of institutions that impact directly and unambiguously on the strategic calculations of actors. The less positivistic approaches, on the other hand, comprise historical institutionalism, comparative political economy, state formation, sociological institutionalism, and constitutionalism. They tend to study institutions with distal effects such as economic institutions (e.g., capital markets, industrial relations), international trade or security regimes, constitutional arrangements, civil-military relations, or any other set of institutions that diffusely and indirectly influences the strategic calculations of actors (Hall and Taylor 1996; Goodin 1996). The differentiation between proximate and distal institutional effects thus could help to refocus the debate from abstract philosophical principles to the more practical question of how much theoretical parsimony and contextual detail are appropriate for analyzing a particular set of institutions.

Institutions and Democracy

Chapters 3 to 6 focused on the electoral and pre-electoral activities of individual parties and demonstrated how voting procedures structured them. The specific focus of these chapters raises the question of their relevance for overall understanding of French and German political history. In other words, how significant is the connection between electoral politics and the overall functioning of democracies? Nonelectoral institutions such as executive-legislative relations, parliamentary procedures, federalism, referenda, or judicial independence also constrain the actions of parties. Moreover, the formation of coalition governments, the legislative decision making, and policy implementation by bureaucrats constitute nonelectoral venues of politics that certainly affect a country's overall political performance. This book's inattention to these nonelectoral institutions and legislative policy-making limits, without preempting, our ability to link our findings to the overall political fortunes of French and German democracy. The strength of the connection between electoral politics and overall democratic performance can be ascertained in two ways: by looking at comparable studies in other countries and by shifting the focus from individual parties to entire party systems.

Comparable studies in other countries emphasize the importance of electoral politics and the organizational characteristics of parties for the overall functioning of democracy. Students of contemporary U.S., Latin American, European, and Japanese politics stress how centrally politicians' legislative conduct is shaped by their electoral considerations. They also point out that the organizational characteristics of parties have a profound impact on policy-making and the overall functioning of democracies (Mayhew 1974; McCubbins and Rosenbluth 1995; Geddes 1994; Ames 1995; Mainwaring 1991). In short, the comparative evidence points to a strong connection between electoral and high politics.

Shifting the focus from individual parties to party systems provides another opportunity for demonstrating the wider importance of electoral politics. This shift is premised on two assumptions. First, the performance of individual parties taken together produces aggregate party-systemic effects (e.g., polarization, fragmentation, volatility) that are observable independently of parties' individual actions. We therefore can investigate to what extent the previously explained actions of individual parties can account for the aggregate characteristics of French and German party systems. Second, the characteristics of party systems are more closely linked to the overall performance of a democracy than the electoral behavior of individual parties. Scholars studying party systems have long equated democratic stability with the attributes of party systems (Sartori 1976; Bartolini and Mair 1990; Downs 1957; Dahl 1966; Powell 1982; Lijphart 1994). The literature on party systems, therefore, allows us to evaluate whether the effects of electoral mechanisms, which we demonstrated for individual parties, also have systematic, cumulative effects at the level of party systems. It allows us to evaluate whether the effects of voting procedures extend beyond the electoral arena.

Electoral mechanisms provide the key explanation for the three differences in the French and German party systems that we discussed in the introduction. The French party system was characterized by considerable continuity, with its established parties retaining in 1939 88.2 percent of the seats they won in 1918. The German party system, in turn, was highly unstable, with established parties maintaining only 44.2 percent of their original strength. The French party system also avoided polarization, with only 5.1 percent of votes going to extremist parties. In Weimar after 1929, extremist parties like the Nazis, the KPD, and the DNVP under Hugenberg won 54.4 percent of the votes. Finally, France's highly fragmented party system was characterized by fluid factionalism, compared to Weimar's impermeable segmentation. It will be remembered that the French and German party systems did not differ in all their characteristics. Compared to other countries, they experienced unusually high levels of fragmentation and volatility. With respect to the differences between the two party systems, the question remains how well they can be explained in terms of how voting procedures structured the electoral and pre-electoral activities of parties.

France's political moderation, stable party system, and fluid factionalism owed much to the innovation induced by its double ballot.[3] As previous chapters demonstrated, this innovation was the consequence of high career uncertainty, which increased turnover of party leaders and made candidate recruitment competitive; it was the result of the low electioneering costs, which limited the ability of interest groups to undermine the policy-making autonomy of politicians; and it owed much to strategic voting, which maximized the electoral leverage of voters. In short, the double ballot made it exceedingly difficult for French politicians to rest on their laurels. It provided them with a reprieve from constant competition in only one way, by creating formidable entry barriers for new start-up parties. The overall effect of the double ballot system therefore was to make competition among and within established parties, rather than the displacement of old, inert parties by new, entrepreneurial ones, the primary mechanism for translating social into political change. It is this overall competitive effect that helps explain the stability of the French party system, its moderation, and fluid factionalism.

The double ballot stabilized the French party system by simultaneously requiring established parties to change continuously while shielding them from start-up parties. The competition among and within established parties assured that changing voter preferences would be represented quickly enough to preempt political opportunities for new parties. Unlike Weimar, the Third Republic witnessed few start-up parties. The most important one was the Catholic Parti démocrate populaire, which successfully tried to capitalize on the URD's intransigent nationalism and lackluster opposition to the Cartel's anticlerical measures (Bourgin et al. 1928, 84–90). As chapters 5 and 6 demonstrate, even when an opportunity arose in the 1930s for the ligues and agricultural protest movements, the high entry barriers protected the stability of the party system.

The double ballot system also preempted the translation of France's social polarization into political polarization. The high level of strategic voting constrained Marin's attempt to exploit anti-German sentiments with an intransigent national course; marginalized the SFIO's revolutionary factions seeking to radicalize workers; contributed to the repeated defection of PCF factions rejecting their party's ideological orthodoxy; and required the ligues to moderate as they sought to enter electoral politics. The double ballot contained political polarization by doing more than just constraining extremist politicians. It also limited the electoral appeal of such politicians by minimizing voter alienation. It did so by assuring that the SFIO, Radicals, and URD defectors innovated sufficiently to offer voters electoral choices that were meaningful enough to avoid their defection to extremist parties. France's high volatility rate provides circumstantial evidence for this interpretation. It indicates that voters were sufficiently dissatisfied to frequently switch parties. But the poor showing of extremist parties suggests established parties offered alternatives that were palatable enough to accommodate such dissatisfied swing voters.

Finally, the double ballot contributed to France's fluid factionalism, thus mitigating the worst consequences of its high level of fragmentation. The need to coordinate withdrawals for runoff elections directly led to the formation of the Bloc national, Union nationale, Cartel des gauches, and Front populaire. The cooperation involved in such electoral alliances exerted an important countervailing effect on the rigid segmentation of the French party landscape. Moreover, the double ballot made it difficult for party leaders to enforce party discipline. This weak party discipline certainly was an important contributing factor to the Third Republic's high level of party fragmentation. But it is important to recall that it facilitated not only defections but also party switching, thus making France's fragmentation more fluid. In chapter 5, we saw that Marin had so little control over candidate recruitment that he was largely powerless to prevent defections from the URD, just as the leaders of the Alliance démocratique could do little to prevent these defectors from joining their ranks. Weak party discipline blurred party lines even more in the legislative arena, where deputies regularly defied party whips and voted across party lines. Ultimately, the weak party discipline made it easier for French politicians to place strictly electoral concerns above the ideological vituperations of party leaders that contributed to the segmentation of German parties. The Third Republic's fragmentation was more like intraparty factional disputes than the organizational manifestation of deeply rooted and divisive social conflicts. Wileman (1988, 14–15) captures the fluidity of France's fragmentation well. "When all the differences of opinion which some political systems resolve inside parties are taken into account, the French system seems no more complex than the various Anglo-Saxon ones. . . . But the profusion of parties . . . have encouraged historians . . . not to take the Third Republic seriously, not to see it being capable of serious progress or reform."

Weimar's polarization, unstable party system, and rigid segmentation, in turn, are closely related to the lack of innovative incentives created by its PR system. This risk aversion was the consequence of low career uncertainty, which limited turnover of party leaders and discouraged the competitive recruitment of candidates; it was the result of high electioneering costs, which facilitated the efforts of economic interest groups to co-opt the parties' agenda setting; and it owed much to low strategic voting, which limited the leverage of voters. Weimar's electoral procedures thus decoupled career ambitions from voters and party members to such an extent that inert politicians faced few immediate political costs. Electoral institutions prevented inertia of politicians in only one way, by facilitating the entry of new parties. The overall effect of the PR system therefore was to make party displacement rather than competition the central mechanism for translating social into political change. Party displacement proved a far less efficient mechanism than competition for accommodating change and consequently contributed to the instability of the Weimar party system, its polarization, and rigid segmentation.

The PR system contributed to the discontinuity of Weimar's party system by providing few incentives for incumbents to continuously adapt to the preferences of voters while simultaneously creating low entry barriers for new parties. It allowed, for example, the SPD to make programmatic choices that were more in accordance with static ideological principles than dynamic electoral expediencies. It prevented bourgeois politicians from swiftly adopting the latest electioneering techniques. And even when parties like the DDP and DVP wanted to formulate more attractive platforms, they were vetoed by their financial backers. This inertia of incumbent parties was the major driving force behind the proliferation of start-up parties. This dynamic was most evident in the bourgeois camp, where in the late 1920s small economic interest parties, regional parties, and peasant parties attracted many DDP, DVP, and DNVP voters. By the 1930s, in turn, these particularistic parties had been largely displaced by the surging NSDAP. Thus, the failure of Weimar's incumbent parties to change resulted in the changing of the party system.

The PR system did little to constrain politicians from exploiting economic grievances for narrow partisan ends and thereby contributing to a swift translation of social into political polarization. Nazis, Communists, and the DNVP under Hugenberg faced few constraints in using the Great Depression to radicalize public opinion. The absence of strategic voting freed these parties from having to pursue a centripetal, median voter strategy. Instead, they could concentrate on a small, radicalized voter segment and try to convert additional voters by politicizing them into partisans. The PR system contributed to polarization in other ways. Party displacement so inefficiently accommodated social change that it contributed to voter alienation. The various small special interest parties to which disgruntled bourgeois voters first flocked had a very short life span. Many of them succumbed to the same inertia afflicting incumbent parties. In effect, these particularistic parties ended up serving as one-time protest vehicles, leaving behind deeply alienated voters more willing than ever to support more radical alternatives.

Finally, the PR system aggravated the effects of Weimar's high fragmentation by turning it into rigid segmentation. Unlike the double ballot, it provided no incentives for forming electoral alliances and hence did not encourage cross-party cooperation. The PR system instead encouraged a go-it-alone strategy. Cooperation on the left was unlikely given the KPD's strict adherence to Moscow's directives and memories of Ebert's repression of the Spartacist uprising in 1918. On the right, Hugenberg succeeded in temporarily uniting the antirepublican forces in the Harzburg Front and the referenda against the Young Plan. But his hope to extend this cooperation into the electoral arena was bitterly disappointed with the quick unraveling of the Front. Even small parties, which had the strongest incentives to cooperate, did not form alliances. The absence of any collaboration did not require politicians to temper their mutual criticisms. Election campaigns therefore were more likely to vilify opponents and thereby strengthen existing political cleavages and obstruct legislative work. Additionally, the PR system contributed to Weimar's segmentation by discouraging party switching and allowing interest groups to veto alliances. By increasing party discipline, the PR system discouraged party defections as well as party switching. As a result, Weimar deputies defecting from a party or being expelled found it difficult to join other parties and ended up forming their own. Chapter 5 illustrated that this was the precise situation faced by deputies leaving the DNVP. Moreover, by increasing the parties' dependence on interest groups, the PR system indirectly allowed these groups to block alliances they deemed a threat to their interests. This is how German big business stopped the DDP's attempts to cooperate with the SPD on various social and economic programs.

This analysis demonstrated that overall characteristics of party systems such as stability, polarization, and type of fragmentation are clearly linked to the actions of individual parties and the institutional constraints under which they operate. The close link between the actions of individual parties and the aggregate characteristics of party systems therefore provides strong evidence that voting procedures affected more than just the pre-electoral and electoral activities. So, while electoral politics might have been a subplot in French and German history, it certainly was much more than a political sideshow. The close link between actions of individual parties and the dynamics of party systems also supports the book's central contention that the innovative incentives created by electoral institutions are central for the proper functioning of democracy. Over the course of our analysis, we encountered reasons to assume that institutions and innovation are especially important in the consolidation of new democracies.

The first chapter documented the entrepreneurial reluctance of French and German politicians. To borrow Margaret Anderson's metaphor (2000), these politicians were still "practicing democracy" regardless of whether or not they accepted it. The principal training ground for democracy was electoral politics. Its institutionally circumscribed ground rules were central in determining how quickly politicians would advance from democratic apprentices to skillful craftsmen mastering the strategic game of competitive politics. The electoral rules became the principal external check on the internal, psychological inertia of politicians and thus played a central role in pressuring politicians to become risk-taking and innovative entrepreneurs. Institutional incentives ultimately determined how quickly political actors were tricked, lured, and cajoled into behaving as genuine agents of voter interests.

More generally, the link between institutions and innovation helps to reconcile the very different assessments that early students of parties like Max Weber, Moisei Ostrogorski, and Robert Michels and later scholars like E. E. Schattschneider, Joseph Schumpeter, Maurice Duverger, and Giovanni Sartori rendered about the impact of parties on democracy. It may be recalled that the first generation of scholars viewed parties as bureaucratic behemoths endangering democracy while the latter generation considered them as entrepreneurial vote-getting machines advancing democracy. This book demonstrated that both generations of scholars were correct. It did so by showing that Germany's bureaucratic, risk-averse parties weakened the Weimar Republic whereas France's more entrepreneurial parties helped preserve the Third Republic. The book thus more generally underscored their conclusion that innovation matters for democracy. It went one step further, however, by showing that institutional incentives determined the innovativeness of parties. It therefore did not have to draw an equally stark conclusion reached by each generation of scholars that parties are either antithetical or integral to democracy. By pointing to institutions, the book revealed that it is not existence or nonexistence of parties that matters but the type of party and the institutional incentives to be innovative and take risks.

Notes

Introduction

1. It is impossible to list all the relevant works. I found particularly insightful Berstein (1980, 1982), Irvine (1979, 1989), Judt (1986), Sirinelli (1992), Childers (1986a), Diehl (1977), Harsch (1993), Jones (1988), Nipperdey (1961), and Schorske (1955).

2. There are two types of macrohistorical explanations. The cross-national ones are mostly written by social scientists. They include Moore (1966); Rueschemeyer, Stephens, and Stephens (1992); Luebbert (1991); and Shefter (1994). National histories, in turn, have been written by sociologists like Dahrendorf (1967) and Lepsius (1973), and most frequently by historians like Blackbourn and Eley (1984); Gerschenkron (1943); Hoffman (1963); Rosanvallon (1992); and Wright (1995). Generally speaking, the historians are more differentiated than social scientists and therefore commit fewer of the above-listed fallacies.

3. Particularly interesting in this respect is the evolution of Hans-Ulrich Wehler's work. He has been and continues to be the most prominent advocate of Germany's baleful exceptionality. His most recent work, while still adhering to the *Sonderweg* position, has significantly softened his position on a number of fronts. For example, he dropped his earlier claim about Germany's organized capitalism, primacy of *Innenpolitik,* and Bonapartism. Interestingly enough, these were the claims that held up least well to the comparisons undertaken by some of his critics (Wehler 1995, vol. 3).

4. The rationale and implications for omitting the Catholic Zentrum are elaborated below. The two countries' Communist parties are excluded because they followed so closely the directives they received from the Third International in Moscow. They consequently remained impervious to national contextual factors as well as the institutional constraints on which this analysis focuses.

5. Before the Laakso-Taagepera index, political scientists expressed fragmentation simply by counting the number of parties and adding ad hoc descriptive qualifications (e.g., one party dominant, two and a half parties, etc.). The Laakso-Taagepera index has the advantage of simultaneously measuring the number of parties as well as their relative electoral size $N_{v(\text{otes})}$ or parliamentary strength $N_{s(\text{eats})}$. The calculations here are based on the parties' parliamentary weight. For the exact formula, see Taagepera and Shugart (1989, 78–79).

6. *Breakaways* (*n*:14): Parti communiste français (1920); Parti communiste unitaire (1929); Kommunistische Partei-Opposition (1929, Alsace); Parti ouvrier et

paysan (1929); Parti socialiste ouvrier-paysan (1937); Parti socialiste français (1919); Parti socialiste de France—Union Jean Jaurès (1933); Parti Camille Pelletan (also Parti Radical-Socialist Camille Pelletan) (1934); Parti frontiste/Front commun (1933); Gauche radical (1924); Fédération radical nationale/Républicains nationaux (1920); Centre démocratique (1932); Indépendents républicains et sociale (1932); Parti republican agraire et sociale (1936).

Start-up parties (*n*:5): Jeune république (n/a); Parti républicaine de reorganisation nationale (1919); Parti démocrate populaire (1924); Parti agraire et paysans français (1928); Parti social français/Croix de Feu (1936).

Counting rule: party has to have won at least one seat. (Sources: various)

7. *Breakaways* (*n*:8): Kommunistische Partei Deutschlands (1919); KPD-Opposition* (1928); Sozialistische Arbeiterpartei Deutschlands* (1931); Deutsch-völkische Freiheitspartei* (1922); Christlich-Nationale Bauern- und Landvolkpartei (1928); Bayerische Volkspartei (1919); Christlicher Volkspartei (1920); Konservative Volkspartei* (1929). [* indicates expulsion]

Start-ups (*n*:8): Jungdeutscher Orden (1930); Sächsisches Landvolk (1928); Polenpartei (1922); Wirtschaftspartei (1925); Volksrechtspartei (1926); Christlich-Sozialer Volksdienst (1929); Landbund (1921); NSDAP (1920).

Counting rule: party has to have won at least one seat. (Falter, Lindenberger, and Schuman 1986)

8. King, Keohane, and Verba implicitly confirm Tarrow's criticism by failing to elaborate on the quote's considerable implications.

9. Arguably, the best-known exceptionalist explanation is the German *Sonderweg* debate, which Daniel J. Goldhagen's recent *Hitler's Willing Executioners* fanned anew. Similar, albeit less acrimonious, debates can be found in British, French, and especially U.S. history.

10. I owe the idea for such configurational analysis to Ira Katznelson.

11. The prolonged dispute over the Duverger law is instructive in this respect. See Sartori (1986) and Riker (1986). For an important recent effort to move beyond this reductionism, see Cox (1997).

12. I owe many thanks to Margaret Anderson for pushing me to address this nettlesome omission and trying to work through its implications.

Chapter 1

1. There is a certain difficulty dating France's introduction of universal (male), free, and fair elections. The Second French Republic first introduced universal male suffrage in 1848 but two years later added a strict three-year residency requirement that disenfranchised most industrial and migrant farm workers (equal to about one-third of France's nine million eligible voters). The residency requirement was revoked in 1851. Furthermore, the Second Empire fielded "official candidates" and assured their election by using government to logistically support its candidates, obstruct its opponents, and manipulate the electoral process. The first genuinely free and universal (male) elections thus took place in 1870. Universal male suffrage in Germany already existed in the North German Federation in 1867

but was extended nationally only after German unification (Huard 1991, 54–55; McPhee 1992, 197–98; Zeldin 1958; Kreuzer 1996).

2. The SFIO only emerged in 1904, from various earlier socialist formations. For simplicity's sake, I will talk about the SFIO when referring to the general development of French socialists from the 1870s onward.

3. In 1891, German socialists changed their name from Socialist Worker's Party to German Social Democratic Party. This name change was meant to indicate a symbolic shift from a class-based to a more universalistic political party. For simplicity, I refer to German socialists prior to 1891 also as SPD.

4. The Reichstag had the right to debate and assent to all bills. The unelected Bundesrat also had to assent to laws (Suval 1985, 32; Craig 1978). It is frequently overlooked that Article 23 of the imperial constitution gave the Reichstag the opportunity to introduce bills. The one thing that the Reichstag could not do was to select or dismiss governments (Anderson, pers. comm.).

5. This differentiation is widely missing in explanations of the European socialist parties. See, for example, Przeworski (1985).

6. The Dreyfus affair culminated between 1898, when Zola wrote "J'accuse," and 1899, when Dreyfus received a presidential pardon. It actually began in 1894 with Dreyfus's conviction and ended in 1906 with his acquittal in a new trial.

7. Curiously enough, political scientists and sociologists have been far more persistent and unanimous than historians in subscribing to exceptionalist interpretations of French and German liberalism (Gerschenkron 1962; Moore 1966; Dahrendorf 1967; Lepsius 1973; Luebbert 1991; Rueschemeyer, Stephens and Stephens 1992). Social scientists pay little attention to how historians have modified these traditional interpretations in recent years. For France, the work by Eugen Weber (1976) has called into question the degree to which France's Great Revolution (1789) actually politicized the countryside and has pushed the onset of popular politics (outside urban and some central settings) to the last decades of the nineteenth century. For the debate Weber's work stimulated, see McPhee (1992) and Weber (1991). For Germany, a wealth of monographs in the last two decades—on regions, on parties, and on classes—have done much to undercut the determinism of the traditional explanations. Even Hans-Ulrich Wehler (1987, 2:774, 776–79), the strongest contemporary advocate of the German *Sonderweg* thesis, has retreated somewhat from his earlier interpretations. He no longer argues about the distinctness of Germany's organized capitalism, the weakening of liberals by the defeat of the 1848 Revolution, and Bismarck's manipulation of deferential voters. Others have gone considerably further and cut the cord between the deficiencies of the Empire and of the Weimar Republic (Anderson 2000, chap. 12; Peukert 1989).

8. The question of whether French liberalism is distinct from other European liberal traditions has been debated with reference to its ideological or socioeconomic characteristics. This debate has been rather inconclusive. I therefore will treat the Parti radical as the rough equivalent of the German liberal parties and eschew a more nuanced differentiation between them. The term *liberal* consequently will be reserved for those political currents and formations from which the

Parti radical finally emerged in 1901. Differentiations are attempted in Hudemann (1988) and Krumeich (1988).

9. Goguel (1946, 34–36) also identifies a distinct radical formation before 1901.

10. The most important ones were the Comité Mascuraud and the Société nationale d'encouragement à l'agriculture (Bardonnet 1960, 228–42, 250–60).

11. The circulation of such inexpensive newspapers rose dramatically, from one million in 1870 to five million in 1890 (Fitch 1992, 59–61).

12. This party broke in turn into its two constituent groups, which formed the Freisinnige Volkspartei and the Freisinnige Vereinigung. They reunited in 1910 in the Fortschrittliche Volkspartei (Sheehan 1978, 191–93).

13. Between 1903 and 1910, Nauman's efforts were concentrated in the Freisinnige Vereinigung and were continued after 1910 in the Fortschrittliche Volkspartei (Sheehan 1978, 265–69).

14. Margaret Anderson points out that the financial burden of public office holding excluded 99 percent of the Prussian population. To overcome this financial obstacle, parties used income from wealthier districts to subsidize office holders from poorer ones. This subsidization across districts "pushed activists toward forming continuous statewide party organizations and led to the greater and greater centralization of fundraising efforts" (Anderson 2000, 348).

15. Margaret Anderson, private communication.

Chapter 2

1. I follow here the European usage of selection and nomination, which differs from the American labeling (Ranney 1968, 141–42).

2. The work on credible commitments draws from the larger economic literature on organization (Moe 1980; North and Weingast 1989).

3. The Third Republic's extremely small physical district size is partly explained by France's late introduction of female suffrage in 1945. By comparison, Britain's districts averaged for 1918–38 42,000 registered voters (Mackie and Rose 1991; Lachapelle, various years).

4. Such voting pacts also occur in regular plurality systems even though they never take on the same importance as in double ballot systems.

5. *Apparentement* is the French word for electoral alliance. Since this feature has been prominently used in France, the literature has adopted the French term. For the various different alliance possibilities, see Cox (1997, 60–62).

6. I classified as large parties DNVP, DVP, Zentrum, KPD, and SPD. All others (except NSDAP) were counted as small (*Statistisches Jahrbuch für das deutsche Reich*, various years).

Chapter 3

1. Some historians have qualified Michels's iron law of oligarchy, which he formulated in 1915. Nipperdey, for example, points out that Michels exaggerated the SPD's organizational ossification by evaluating its governance against a highly

participatory conception of democracy. His critique of social democracy also was influenced by syndicalism, to which he became exposed when teaching and lecturing in France (Nipperdey 1961, 334, 389–90; Schorske 1955, 116–45; Buse 1990; Mitzman 1987, 282–310).

2. Lindeman (1974, 73, 22–25), for example, attributes this stunning defeat (3,208 voted yes, 1,002 voted no) to two factors. First, he makes much of the ability of Frossard and Chochin (the SFIO's two delegates to and ardent advocates of the Third International) and Loriot's Comité pour la Troisième internationale to convince the party's membership. Yet he also claims that delegates seemed less concerned about the issue of joining the Third International and more intent on expressing their disaffection with the leadership's support for the war and growing control over party affairs.

3. Unfortunately, no reliable figures could be found for the size of the prewar bureaucracy. Nipperdey (1961, 327) reports 100 salaried employees in all the district organizations in 1913. He does not mention the figures for regional and national organizations.

4. Prior to 1918, the SPD's regional organization corresponded to the pre-1914 administrative districts (*Regierungsbezirke*), which also formed the basis for the post-1918 electoral districts. So the SPD already had an organizational presence prior to 1914 where the new Weimar electoral system would require one. What the new PR system did, however, was to vastly increase the importance of the regional districts and diminish that of local district associations (Hunt 1964, 46–48).

5. Figures for new deputies have been calculated as the percentage of the total elected deputies. Sources: Schwarz (1965); Jolly (1960–72); Lachapelle (1919–36).

6. This calculation is based on those districts where SFIO and Radicals came in second or lower on the first ballot. In 170 (70.5 percent) of these districts, the SFIO's candidates withdrew, and in 69 (29.5 percent) they refused to withdraw. The figures for the Radicals are 88 (53 percent) and 78 (47 percent) respectively. The SFIO was the largest party in 196 districts (157 for Radicals) after the first ballot and did not contest 67 districts (244 for Radicals). In 67 districts (4 for Radicals), there was no runoff because one party obtained an absolute majority on the first ballot (Lachapelle 1936).

7. The Front united, besides the SPD, the Reichsbanner, the ADGB, the Allgemeiner freier Angestelltenbund, the Allgemeiner Beamtenbund, and the Arbeiter Turn- und Sportverband. It failed, however, in its objective to also include other bourgeois, republican organizations (Schaefer 1990, 311–13).

8. The SPD adopted a modern campaign style at the national level for the first time in the 1933 election (its functionaries decried it as Americanization) (Schaefer 1990, 338–44, 352).

Chapter 4

1. Turner (1984) further argues that German historiography generally overestimates the organizational cohesion of big business.

Chapter 5

1. The URD is the direct successor to the Fédération républicaine. The traditional French right generally was so loosely organized that certain of its political formations have until today eluded scholarly analysis. I consequently confine myself to the URD, which is the largest, most cohesive, and only well-researched French conservative party. The Alliance démocratique, for example, has received no scholarly attention except for a dissertation (Wileman 1988).

2. The internal politics contributing to the various defections were too Byzantine to be recounted here. I therefore limit myself at this point to strict chronology of the various defections. I will add more details whenever the analysis requires it.

DNVP's defection chronology. Before the May 26, 1929, election, three DNVP deputies left the party to form the Christlich-Nationale Bauern- und Landvolkpartei (CNBLP). Three months after the election, they were joined by 10 more DNVP defectors. In December 1929, a group of 12 deputies led by Gottfried Treviranus left the DNVP. Shortly before September 1930, a faction of 29 deputies led by Martin Schiele and Count Kuno Westarp broke with Hugenberg. The last two defecting groups either joined the CNBLP or the newly founded, smaller, and even more short-lived Konservative Volkspartei (Wende 1981; Jones 1988).

URD's defection chronology. Between the 1928 and 1932 elections, 10 URD deputies switched in 1930 to the Alliance démocratique, six did in 1931, and five in 1932. Eighteen more deputies left the URD in 1932, forming the so-called Groupe Pernot, which closely aligned itself with the Alliance (Bomier-Landowski 1951, 83–85; *Journal officiel,* various years).

3. The loss of 36 seats does not count the three defections the DNVP experienced before the 1928 election.

4. The Parti démocrate populaire emerged after the 1924 election to defend Catholic interests against the anticlerical legislation of the Cartel. It adopted a Christian democratic platform and never succeeded in winning more than 8 to 10 seats (Delbreil 1990).

5. The Parti frontiste was founded in 1937 by Bergery on a nationalist and leftist political agenda; it elected two deputies in 1936. Bergery increasingly moved rightward and eventually became a sympathizer of Doriot's Parti populaire français (Burrin 1986, 225–27).

6. The Landvolk*bewegung* was concentrated in Schleswig-Holstein and should not be confused with the Landvolk*partei,* whose full name was the Christlich-Nationale Bauern- und Landvolkpartei (Christian-National Peasants' and Farmers' Party). The latter emerged from the conservative Reichslandbund.

Chapter 6

1. This post hoc, ergo prompter hoc fallacy is strikingly reflected in historical research. German historiography on the far right concentrates almost exclusively on the NSDAP, while French research consists of a motley collection of single movement or regional studies.

Conclusion

1. These two methodological modifications are not meant to evaluate how much contextual factors bias institutional regularities. Such a course of action is not feasible. We saw that the interwar historical contingencies varied with each party: conservatives facing the agricultural crisis, liberals grappling with inflation, socialists confronting fascism and mass unemployment, and paramilitary groups dealing with political stability. These contexts simply are too different and idiosyncratic to be conceptualized as meaningful variables within a given country. In other words, the party-specific contexts are so varied that it is impossible to analyze how much party innovation was induced by the agricultural crisis compared to, say, inflation. The noncomparability of different contexts thus prevents inquiring how much variance in party innovation they explain compared to institutions. The two methodological modifications have a more limited purpose. They are meant to provide different angles for analyzing how contextual factors modify and interact with institutions. It follows the rationale of mechanism-based explanations of not measuring "the strength . . . of the relationship between the entities of interest but to address a further and deeper problem: how (i.e., through what process) was the relationship brought about?" (Hedström and Swedberg 1998b, 10).

2. The parsing has to be limited to institutional variables. It cannot be extended to contextual factors since they are too varied and contingent. The introduction discusses this unsystematic nature of contextual factors in greater detail.

3. The following institutional and choice-theoretic explanation differs from the ones commonly provided by the party system literature. This literature attributes the aggregate characteristics of party systems to societal cleavage structures, systemic imperatives of the party system itself, or the strategic interaction among parties (Bartolini and Mair 1990; Sartori 1976).

Bibliography

Note: Works specific to France and Germany follow the section on General Works.

General Works

Aldrich, John. 1995. *Why Parties? The Origins and Transformation of Party Politics in America.* Chicago: University of Chicago Press.

Ames, Barry. 1995. "Electoral Strategy under Open-List Proportional Representation." *American Journal of Political Science* 39, no. 2: 406–33.

Amy, Douglas. 1993. *Real Choices/New Voices.* New York: Columbia University Press.

Barry, Brian. 1970. *Sociologists, Economists, and Democracy.* Chicago: University of Chicago Press.

Bartolini, Stefano. 1984. "Institutional Constraints and Party Competition in the French Party System." *West European Politics* 7: 103–27.

Bartolini, Stefano, and Peter Mair. 1990. *Identity, Competition, and Electoral Availability.* Cambridge: Cambridge University Press.

Beer, Samuel. 1982. *Britain against Herself: The Political Contradictions of Collectivism.* New York: Norton.

Black, Gordon. 1972. "A Theory of Political Ambition: Career Choices and the Role of Structural Incentives." *American Political Science Review* 66 (March): 144–59.

Burnham, Walter Dean. 1994. "Pattern Recognition and 'Doing' Political History: Art, Science, or Bootless Enterprise." In *The Dynamics of American Politics,* edited by Lawrence Dodd and Calvin Jillson, 59–82. Boulder: Westview.

Cain, Bruce, John Ferejohn, and Morris Fiorina. 1987. *The Personal Vote: Constituency Service and Electoral Independence.* Cambridge: Harvard University Press.

Canon, David. 1990. *Actors, Athletes, and Astronauts: Political Amateurs in the United States Congress.* Chicago: University of Chicago Press.

Carey, John, and Matthew Soberg Shugart. 1996. "Incentives to Cultivate a Personal Vote: A Rank Ordering of Electoral Formulas." *Electoral Studies* 14, no. 1 (January): 417–39.

Clark, Peter, and J. Q. Wilson. 1961. "Incentive Systems." *Administrative Science Quarterly* 6, no. 2 (September): 129–66.

Cohen, Morris. 1947. *The Meaning of Human History.* LaSalle: Open Court.

Cohen, Youssef. 1994. *Radicals, Reformers, and Reactionaries.* Chicago: University of Chicago Press.

Collier, Ruth Berins, and David Collier. 1991. *Shaping the Political Arena: Critical Junctures, the Labor Movement, and Regime Dynamics in Latin America.* Princeton: Princeton University Press.

Cox, Gary. 1987. *The Efficiency Secret.* Cambridge: Cambridge University Press.

———. 1990. "Centripedal and Centerfugal Incentives in Electoral Systems." *American Journal of Political Science* 34, no. 4 (November) 903–35.

———. 1997. *Making Votes Count: Strategic Coordination in the World's Electoral Systems.* Cambridge: Cambridge University Press.

Cox, Gary, and Mathew McCubbins. 1993. *Legislative Leviathan: Party Government in the House.* Berkeley: University of California Press.

Curtis, Gerald. 1971. *Electoral Campaigning Japanese Style.* New York: Columbia University Press.

Dahl, Robert. 1966. "Patterns of Opposition." In *Political Oppositions in Western Democracies,* edited by Robert Dahl, 332–48. New Haven: Yale University Press.

Downs, Anthony. 1957. *An Economic Theory of Democracy.* New York: Harper and Row.

Duverger, Maurice. 1951. *Les Partis politiques.* Paris: Armand Colin.

Eggertsson, T. 1990. *Economic Behavior and Institutions.* Cambridge: Cambridge University Press.

Elster, Jon. 1983. *Explaining Technical Change.* Cambridge: Cambridge University Press.

———. 1989a. *The Cement of Society.* Cambridge: Cambridge University Press.

———. 1989b. *Nuts and Bolts for the Social Sciences.* Cambridge: Cambridge University Press.

Epstein, David, David Brady, Sadafumi Kawato, and Sharyn O'Halloran. 1997. "A Comparative Approach to Legislative Organization: Careerism and Seniority in the United States and Japan." *American Journal of Political Science* 41, no. 3 (July): 965–88.

Epstein, Leon. [1967] 1980. *Political Parties in Western Democracies.* New Brunswick, N.J.: Transaction Books.

Ferejohn, John. 1991. "Rationality and Interpretation." In *The Economic Approach to Politics,* edited by Kirsten Renwick Monroe, 279–305. New York: HarperCollins.

Fisichella, Domenico. 1984. "The Double Ballot System as a Weapon against Anti-system Parties." In *Choosing an Electoral System,* edited by Arend Lijphart and Bernard Grofman, 181–85. New York: Praeger.

Fowler, Linda. 1994. "Political Entrepreneurs, Governing Processes, and Political Change." In *New Perspectives on American Politics,* edited by Lawrence Dodd and Calvin Jillson, 291–310. Washington, D.C.: C. Q. Press.

Geddes, Barbara, 1994. *Politician's Dilemma: Building State Capacity in Latin America.* Berkeley: University of California Press.

Gerschenkron, Alexander. 1962. *Economic Backwardness in Historical Perspective.* Cambridge: Harvard University Press.

Goodin, Robert. 1996. "Institutions and Their Design." In *The Theory of Institutional Design,* edited by Robert Goodin, 1–51. Cambridge: Cambridge University Press.

Granovetter, Mark. 1985. "Economic Action and Social Structure: The Problem of Embeddedness." *American Journal of Sociology* 91, no. 3 (November): 483–87.

Hall, Peter, and Rosemary Taylor. 1996. "Political Science and the Three New Institutionalisms." *Political Studies* 44:936–57.

Hardin, Russell. 1982. *Collective Action.* Baltimore: Johns Hopkins University Press.

Hedström, Peter, and Richard Swedberg, eds. 1998a. *Social Mechanisms: An Analytical Approach to Social Theory.* Cambridge: Cambridge University Press.

Hedström, Peter, and Richard Swedberg. 1998b. "Social Mechanisms: An Introductory Essay." In *Social Mechanisms: An Analytical Approach to Social Theory,* edited by Peter Hedström and Richard Swedberg, 1–31. Cambridge: Cambridge University Press.

Hermens, F. A. 1941. *Democracy or Anarchy? A Study of Proportional Representation.* South Bend, Ind.: University of Notre Dame Press.

Immergut, Ellen. 1992. "The Rules of the Game: The Logic of Health Policy-Making in France, Switzerland, and Sweden." In *Structuring Politics,* edited by Sven Steinmo, Kathleen Thelen, and Frank Longstreth, 57–89. Cambridge: Cambridge University Press.

Kalyvas, Stathis. 1996. *The Rise of Christian Democracy.* Ithaca: Cornell University Press.

Katz, Richard. 1980. *A Theory of Parties and Electoral Systems.* Baltimore: Johns Hopkins University Press.

———. 1986. "Intraparty Preference Voting." In *Electoral Laws and Their Political Consequences,* edited by Bernard Grofman and Arend Lijphart, 85–103. New York: Agathon Press.

Katz, Richard, and Peter Mair. 1995. "Changing Models of Party Organization and Party Democracy." *Party Politics* 1, no. 1: 5–28.

Katznelson, Ira. 1992. "The State to the Rescue? Political Science and History Reconnect." *Social Research* 59, no. 4 (winter): 719–37.

———. 1997. "Structure and Configuration in Comparative Politics." In *Comparative Politics: Rationality, Culture, and Structure,* edited by Mark Lichbach and Alan Zuckerman, 81–131. Cambridge: Cambridge University Press.

King, Gary, Robert Keohane, and Sidney Verba. 1994. *Designing Social Inquiry: Scientific Inference in Qualitative Research.* Princeton: Princeton University Press.

Kirchheimer, Otto. 1966. "The Transformation of the Western European Party Systems." In *Political Parties and Political Development,* edited by Joseph LaPalombara and Myron Weiner, 177–200. Princeton: Princeton University Press.

Kiser, Edgar. 1996. "The Revival of Narrative in Historical Sociology: What Rational Choice Theory Can Contribute." *Politics and Society* 24, no. 3 (September): 249–71.

Kreuzer, Marcus. 1998. "Electoral Institutions, Political Organization, and Party Development: French and German Socialists and Mass Politics." *Comparative Politics* 30, no. 3 (April): 273–92.

———. 1999. "Money, Votes, and Political Leverage: Explaining the Electoral Performance of Liberals in Interwar France and Germany." *Social Science History* 23, no. 2 (summer): 211–40.

———. 2000. "Electoral Mechanisms and Electioneering Incentives: Vote-Getting Strategies of Japanese, French, British, German, and Austrian Conservatives." *Party Politics* 6, no. 4: 487–504.

Leibholz, Gerhard. 1951. "Die verfassungsrechliche Stellung und innere Ordnung der Parteien." In *Verhandlungen des 38 deutschen Juristentages,* edited by Ständige Deputation des deutschen Juristentages, C2–C43. Tübingen: Mohr.

———. 1967. "Die Grundlagen des modernen Wahlrechts [1931]." In *Strukturprobleme der modernen Demokratie.* Karlsruhe: C. F. Müller.

Levi, Margaret. 1981. "The Predatory Theory of Rule." *Politics and Society* 10, no. 4: 431–65.

Lichbach, Mark. 1997. "Social Theory and Comparative Politics." In *Comparative Politics: Rationality, Culture, & Structure,* edited by Mark. I. Lichbach and Alan Zuckerman, 239–76. Cambridge: Cambridge University Press.

Lijphart, Arend. 1990. "The Political Consequences of Electoral Laws." *American Political Science Review* 84, no. 2 (June): 481–96.

———. 1994. *Electoral Systems and Party Systems: A Study of Twenty-seven Democracies, 1945–1990.* Oxford: Oxford University Press.

Lipset, Seymour Martin. 1983. "Radicalism or Reformism: The Sources of Working-Class Politics." *American Political Science Review* 77, no. 1 (March): 1–18.

Lipset, Seymour M., and Stein Rokkan. 1967. "Cleavage Structures, Party Systems, and Voter Alignment: An Introduction." In *Party Systems and Voter Alignments,* edited by Seymour M. Lipset and Stein Rokkan, 1–64. New York: Free Press.

Luebbert, Gregory. 1991. *Liberalism, Fascism, or Social Democracy.* New York: Oxford University Press.

Mackie, Thomas, and Richard Rose. 1991. *The International Almanac of Electoral History.* Washington, D.C.: Congressional Quarterly.

Maier, Charles. 1975. *Recasting Bourgeois Europe: Stabilization in France, Germany, and Italy in the Decade after World War I.* Princeton: Princeton University Press.

———. 1987. *In Search of Stability.* Cambridge: Cambridge University Press.

Mainwaring, Scott. 1991. "Politicians, Parties, and Electoral Systems." *Comparative Politics* 24, no. 1 (October): 21–43.

Mainwaring, Scott, and Timothy Scully, eds. 1995. *Building Democratic Institutions: Party Systems in Latin America.* Stanford: Stanford University Press.

Mann, Michael. 1995. "Sources of Variation in Working-Class Movements in Twentieth Century Europe." *New Left Review,* no. 212 (July/August): 15–52.

March, James, and Johan Olsen. 1984. "The New Institutionalism." *American Political Science Review* 78, no. 3 (September): 734–49.

Mayhew, David., 1974. *Congress: The Electoral Connection.* New Haven: Yale University Press.

McCubbins, Mathew, and Frances Rosenbluth. 1995. "Party Provision for Personal Politics: Dividing the Vote in Japan." In *Structure and Policy in Japan and the United States,* edited by Peter Cowhey and Mathew McCubbins, 35–55. Cambridge: Cambridge University Press.

McDonald, Terrence J., ed. 1996. *The Historic Turn in the Human Sciences.* Ann Arbor: University of Michigan Press.

Michels, Robert. [1915] 1959. *Political Parties.* New York: Dover.

Moe, Terry. 1980. *The Organization of Interests.* Chicago: University of Chicago Press.

Monroe, Kristen R. 1991. "The Theory of Rational Action." In *The Economic Approach to Politics,* edited by Kristen R. Monroe, 1–52. New York: Harper-Collins.

Moore, Barrington. 1966. *The Social Origins of Dictatorship and Democracy.* Boston: Beacon Hill.

Morlok, Martin. 1990. "Die Innere Ordnung der Parteien." In *Parteienrecht im europäischen Vergleich,* edited by Dimitris Tsatsos, Dian Schefold, and H.-P Schneider, 304–35. Baden-Baden: NOMOS.

North, Douglass. 1990. *Institutions, Institutional Change, and Economic Performance.* Cambridge: Cambridge University Press.

North, Douglass, and Barry Weingast. 1989. "Constitutions and Commitment: The Evolution of Institutions Governing Public Choice in Seventeenth-Century England." *Journal of Economic History* 44, no. 4 (December): 803–32.

Offe, Claus. 1990. "Reflections on the Institutional Self-Transformation of Movement Politics: A Tentative Stage Model." In *Challenging the Political Order,* edited by Russell Dalton and Manfred Kuechler, 232–50. New York: Oxford University Press.

Olson, Mancur. 1965. *The Logic of Collective Action.* Cambridge: Harvard University Press.

Pierson, Paul. 1996. "The Path to European Integration: A Historical Institutionalist Analysis." *Comparative Political Studies* 29, no. 2 (April): 123–63.

Poguntke, Thomas. 1987. "The Organization of a Participatory Party—The German Greens." *European Journal of Political Research* 15, no. 6: 609–33.

Pollock, James. 1932. *Money and Politics Abroad.* New York: Knopf.

Popkin, Samuel. 1995. "Information Shortcuts and the Reasoning Voter." In *Information, Participation, and Choice,* edited by Bernard Grofman, 17–36. Ann Arbor: University of Michigan Press.

Popper, Karl. 1988. "The Open Society and Its Enemies Revisited." *Economist,* April 23, 19–22.

Powell, Bingham. 1982. *Contemporary Democracies.* Cambridge: Harvard University Press.

Przeworski, Adam. 1985. "Social Democracy as a Historical Phenomenon." In *Capitalism and Social Democracy,* 7–46. Cambridge: Cambridge University Press.

———. 1986. "Some Problems in the Study of the Transition to Democracy." In

Transitions from Authoritarian Rule: Comparative Perspectives, edited by Guillermo O'Donnell et al., 47–63. Baltimore: Johns Hopkins University Press.

———. 1991. *Democracy and the Market.* Cambridge: Cambridge University Press.

Przeworski, Adam, and John Sprague. 1986. *Paper Stones: A History of Electoral Socialism.* Chicago: University of Chicago Press.

Przeworski, Adam, and Henry Teune. 1970. *The Logic of Comparative Social Inquiry.* New York: John Wiley.

Quattrone, G. A., and A. Tversky. 1988. "Contrasting Rational and Psychological Analyses of Political Choice." *American Political Science Review* 82, no. 3 (September): 719–36.

Rae, Douglas. 1967. *The Political Consequences of Electoral Laws.* New Haven: Yale University Press.

Ragin, Charles. 1992. "Introduction: Cases of 'What Is a Case?'" In *What Is a Case?* 1–15. Cambridge: Cambridge University Press.

Ranney, Austin. 1968. "Candidate Selection and Party Cohesion in Britain and the United States." In *Approaches to the Study of Party Organization,* edited by William Crotty, 139–57. Boston: Allyn and Bacon.

Renwick Monroe, Kirsten. 1991. "The Theory of Rational Action." In *The Economic Approach to Politics,* edited by Kirsten Renwick Monroe, 1–32. New York: HarperCollins.

Riker, William. 1986. "Duverger's Law Revisited." In *Electoral Laws and Their Political Consequences,* edited by Bernard Grofman and Arend Lijphart, 19–43. New York: Agathon Press.

———. 1990. "Heresthetic and Rhetoric in the Spatial Model." In *Advances in the Spatial Theory of Voting,* edited by James Enelow and Melvin Hinich, 46–63. Cambridge: Cambridge University Press.

Rokkan, Stein. 1966. "Electoral Mobilization, Party Competition, and National Integration." In *Political Parties and Political Development,* edited by Joseph LaPalombara and Myron Weiner, 241–67. Princeton: Princeton University Press.

———. 1968. "The Structuring of Mass Politics in Smaller European Democracies." *Comparative Studies in Society and History* 10, no. 2 (January): 173–210.

Rueschemeyer, Dietrich, Evelyne Huber Stephens, and John Stephens. 1992. *Capitalist Development and Democracy.* Chicago: University of Chicago Press.

Rustow, Dankwart. 1970. "Transitions to Democracy." *Comparative Politics* 2, no. 2 (January): 337–63.

Sartori, Giovanni. 1968. "Political Development and Political Engineering." In *Public Policy,* vol. 17, edited by J. D. Montgomery and Albert O. Hirschman, 261–98. Cambridge: Cambridge University Press.

———. 1969. "From the Sociology of Politics to Political Sociology." In *Politics and the Social Sciences,* edited by Seymour Martin Lipset, 65–100. New York: Oxford University Press.

———. 1976. *Parties and Party Systems.* Cambridge: Cambridge University Press.

————. 1986. "The Influence of Electoral Systems." In *Electoral Laws and Their Political Consequences,* edited by Bernard Grofman and Arend Lijphart, 43–68. New York: Agathon Press.

————. 1987. *The Theory of Democracy Revisited.* Chatham: Chatham House.

————. 1994. *Comparative Constitutional Engineering.* New York: New York University Press.

Scarrow, Susan. 1995. *Parties and Their Members: Organizing for Victory in Britain and Germany.* Oxford: Oxford University Press.

Schattschneider, E. E. [1942] 1970. *Party Government.* Westport, Conn.: Greenwood Publications.

Schlesinger, Joseph. 1975. "The Primary Goals of Political Parties: A Clarification of Positive Theory." *American Political Science Review* 69, no. 3 (September): 840–49.

————. 1984. "On the Theory of Party Organization." *Journal of Politics* 46:369–400.

Schorske, Carl. 1980. *Fin de Siècle Vienna.* New York: Vintage.

Schumpeter, Joseph. [1943] 1987. *Capitalism, Socialism, and Democracy.* London: Unwin.

Sewell, William. 1996. "Three Temporalities: Toward an Eventful Sociology." In *The Historic Turn in the Human Sciences,* edited by Terrence J. McDonald, 245–80. Ann Arbor: University of Michigan Press.

Shefter, Martin. 1994. *Political Parties and the State.* Princeton: Princeton University Press.

Shvetsova, Olga. 1998. "Assessing the Severity of the Endogeneity Problem in Institutional Selection: The Case of Eastern Europe." Paper prepared for Mid-western Political Science Association. Chicago, April 24–26.

Simmons, Beth. 1994. *Who Adjusts? Domestic Sources of Foreign Economic Policy during the Interwar Years.* Princeton: Princeton University Press.

Simon, Herbert. 1985. "Human Nature in Politics: The Dialogue between Psychology and Political Science." *American Political Science Review* 79, no. 2 (June): 293–304.

Skocpol, Theda. 1979. *States and Social Revolutions.* Cambridge: Cambridge University Press.

Soberg, Matthew, and John Carey. 1992. *Presidents and Assemblies.* Cambridge: Cambridge University Press.

Strom, Kaare. 1990. "A Behavioural Theory of Competitive Political Parties." *American Journal of Political Science* 34, no. 2 (May): 277–300.

Taagepera, Rein, and Matthew Shugart. 1989. *Seats and Votes.* New Haven: Yale University Press.

Tarrow, Sidney. 1995. "Bridging the Quantitative-Qualitative Divide in Political Science." *American Political Science Review* 89, no. 2 (June): 471–74.

Taylor, Michael. 1993. "Structure, Culture, and Action in the Explanation of Social Change." In *Politics and Rationality,* edited by William James Booth, Patrick James, and Hudson Meadwell, 89–131. Cambridge: Cambridge University Press.

Thelen, Kathleen, and Sven Steinmo. 1992. "Historical Institutionalism in Comparative Politics." In *Structuring Politics,* edited by Sven Steinmo, Kathleen Thelen, and Frank Longstreth, 1–32. Cambridge: Cambridge University Press.

Tsatsos, Dimitris, Dian Schefold, and Hans-Peter Schneider, eds. 1990. *Parteienrecht im Europäischen Vergleich.* Baden-Baden: Nomos.

Tsebelis, George. 1990. *Nested Games: Rational Choice in Comparative Politics.* Berkeley: University of California Press.

Weber, Max. 1946. "Politics as a Vocation." In *From Max Weber,* edited by H. H. Gerth and C. Wright Mills, 77–128. Oxford: Oxford University Press.

Weyland, Kurt. 1996. "Risk Taking in Latin American Economic Restructuring: Lessons from Prospect Theory." *International Studies Quarterly* 40, no. 2 (June): 29–52.

Wilson, James Q. 1973. *Political Organization.* New York: Basic Books.

Zimmerman, Ekkart. 1987. "Government Stability in Six European Countries during the World Economic Crisis of the 1930s." *European Journal of Political Research* 15:23–52.

France

Agulhon, Maurice. [1973] 1983. *The Republican Experiment, 1848–1852,* trans. Janet Lloyd. Cambridge: Cambridge University Press.

Albertini, Rudolf von. 1961. "Parteiorganisation und Parteibegriff in Frankreich, 1789–1940." *Historische Zeitschrift* 193:529–600.

Baker, D. N. 1971. "The Politics of Socialist Protest in France: The Left-Wing of the Socialist Party, 1921–39," *Journal of Modern History* 43, no. 1 (March): 2–40.

Bardonnet, Daniel. 1960. *Evolution de la structure du Parti radical.* Paris: Editions Montechretion.

Barral, Pierre. 1962. *Le Départment de l'Isère sous la Troisième république, 1870–1940.* Paris: Colin-FNSP 115.

Bergeron, Francis. 1985. *Les Droites dans la rue: Nationaux et Nationalistes sous la Troisième république.* Paris: DMM.

Bergounioux, Alain. 1983/84. "L'évolution doctrinale du socialisme français dans l'entre deux-guerres." In *L'Internationale Operaia e Socialista tra la due guerre: Annali* (Fondazione Giangiacome Feltrinelli) 23, 1158–87. Milano: Feltrinelli.

Bergounioux, Alain, and Gérard Grunberg. 1992. *Le long remords du pouvoir: Le Parti socialiste français—1905–1992.* Paris: Fayard.

Berstein, Gisèle, and Serge Berstein. 1987. *La Troisième république.* Paris: MA Edition.

Berstein, Serge. 1978. "Les conceptions du parti radical en matière politique économique exterieur." *Relations Internationales* 13 (spring): 71–89.

———. 1980. *Histoire du Parti radical.* Vol. 1. Paris: Presse de FNSP.

———. 1982. *Histoire du Parti radical.* Vol. 2. Paris: Presse de FNSP.

———. 1992. "La Ligue." In *Histoire des droites en France,* vol. 2, edited by Jean-François Sirinelli, 61–113. Paris: Gallimard.

Bomier-Landowski, Alain. 1951. "Les Groupes parlementaires de L'Assemblée nationale et de la Chambre des députes de 1871 à 1940." In *Sociologie Electorale,* edited by François Goguel and Georges Dupeux, 75–89. Paris: Fondation Nationales des Sciences Politiques.

Bouet, Aurélien. 1996. "Jacques Kayser: Un radical de gauche." *Revue d'Histoire Moderne et Contemporaine* 43, no. 1:119–36.

Bourgin, G., J. Carrère, and A. Guérin. 1928. *Manuel des partis politiques en France.*

Burns, Michael. 1984. *Rural Society and French Politics: Boulangism and the Dreyfus Affair, 1886–1900.* Princeton: Princeton University Press.

Burrin, Philippe. 1986. *La Dérive fasciste: Doriot, Déat, Bergery, 1933–45.* Paris: Editions du Seuil.

Charnay, Jean Paul. 1964. *Les Scrutins politiques en France de 1815 à 1962.* Paris: Colin-FNSP 132.

Cleary, M. C. 1989. *Peasants, Politicians, and Producers: The Organization of Agriculture in France since 1918.* Cambridge: Cambridge University Press.

Coston, Henry. 1967. *Dictionnaire de la politique française.* Paris: La Librairie française.

Cotteret, Jean Marie. 1960. *Lois électorales et inégalité de représentation en France, 1936–60.* Paris: Colin-FNSP 107.

Delbreil, Jean Claude. 1960. *Centrism et démocratie chrétienne en France: Le Parti démocratique populaires des origines au MRP (1919–44).* Paris: Publications de la Sorbonne.

Duverger, Maurice, and J. K. Seurin. 1955. "Le Statut juridique des parties politiques en France." *Annales de la Faculté de Droit de Bourdeaux* 6, no. 1: 93–115.

Fitch, Nancy. 1992. "Mass Culture, Mass Parliamentary Politics, and Modern Anti-semitism: The Dreyfus Affaire in Rural France." *American Historical Review* 97, no. 1 (February): 55–95.

Florin, Jean-Pierre. 1974. "Le Radicalism-Socialism dans le Département du Nord (1914–36)." *Revue Française de Science Politique* 24, no. 2 (April): 236–76.

Garrigou, Alain. 1992. *La Vote et la vertu: Comment les Français sont devenues électeurs.* Paris: Presse de la Fondation Nationale des Sciences Politiques.

Gerber, John. 1990. "Dissident Communist Groups in France, 1920–39." *Third Republic* 9:1–62.

Goguel, François. 1946. *La Politique des parties sous la Troisième république.* Paris: Editions du Seuil.

———. 1977. "Les Élections législatives et sénatorielles partielles." In *Edouard Daladier, Chef de gouvernement,* edited by René Remond and J. Bourdin, 45–55. Paris: Fondation Nationale des Sciences Politiques.

Goodfellow, Samuel. 1992. "Fascism in Alsace, 1918–45." Dissertation, Indiana University.

Graham, B. D. 1994. *Choice and Democratic Order: The French Socialist Party, 1937–1950.* Cambridge: Cambridge University Press.

Greene, N. 1969. *Crisis and Decline: The French Socialist Party in the Popular Front Era.* Ithaca: Cornell University Press.

Haig, Robert. 1929. *The Public Finances of Postwar France.* New York: Columbia University Press.

Haupt, Heinz-Gerhard. 1986. "Staatliche Bürokratie und Arbeiterbewegung: Zum Einfluss der Polizei auf die Konstituierung von Arbeiterbewegung und Arbeiterklasse in Deutschland und Frankreich zwischen 1848 und 1890." In *Arbeiter und Bürger im 19. Jahrhundert,* edited by Jürgen Kocka, 219–54. Munich: Oldenbourg.

Hoffman, Stanley. 1963. "Paradoxes of the French Political Community." In *In Search of France,* edited by Stanley Hoffman et al., 1–117. New York: Harper.

Huard, Raymond. 1991. *Le Suffrage universel en France, 1848–1946.* Paris: Aubier.

Hudemann, Rainer. 1988. "Politische Reform und gesellschaftlicher Status quo: Thesen zum französischen Liberalismus im 19. Jahrhundert." In *Liberalismus im 19. Jahrhundert,* edited by Dieter Langewiesche, 332–52. Göttingen: Vandenhoeck und Ruprecht.

Irvine, William. 1979. *French Conservatism in Crisis: The Republican Federation of France in the 1930s.* Baton Rouge: Louisiana State University Press.

———. 1989. *The Boulanger Affair Reconsidered.* New York: Oxford University Press.

———. 1991. "Fascism in France and the Strange Case of the Croix de Feu." *Journal of Modern History* 63, no. 2 (June): 271–95.

Jackson, Julian. 1985. *The Politics of Depression in France, 1932–36.* Cambridge: Cambridge University Press.

Jankowski, Paul. 1989. *Communism and Collaboration: Simon Saviani and Politics in Marseille, 1919–44 .* New Haven: Yale University Press.

Jeanneney, Jean-Noel. 1976. *François Wendel en République.* Paris: Editions du Seuil.

———. 1981. *L'argent cachet: Milieu d'affaires et pouvoirs politiques dans la France du XX siècle.* Paris: Fayard.

Jolly, Jean, ed. 1960–72. *Dictionnaire des parlementaires français.* Vols. 1–7. Paris: PUF.

Journal officiel de la République française. Paris, various years.

Jouvenel, Robert de. 1914. *La République des camarades.* Paris: B. Grasset.

Judt, Tony. 1976. "The French Socialists and the Cartel des Gauches of 1924." *Journal of Contemporary History* 11, nos. 2–3 (July): 199–216.

———. 1986. *Marxism and the French Left.* Oxford: Oxford University Press.

Keiger, J. K. V. 1997. *Raymond Poincaré.* Cambridge: Cambridge University Press.

Kergoat, Jacques. 1986. *La France du Front populaire.* Paris: La Découverte.

Kheitmi, Mohammed Rechid. 1964. *Les Partis politiques et le droit positif français.* Paris: Librairie Général du Droit.

Kreuzer, Marcus. 1996. "Democratization and Changing Methods of Electoral Corruption in France from 1815 to 1914." In *Political Corruption in Europe and Latin America,* edited by Walter Little and Eduardo Posada-Carbó, 97–114. London: Macmillan.

Kreuzer, Marcus, and Ina Stephan. 1999. "Frankreich: Zwischen Wahlkreishonoratioren und nationalen Technokraten." In *Politik als Beruf,* edited by Jens Borchert, 161–85. Opladen: Leske und Budrich.

Krumeich, Gerd. 1988. "Der politische Liberalismus im parlamentarischen System Frankreichs vor dem Ersten Weltkrieg." In *Liberalismus im 19. Jahrhundert,* edited by Dieter Langewiesche, 353–66. Göttingen: Vandenhoeck und Ruprecht.

Kuisel, Richard. 1967. *Ernest Mercier: A French Technocrat.* Berkeley: University of California Press.

Lachapelle, Georges. 1919, 1924, 1928, 1932, 1936. *Elections legislatives.* Paris: Georges Roustan.

Lachs, Fritz. 1927. "Parteien und Wirtschaftsverbände im modernen Frankreich." *Archiv für Politik und Geschichte* 9, no. 2:110–24.

Larmour, Peter. 1964. *The French Radical Party in the 1930s.* Stanford: Stanford University Press.

Le Béguec, Gilles. 1992. "Le parti." In *Histoire des droites en France,* vol. 2, edited by Jean-François Sirinelli, 13–59. Paris: Gallimard.

Le Béguec, Gilles, and Jacques Prévotat. 1992. "1898–1919: L'éveil à la modernité politique." In *Les Droites françaises,* edited by Jean-François Sirinelli, 383–506. Paris: Gallimard.

Levillain, Philippe. 1992. "Les Droites en République." In *Les Droites françaises,* edited by Jean-François Sirinelli, 276–382. Paris: Gallimard.

Lindeman, Albert. 1974. *The Red Years.* Berkeley: University of California Press.

Machefer, Philippe. 1970. "L'Union des droites: Le PSF et le Front de la liberté, 1936–37." *Revue d'Histoire Moderne et Contemporaine* 18 (January–March): 112–26.

———. 1974. *Ligues et fascismes en France (1919–39).* Paris: PUF.

Marcus, John T. 1958. *French Socialism in the Crisis Years, 1933–36.* New York: Praeger.

Magraw, Roger. 1992. *Workers and the Bourgeois Republic.* Oxford: Blackwell.

McPhee, Peter. 1992. *The Politics of Rural France: Political Mobilization in the French Countryside, 1846–1852.* Oxford: Clarendon Press.

Müller, Klaus Jürgen. 1980. "Protest—Modernisierung—Integration: Bemerkungen zum Problem faschistischer Phenomene in Frankreich, 1924–32." *Francia* 8:465–524.

———. 1990. "Fascism in France." In *France and Germany in an Age of Crisis, 1900–60,* edited by Hain Shamir. Leiden: E. J. Brill.

Nogaro, B. 1925. "La politique financière du Parti radical." *Revue Politique et Parlementaire,* November.

Noland, Aron. [1953] 1970. *The Founding of the French Socialist Party.* Cambridge: Harvard University Press.

Nord, Philip. 1995. *The Republican Moment: Struggles for Democracy in 19th Century France.* Cambridge: Harvard University Press.

Passmore, Kevin. 1993. "The French Third Republic: Stalemate Society or Cradle of Fascism?" *French History* 7, no. 4 (December): 417–49.

———. 1997. *From Liberalism to Fascism: The Right in a French Province, 1928–39.* Cambridge: Cambridge University Press.

Paxton, Robert. 1972. *Vichy France*. New York: Columbia University Press.

———. 1997. *French Peasant Fascism: Henry Dorgères's Greenshirts and the Crisis of French Agriculture, 1929–39*. Oxford: Oxford University Press.

Pinol, Jean-Luc. 1992. "1919–58: Le Temps des droites?" In *Histoire des droites en France,* vol. 2, edited by Jean-François Sirinelli, 291–391. Paris: Gallimard.

Quellien, Jean. 1986. *Bleus, Blancs, Rouges: Politique et elections dans le Calvados, 1870–1939*. Caen: Annales de Normandie.

Rebérioux, Madeleine. 1975. *La République radicale? 1898–1914*. Paris: Le Seuil.

Rosanvallon, Pierre. 1992. *Le Sacre du citoyen*. Paris: Gallimard.

Rousselier, Nicolas. 1992. "La Contestation du modèle républicain dans les années 30." In *Le modèle républicain,* edited by Serge Berstein and Odile Rudelle, 319–36. Paris: Presse Universitaire de France.

Russo, Henri. 1991. *The Vichy Syndrome*. Cambridge: Harvard University Press.

Saposs, David. 1931. *The Labor Movement in Postwar France*. New York: Columbia University Press.

Schlesinger, Mildred. 1974. "The Development of the Radical Party in the Third Republic: The New Radical Movement, 1926–32." *Journal of Modern History* 46:476–501.

———. 1978. "The Cartel des Gauches: Precursor of the Front Populaire." *European Studies Review* 8, no. 2 (April): 211–35.

———. 1989. "Legislative Governing Coalitions in Parliamentary Democracies: The Case of the French Third Republic." *Comparative Political Studies* 22, no. 1 (April): 33–65.

Schuker, Stephen. 1976. *The End of French Permanence in Europe: The Financial Crisis of 1924 and the Negotiation of the Dawes Plan*. Chapel Hill: University of North Carolina Press.

Sirinelli, Jean-François, ed. 1992. *Histoire des droites en France*. 3 vols. Paris: Gallimard.

Soucy, Robert. 1986. *French Fascism: The First Wave, 1924–33*. New Haven: Yale University Press.

———. 1995. *French Fascism: The Second Wave, 1933–39*. New Haven: Yale University Press.

Sternhell, Zeev. 1978. *La Droite révolutionnaire: Les origines françaises du fascisme, 1885–1914*. Paris: Seuil.

———. 1984. "Emmanuel Mounier et la contestation de la démocratie libérale dans la France des années trente." *Revue Française de Science Politique* 34, no. 6 (December): 1141–81.

———. 1986. *Neither Right nor Left: Fascist Ideology in France*. Berkeley: University of California Press.

Viple, Jean-François. 1967. *Sociologie politique de l'Allier: La Vie politique et les élections sous la Troisième république*. Paris: Pichon.

Weber, Eugen. 1976. *Peasants into Frenchmen: The Modernization of Rural France, 1870–1914*. Stanford: Stanford University Press.

———. 1991. *My France: Politics, Culture, Myth*. Cambridge: Belknap Press of Harvard University Press.

Weinreis, Hermann. 1986. *Liberal oder autoritäre Republik?* Göttingen: Muster-Schmidt.

Wileman, Donald. 1988. *L'Alliance Républicaine Démocratique: The Dead Center of French Politics, 1901–1947.* Ph.D. diss., York University, Toronto.

———. 1994. "What the Market Will Bear: The French Cartel Elections of 1924." *Journal of Contemporary History* 29, no. 3 (July): 483–500.

Williams, Philip. 1958. *Politics in Postwar France.* 2d ed. London: Longmans.

Wohl, Robert. 1966. *French Communism in the Making: 1914–24.* Stanford: Stanford University Press.

Wolf, Dieter. 1967. *Die Doriotbewegung.* Stuttgart: Deutsche Verlagsanstalt.

Wright, Gordon. 1995. *France in Modern Times.* 5th ed. New York: Norton.

Zeldin, Theodore. 1958. *The Political System of Napoleon III.* New York: Norton.

———. 1973. *France, 1848–1945: Politics and Anger.* Oxford: Oxford University Press.

Ziebura, Gilbert. 1967. *Léon Blum et le Parti socialiste, 1872–1934.* Paris: FNSP-Armand Colin.

Germany

Abraham, David. 1981. *The Collapse of the Weimar Republic.* Princeton: Princeton University Press.

Albertin, Lothar. 1972. *Liberalismus und Demokratie am Anfang der Weimarer Republik.* Düsseldorf: Droste Verlag.

———. 1981. "Der unzeitige Parlamentarismus der Liberalen." In *Politische Parteien auf dem Weg zur parlamentarischen Demokratie in Deutschland,* edited by Lothar Albertin and Werner Link, 31–62. Düsseldorf: Droste Verlag.

Anderson, Margaret L. 1993. "Voters, Junker, Landrat, Priest: The Old Authorities and the New Franchise in Imperial Germany." *American Historical Review* 98, no. 4 (December): 1448–74.

———. 2000. *Practicing Democracy: Elections and Political Culture in Imperial Germany.* Princeton: Princeton University Press.

Berghahn, Volker. 1966. *Der Stahlhelm, Bund der Frontsoldaten, 1918–35.* Düsseldorf: Droste Verlag.

Bergman, Theodor. 1984. "Das Zwischenfeld der Arbeiterbewegung zwischen SPD und KPD, 1928–33." In *Kampflose Kapitulation,* edited by Manfred Scharrer, 162–82. Reinbeck: Rowohlt.

Berman, Sheri. 1998. *The Social Democratic Moment: Ideas and Politics in the Making of Interwar Europe.* Cambridge: Harvard University Press.

Blackbourn, David, and Geoff Eley. 1984. *The Peculiarities of German History.* Oxford: Oxford University Press.

Bracher, Dieter. 1970. *The German Dictatorship.* New York: Praeger.

Bracher, Karl Dietrich. 1955. *Die Auflösung der Weimarer Republik.* Düsseldorf: Droste Verlag.

Braunthal, Gerard. 1978. *Socialist Labor and Politics in Weimar Germany.* Hamden: Anchor Press.

Brustein, William. 1996. *The Logic of Evil: The Social Origin of the Nazi Party, 1925–33.* New Haven: Yale University Press.

Brustein, William, and Jürgen Falter. 1994. "The Sociology of Nazism." *Rationality and Society* 6, no. 3 (July): 369–99.

Buse, Dieter. 1990. "Party Leadership and Mechanisms of Unity: The Crisis of the German Social Democratic Party Reconsidered, 1910–14." *Journal of Modern History* 62, no. 3 (September): 477–502.

Butzer, Hermann. 1999. *Diäten und Freifahrt im Deutschen Reichstag.* Düsseldorf: Droste.

Chanady, Attilla. 1967. "The Disintegration of the DNVP, 1924–30." *Journal of Modern History* 39:65–90.

Childers, Thomas. 1976. "The Social Bases of the National Socialist Vote." *Journal of Contemporary History* 11, no. 4 (October): 17–42.

———. 1985. "Interest and Ideology: Anti-system Politics in the Era of Stabilization, 1924–28." In *Die Nachwirkungen der Inflation auf die deutsche Geschichte, 1924–33,* edited by Gerald Feldman, 1–20. Munich: Oldenbourg.

———, ed. 1986a. *The Formation of the Nazi Constituency.* London: Croom Helm.

Childers, Thomas. 1986b. "The Limits of National Socialist Mobilization: The Election of November 1932 and the Fragmentation of the Nazi Constituency." In *The Formation of the Nazi Constituency, 1919–33,* edited by Thomas Childers, 232–59. London: Croom Helm.

Craig, Gordon. 1978. *Germany, 1866–1945.* Oxford: Oxford University Press.

Dahrendorf, Ralf. 1967. *Society and Democracy in Germany.* New York: Norton.

Diehl, James. 1977. *Paramilitary Politics in Weimar Germany.* Bloomington: Indiana University Press.

Dörr, Manfred. 1964. "Deutschnationale Volkspartei 1925 bis 1928." Dissertation, Marburg.

Eichenrode, Dieter. 1990. "Parteiorganization und Wahlkampfe der Sozialdemokraten in Berlin." In *Aufstieg der Arbeiterbewegung,* edited by Gerhard Ritter, 125–39. Munich: Oldenbourg.

Eley, Geoff. 1991. *Reshaping the German Right: Radical Nationalism and Political Change after Bismarck.* Ann Arbor: University of Michigan Press. Original edition, New Haven: Yale University Press, 1980.

———. 1991. "Die Umformierung der Rechten: Der radikaler Nationalismus und der Deutsche Flottenverein, 1898–1908." In *Wilhelminismus, Nationalismus, Faschismus,* 144–74. Münster: Verlag Dampfboot.

———. 1993. "Anti-semitism, Agrarian Mobilization, and the Conservative Party: Radicalism and Containment in the Founding of the Agrarian League, 1890–93." In *Between Reform, Reaction, and Resistance: Studies in the History of German Conservatism from 1789 to 1945,* edited by Larry Eugene Jones and James Retallack, 187–228. Providence: Berg.

Evans, Richard. 1985. "The Myth of Germany's Missing Revolution." *New Left Review* 149 (January/February): 67–94.

Falter, Jürgen. 1991. *Hitler's Wähler.* Munich: Beck.

Falter, Jürgen, Thomas Lindenberger, and Siegfried Schuman. 1986. *Wahlen und Abstimmungen in der Weimarer Republik.* Munich: Beck.

Faul, Erwin. 1964. "Verfemung, Duldung und Annerkennung des Parteiwesens in der Geschichte des Politischen Denkens." *Politische Vierteljahresschrift* 5:60–80.

Fritzsche, Peter. 1990. *Rehearsal for Fascism.* New York: Oxford University Press.

Fromme, Friedrich Karl. 1960. *Von der Weimarer Verfassung zum Bonner Grundgesetz.* Tübingen: Mohr.

Gates, Robert. 1974. "German Socialism and the Crisis of 1929–33." *Central European History* 7:332–59.

Gerschenkron, A. 1943. *Bread and Democracy in Germany.* Berkeley: University of California Press.

Gessner, Dieter. 1976. *Agrarverbände in der Weimarer Republik: Wirtschaftliche und soziale Voraussetzungen agrarkonservativer Politik bevor 1933.* Düsseldorf: Droste.

Gies, Horst. 1967. "NSDAP und landwirtschaftliche Organisationen in der Endphase der Weimarer Republik." *Vierteljahreshefte für Zeitgeschichte* 15:341–76.

Groh, Dieter. 1974. "Die Sozialdemokratie im Verfassungsystem des Zweiten Reiches." In *Sozialdemokratie zwischen Klassenbewegung und Volkspartei,* edited by Hans Mommsen, 62–83. Frankfurt: Fischer.

Gusy, Christoph. 1993. *Die Lehre vom Parteienstaat in der Weimarer Republik.* Baden-Baden: Nomos Verlag.

Harsch, Donna. 1993. *Social Democracy and the Rise of Fascism.* Chapel Hill: University of North Carolina Press.

Heberle, Rudolf. [1932] 1963. *Landbevölkerung und Nationalsozialismus: Eine soziologische Untersuchung der politischen Willensbildung in Schleswig Holstein, 1918–32.* Stuttgart: Deutsche Verlagsanstalt.

Heineman, Ulrich. 1985. "Linksopposition in der Sozialdemokratie und die Erfahrung der SAP in der Weimarer Republik." In *L'Internationale Operaia e Socialista tra la due guerre: Annali* (Fondazione Giangiacome Feltrinelli) 23 (1983/84): 497–526. Milano: Feltrinelli.

Hermens, F. A. 1936. "Proportional Representation and the Breakdown of German Democracy." *Social Research* 3, no. 4 (November): 411–33.

Holzbach, Heidrun. 1981. *Das "System Hugenberg": Die Organisation bürgerlicher Sammlungspolitik vor dem Aufstieg der NSDAP.* Stuttgart: Deutsche Verlagsanstalt.

Hunt, Richard. 1964. *German Social Democracy, 1918–33.* New Haven: Yale University Press.

Jonas, Erasmus. 1965. *Die Volkskonservativen, 1928–33.* Düsseldorf: Droste.

Jones, Larry Eugene. 1974. "The Crisis of White Collar Interest Politics." In *Industrielles System und politische Entwicklung in der Weimarer Republik,* edited by Hans Mommsen, Dietmar Petzina, and Bernard Weisbrod, 811–22. Düsseldorf: Droste Verlag.

———. 1985. "In the Shadow of Stabilization: German Liberalism and the Legitimacy Crisis of the Weimar Party System, 1924–30." In *Die Nachwirkungen der Inflation auf die deutsche Geschichte, 1924–33,* edited by Gerald Feldman, 21–42. Munich: Oldenbourg.

————. 1986. "Crisis and Realignment: Agrarian Splinter Parties in the Late Weimarer Republic, 1928–33." In *Peasants and Lords in Modern Germany,* edited by Robert Moeller, 198–232. Boston: Allen and Unwin.

————. 1988. *German Liberalism and the Dissolution of the German Party System, 1918–33.* Chapel Hill: University of North Carolina Press.

————. 1992. "The Greatest Stupidity of My Life: Alfred Hugenberg and the Formation of the Hitler Cabinet, January, 1933." *Journal of Contemporary History* 27, no. 1 (January): 63–88.

Kehr, E. 1970. *Primat der Innenpolitik.* Frankfurt: Suhrcamp.

Kühne, Thomas. 1993. *Dreiklassenwahlrecht und Wahlkulture in Preussen, 1867–1914: Landstagswahlen zwischen korporative Tradition und politische Massenmarkt.* Düsseldorf: Droste.

Lepsius, Rainer. 1973. "Parteiensystem und Sozialstruktur: Zum Problem der Demokratisierung der deutschen Gesellschaft." In *Deutsche Parteien vor 1918,* edited by Gerhard Ritter, 56–80. Köln: Kiepenheuer und Witsch.

Liebe, Werner. 1956. *Die Deutschnationale Volkspartei, 1918–24.* Düsseldorf: Droste.

Maier, Charles. 1988. *The Unmasterable Past.* Cambridge: Harvard University Press.

Matthias, Erich, and Rudolf Morsey. 1960. "Die deutsche Staatspartei." In *Das Ende der Parteien,* edited by Erich Matthias and Rudolf Morsey, 31–97. Düsseldorf: Droste.

Mitzman, Arthur. 1987. *Sociology and Estrangement: Three Sociologists in Imperial Germany.* New Brunswick. N.J.: Transaction Books.

Mommsen, Hans. 1974. "Die Sozialdemokratie in der Defensive: Der Immobilismus der SPD und der Aufstieg des Nationalsozialismus." In *Sozialdemokratie zwischen Klassenbewegung und Volkspartei,* edited by Hans Mommsen, 106–33. Frankfurt: Fischer.

Mühlberger, Detlef. 1986. "Central Control versus Regional Autonomy: A Case Study of Nazi Propaganda in Westphalia, 1925–32." In *The Formation of the Nazi Constituency,* edited by Thomas Childers, 64–103. London: Croom Helm.

Neumann, Sigmund. [1932] 1965. *Die Parteien der Weimarer Republik.* Stuttgart: Kohlhammer.

Nipperdey, Thomas. 1958. "Die Organisation der bürgerlichen Parteien vor 1918." *Historische Zeitschrift* 185 (1958): 550–602.

————. 1961. *Die Organisation der deutschen Parteien vor 1918.* Düsseldorf: Droste.

————. 1993. *Deutsche Geschichte, 1966–1918.* Vol. 2. Munich: C. H. Beck.

Oberreuter, Heinrich. 1990. "Politische Parteien: Stellung und Funktion im Verfassungssystem der BRD." In *Parteien in der Bundesrepublik,* edited by Alf Mintzel and H. Oberreuter, 15–49. Bonn: Bundeszentrale für politische Bildung.

Orlow, Dietrich. 1969. *The History of the Nazi Party, 1919–33.* Vol. 1. Pittsburgh: University of Pittsburgh Press.

Peukert, Detlev. 1989. *The Weimar Republic.* New York: Hill and Wang.

Pollock, James Kerr. 1934. "German Election Administration." In *Aspects of German Political Institutions,* edited by Lindsay Rogers, 1–71. New York: Columbia University Press.

Portner, Ernst. 1965. "Der Ansatz zur demokratischen Massenpartei im deutschen Liberalismus." *Vierteljahresheft für Zeitgeschichte* 13:15–61.

Pridham, Geoffrey. 1973. *Hitler's Rise to Power: The Nazi Movement in Bavaria, 1923–1933.* London: Hart-Davis MacGibbon.

Pyta, Wolfram. 1989. *Gegen Hitler. Auseinandersetzung der deutschen Sozialdemokratie mit der NSDAP in der Weimarer Republik.* Düsseldorf: Droste.

Retallack, James. 1988. *Notables of the Right: The Conservative Party and Political Mobilization in Germany, 1876–1918.* London: Unwin Hyman.

Richter, Michaela. 1986. "Resource Mobilization and Legal Revolution: The National Socialist Tactics in Franconia." In *The Formation of the Nazi Constituency,* edited by Thomas Childers, 104–30. London: Croom Helm.

Ritter, Gerhard. 1970. "Kontinuität und Umformung des deutschen Parteiensystem, 1918–20." In *Entstehung und Wandel der modernen Gesellschaft,* edited by Gerhard Ritter, 342–83. Berlin: de Gruyter.

———. 1979. "Die sozialistischen Parteien in Deutschland zwischen Kaiserreich und Republik." In *Staat und Gesellschaft im politischen Wandel,* edited by Werner Pols, 100–155. Stuttgart: Klett-Cotta.

Roth, Günther. 1963. *The Social Democracy in Imperial Germany.* Totowa, N.J.: Transaction.

Schaefer, Rainer. 1990. *SPD in der Ära Brüning: Tolerierung oder Mobilisierung?* Frankfurt: Campus.

Schanbacher, Eberhard. 1982. *Parlamentarische Wahlen und Wahlsystem in der Weimarer Republik.* Düsseldorf: Droste Verlag.

Schneider, Werner. 1978. *Die deutsche Demokratische Partei in der Weimarer Republik, 1925–30.* Munich: Fink.

Schorske, Carl. 1955. *German Social Democracy, 1905–17: The Development of the Great Schism.* New York: Harper.

Schwarz, Max. 1965. *Biographisches Handbuch des Reichstages.* Hannover: Verlag für Literatur und Zeitgeschehen.

Sheehan, James. 1978. *German Liberalism in the 19th Century.* Chicago: University of Chicago Press.

Southern, David. 1981. "The Impact of Inflation: Inflation, the Courts, and Revaluation." In *Social Change and Political Development in Weimar Germany,* edited by Richard Bessel and E. J. Feuchtwanger, 55–77. Totowa, N.J.: Croom Helm.

Statistisches Jahrbuch für das deutsche Reich. Various years. Stuttgart: Kohlhammer.

Stern, Fritz. 1975. "The Political Consequences of the Unpolitical German [1957]." In *The Failure of Illiberalism,* edited by Fritz Stern, 3–32. Chicago: University of Chicago Press.

Suval, Stanley. 1985. *Electoral Politics in Wilhelmine Germany.* Chapel Hill: University of North Carolina Press.

Tracey, Donald. 1975. "The Development of the National Socialist Party in Thuringia, 1926–30." *Central European History* 8:23–41.

Turner, Henry A. 1984. *German Big Business and the Rise of Hitler.* Oxford: Oxford University Press.

Wehler, Hans-Ulrich. 1971. *Das deutsche Kaiserreich.* Göttingen: Vandenhoeck.

———. 1987. *Deutsche Gesellschaftsgeschichte.* Vol. 2, *Von der Reformära bis zur industriellen und politischen 'Deutschen Doppelrevolution,' 1815–1845/49.* Munich: Beck.

———. 1995. *Deutsche Gesellschaftsgeschichte.* Vol. 3, *Von der 'Deutschen Doppelrevolution' bis zum Beginn des Ersten Weltkrieges, 1849–1914.* Munich: Beck.

Wende, F., ed. 1981. *Lexikon zur Geschichte der Parteien in Europa.* Stuttgart: Kroener.

Winkler, Heinrich. 1982. "Klassenbewegung oder Volkspartei? Zur sozialdemokratischen Programmdebatte, 1920–25." *Geschichte und Gesellschaft* 8, no. 1: 9–54.

———. 1991. "Klassenkampf versus Koalition: Die französischen Sozialisten und die Politik der deutschen Sozialdemokraten, 1928–33." *Geschichte und Gesellschaft* 17, no. 2: 182–219.

Zeender, John. 1963. "The German Catholics and the Presidential Election of 1925." *Journal of Modern History* 35, no. 4 (December): 255–75.

Author Index

Subject Index